HEIRLOOM
COUNTRY GARDENS

HEIRLOOM COUNTRY GARDENS

Timeless Treasures *for* Today's Gardeners

SARAH WOLFGANG HEFFNER

RODALE

RODALE

WE **INSPIRE** AND **ENABLE** PEOPLE TO IMPROVE
THEIR LIVES AND THE WORLD AROUND THEM

Editors: CHRISTINE BUCKS AND NANCY J. ONDRA
Cover and Interior Book Designer: MARTA M. STRAIT
Layout Designer: DONNA ROSSI
Computer Graphics Specialist: DALE MACK
Front Cover and Interior Illustrator: HELEN SMYTHE
Calligrapher: ELIZA S. HOLLIDAY
Photography Editors: LYN HORST AND JAMES A. GALLUCCI
Copy Editor: ERANA BUMBARDATORE
Researcher: HEIDI A. STONEHILL
Manufacturing Coordinator: PATRICK T. SMITH
Indexer: LINA BURTON
Editorial Assistance: KERRIE CADDEN AND SUSAN NICKOL
Project and Garden Designer: SARAH WOLFGANG HEFFNER

RODALE ORGANIC GARDENING BOOKS
Executive Editor: Ellen Phillips
Managing Editor: Fern Marshall Bradley
Executive Creative Director: Christin Gangi
Art Director: Patricia Field
Production Manager: Robert V. Anderson Jr.
Studio Manager: Leslie M. Keefe
Associate Copy Manager: Jennifer Hornsby
Manufacturing Manager: Mark Krahforst

Library of Congress Cataloging-in-Publication Data

Heffner, Sarah Wolfgang, date.
    Heirloom country gardens : timeless treasures for today's gardeners / Sarah Wolfgang Heffner.
        p.   cm.
    Includes bibliographical references and index.
    ISBN 0–87596–818–X (hardcover)
    1. Organic gardening. 2. Heirloom varieties (Plants)
I. Title.
SB453.5 .H45 2000
635'.0484—dc21   99–6748

Distributed in the book trade by St. Martin's Press

2 4 6 8 10 9 7 5 3 1   hardcover

To the memory of my mother, Laura Wolfgang,
who instilled in me the love of gardening.

CONTENTS

Part Two:

Part Three:

My Heirloom Country Garden

I come from a long line of country gardeners: My mother, aunts, and grandparents all had wonderful gardens full of vegetables, flowers, and fruit. My mother always grew huge vegetable gardens, saved tomato seeds, took geranium cuttings in the fall, and put up vast amounts of produce. My aunts arranged beautiful bouquets with flowers from their own gardens for church functions. My grandfather had brooms made for each family at Christmas from his own broom corn. Growing up surrounded by gardeners, it was natural for me to develop a passion for gardening. I admit that as a youth I grumbled when picking beans and I threw my share of tomatoes at my brother, but I have always loved old-time country gardens.

Now, as a forty-something gardener in a world of harried schedules, lots of responsibilities, and increasing suburbia in my beloved farm valley, an old-fashioned garden continues to mean bounty and beauty to me, just as it did to my grandparents and their grandparents. But it's also more than that—it's a haven where I can unwind from a hectic day and lose myself in the pleasures of long-loved plants.

In the process of researching and writing this book, I've had a wonderful time learning from other gardeners, past and present. I've discovered many "new old" plants, crafts, and recipes I'd like to try, and I've developed an even greater appreciation for the skills of gardeners of times past. In the following pages, I'll share some of my favorite discoveries with you, so you can also enjoy the peace and plenty of this time-tested style of gardening.

If you're looking for a retreat from a busy lifestyle, a way to enjoy the tastiest fruits and vegetables, or simply an attractive, easy-care landscape, give an heirloom country garden a try. It's a great way to bring a touch of the country into any backyard!

Sarah Wolfgang Heffner

Sarah Wolfgang Heffner

How to Use This Book

This book tells you how to grow and enjoy an heirloom country garden—a garden filled with old-fashioned charm and a sense of history. Whether you'd like to grow a few heirloom vegetables or an entire kitchen garden, an apple from George Washington's time or an orchard full of them, a cottage garden or a formal parlor garden, in this book, you'll find what you need to succeed.

In the first part of this book, learn about the different styles of heirloom gardens in "Heirloom Gardens Then and Now," starting on page 3. "A Sampler of Heirloom Garden Designs," starting on page 17, shows you how to incorporate those styles into wonderful garden plans that you can use to create your own old-fashioned garden.

To make it easier to grow the heirloom garden of your dreams, I've included several chapters in the second part of this book on the specific plant types, including "Heirloom Vegetables: A Gardener's Guide," starting on page 49, "Antique Flowers: Lore and Romance," starting on page 85, "Herbs with a History," starting on page 129, and "Flavorful Old-Time Fruits and Berries," starting on page 149. Each of these chapters includes an A-to-Z gallery of the best heirlooms available today, so you can learn their history, as well as how to grow them.

If you're looking for more general inspiration on creating and enjoying your old-time country garden, the third part of this book is for you. "Growing Great Gardens Grandma's Way," starting on page 167, has the information you need to maintain a lush, gorgeous, productive garden all season long. Complete the old-time garden look with a selection of authentic projects, such as a rustic grape arbor or a dried flower press. You'll find step-by-step instructions for these projects and a variety of great garden crafts in "Garden Projects for That Country Look," starting on page 193. And when you're ready to enjoy the fruits (and vegetables!) of your labor, turn to "Favorite Old-Time Recipes," starting on page 207, to learn how to prepare wonderful regional delicacies that evolved with America's gardens—from delicious Native American corn soup to Pennsylvania German fruit pies.

Once you've been bitten by the old-time gardening bug, you'll want to learn even more, so I've included "Resources for Heirloom Country Gardens," starting on page 226. Here's where you'll find listings of historical gardens, seed-saving organizations, and seed and plant companies that supply heirloom varieties. Dig in!

Part One

CREATING AN HEIRLOOM COUNTRY GARDEN

Heirloom plants and garden styles are wonderful because they carry fascinating stories with them. In this section, you'll find a brief history of American garden styles, plus some regional garden specialties. There's also a chapter of garden designs, where you'll find inspiration for your own heirloom kitchen, herb, fruit, or flower garden.

CHAPTER

O N E

Heirloom Gardens
Then and Now

What's so special about heirloom country gardens? There are as many answers as there are gardeners! For some, it's the tidy beauty of a carefully planned kitchen garden or the carefree bounty of blooms in a charming cottage garden. For others, it's a lifestyle of growing plants the old-fashioned way, without relying on pesticides, herbicides, and other new-fangled chemical concoctions.

For many gardeners, the draw is the romance of the folklore surrounding the plants and the sense of connection with gardeners who have gone before you. And if you enjoy cooking or crafts, you can enjoy and share the bounty of your garden by experimenting with old-time recipes and projects, from herbal teas to pressed-flower designs.

Whatever attracts you to heirloom country gardens, you're in for a treat if you plant one. You'll enjoy the unforgettable flavor and unique shapes and patterns of heirloom vegetables and fruits—and learn the wonderful stories behind them. Your yard will look great all season long, full of beautiful, sturdy, old-fashioned flowers. And just think of the fun you'll have telling friends and neighbors about your luscious 'Moon and Stars' watermelons and pretty 'Grandpa Ott's' morning glories!

OPPOSITE: Hardy perennials and native plants shape the informal beauty of a cottage garden.

3

Early Times in America's Gardens

When you're ready to start planning your heirloom country garden, you have a long history to draw from for inspiration. America's earliest gardens didn't have much room for romance—they were primarily used for food and medicinal herb production—though both Native Americans and European settlers grew a few flowers. Gardens containing a mixture of vegetables, herbs, and flowers continued into the 1800s and even into this century. Hand-dug beds were outlined with paths and enclosed with picket fences or decorative iron fences. Just like today's dedicated gardeners, old-time gardeners constructed coldframes from old window glass to harden-off the tender seedlings that they had raised on their windowsills. Wood ashes and manure were used for fertilizer by yesterday's (and today's) organic gardeners.

Early flower gardening was usually confined to the parlor garden. In the late 1700s, this was a "best-foot-forward" formal garden where you could walk with your friends and admire favorite plants. Typically around 36 × 24 feet in size, this garden was usually located to the front of the house in the New England states and to the back or along the side of the property in the mid-Atlantic and Southern states. Parlor gardens were laid out in beds with central and side paths. The beds were planted with the owner's favorite combinations of flowers and herbs and were enclosed by a fence.

FOOD AND FLOWERS

By the early 1800s, food production was still an important priority for gardeners, but flower gardening was becoming increasingly popular. American gardening was coming into its own. Most country homesteads had lilacs and roses in their yards. Lilacs (*Syringa vulgaris*) were popular shrubs for landscaping the outhouse—for obvious reasons! Other favorite shrubs included bridal wreath (*Spiraea prunifolia*), forsythias (*Forsythia* spp.), and hydrangeas (*Hydrangea arborescens* and *H. paniculata*).

Flowers played an important role in these landscapes, too. Spring bulbs included daffodils (*Narcissus* spp.), grape hyacinths (*Muscari* spp.), Siberian iris (*Iris sibirica*), and tulips (*Tulipa* spp.). Annuals included China aster (*Callistephus chinensis*), four-o'clocks (*Mirabilis jalapa*), larkspur (*Consolida ambigua*), marigolds (*Tagetes* spp.), rose moss (*Portulaca grandiflora*), sunflower (*Helianthus annuus*), sweet alyssum (*Lobularia maritima*), and zinnias (*Zinnia elegans*). Popular perennials and biennials included bleeding heart (*Dicentra spectabilis*), Canterbury bells (*Campanula medium*), foxgloves (*Digitalis* spp.), phlox (*Phlox* spp.), primroses (*Primula* spp.), sweet William (*Dianthus barbatus*), and violets (*Viola* spp.). Seed companies and plant nurseries flourished. Many horticultural societies formed at this time, and gardening periodicals were popular.

Working-class Americans in the early 1800s lived in modest cottages on small plots of land, but these small plots still provided a surprising amount of gardening space. (Lawns had not yet come into their own, so more of the property was available for use.) Vegetable plots were sited at the rear of the property, while flower gardens were placed where passersby could see them. Even fruit gardens were included in these yards. *The Cottage Garden,* an 1848 text by Walter Eldenfield, specifies that a small village lot have a one-eighth acre garden that contains 8 fruit trees, 6 currant and 6 raspberry bushes, 4 gooseberry bushes, 50 strawberry plants, 6 flowering shrubs, 12 roses, 2 grapevines, 2 "street shade trees," and 12 climbing plants.

VICTORIAN GARDENING

Victorians loved flowers and planted them in their home landscapes. Perennial and annual beds bordered the sides of their homes, and vines such as clematis (*Clematis* spp.), wisterias (*Wisteria* spp.), scarlet runner bean (*Phaseolus coccineus*), and morning glories (*Ipomoea* spp.) twined around their porches. But in spite of the flower plantings and vines, Victorian home landscaping would be considered stark by contemporary standards. Shrubs and trees were used to accent the property, but not as foundation plantings around the house.

Floral hobbies were also popular with Victorians. Houseplants, including hanging baskets of ivies and ferns, were displayed in elaborate window gardens. Glass terrariums were popular as "Wardian cases" or "winter gardens." Wealthier gardeners collected orchids. Flower arranging was also popular at this time.

Toward the last quarter of the 1800s, a romantic, nostalgic view of gardening became popular. Garden writers and magazines advocated old-time cottage gardens of hardy perennials, annuals that would reseed, and Native American plants. Gertrude Jekyll, the famous English garden designer and author, promoted flower gardens of perennials and annuals grown in a cottage-garden style as an antidote to the colorful "bedding out" planting schemes of masses of annuals that was a holdover from Victorian times. American gardeners gravitated to this idea. The New York State exhibit in the 1893 World's Columbian Exposition in Chicago featured a 2,500-square-foot garden that was a collection of old-time flowers including hollyhocks, foxgloves, phlox, zinnias, tiger lilies, climbing roses, and golden honeysuckles, among many other old-fashioned favorites.

By the late 1800s, a golden age of gardening flourished. The seed industry and nursery trades were thriving, and periodicals and garden books abounded. The gardener-as-consumer had arrived. Artists used old-time gardens as a popular theme for painting. Homeowners gardened for many of the same reasons we enjoy gardening today. Country folk gardened for their provisions and enjoyment, while town and suburban dwellers relaxed and escaped the everyday humdrum in their little "heaven on earth."

Today, we are also in a golden age of gardening. Gardening is the number one leisure-time activity, and we have excellent periodicals, garden books, and even the Internet in this information age! And while most of us no longer raise all of our own produce, we are much like our Victorian counterparts in that our gardens provide relaxation, beauty, and healthy, flavorful foods.

Regional Heirloom Garden Styles

While wide-sweeping trends certainly had an effect on America's old-time gardens, local influences played a major part in developing their regional flavors. Gardeners in past times had to rely on materials and plants that were readily available, so it's not surprising that crops and garden accessories varied from place to place. Gardens also reflected the cultural heritage of the people that created them. And climate played a role in determining gardening styles, just as it does today.

When you're planning an heirloom garden for your yard, you'll want to keep these regional differences in mind. There's no rule that says you can't have a New England kitchen garden in Florida or a knot garden in Nebraska. But if you want to create a garden that's true to the history of your area, you'll want to lean heavily toward the styles and plants that were native in your region.

New England and New York Gardens

For the early European settlers in this region, gardening was a matter of survival, rather than of pleasure. The men cleared land to plant field crops, while the women were primarily vegetable and herb gardeners, growing these practical plants in kitchen gardens. When choosing a site for their garden, they looked for good soil and a southern exposure for maximum sun. They laid their gardens out in raised beds linked by pathways and enclosed by fencing for protection from wind damage and wandering animals. The packed-earth or grassy paths were just wide enough for one person and were occasionally covered with gravel or clamshells. The raised beds were held in place by cut saplings or planks laid directly on the ground.

Kitchen gardens varied in size and shape and were planted with vegetables, herbs, and flowers together without regard for size or type. Low plants like boxwoods (*Buxus* spp.), hyssop (*Hyssopus officinalis*), pinks (*Dianthus* spp.), and thrifts (*Armeria* spp.) were sometimes used to edge the beds and keep the soil in place. While the emphasis was on growing sufficient food to survive, a bit of beauty provided pleasure for our long-ago gardening counterparts. Herbs were an essential part of New England gardens and had many uses, from medicinal preparations and food preservation to dyeing cloth and warding off vermin.

Traveling south, the Dutch and French Huguenots in New York followed their

GARDENING WITH THE THREE SISTERS

THE THREE MAINSTAYS OF NEW ENGLAND gardens—maize (corn), beans, and squash—were all adopted from Native Americans. These three vegetables, called "the three sisters" in the Iroquois story of creation, were grown together: The tall flint (meal) corn provided support for the pole beans, while the squash vines covered the ground, suppressing weeds and conserving soil moisture. This trio of crops provided good nutrition for the early settlers, whose food supplies were often limited.

This simple plant grouping is still worth growing today, since it makes efficient use of garden space while minimizing weeding. Create your own three sisters garden with the traditional flint corn, pole beans, and squash, or customize the combination to fit your particular needs. To make a fun, old-time garden for kids, for instance, you could grow popcorn with scarlet runner beans and miniature pumpkins. Or, if you love sweet corn, substitute it for the flint corn.

Try the three sisters grouping of corn, beans, and squash in your own garden to enjoy a generous harvest from a small space.

Narrow paths allow more room for crops and flowers, while the picket fence helps keep marauding animals at bay.

New England Kitchen Gardens

A perennially popular garden design, important features of a New England kitchen garden include:

✳ Raised beds of varying shapes and sizes. Design them based on the site and what you want to plant.

✳ Mixed plantings of vegetables, flowers, and herbs.

✳ Narrow pathways of gravel, grass, clamshells, or sod.

✳ Wooden picket fencing around the garden.

heritage with more formal and elaborate kitchen gardens. Kitchen gardens were laid out in a very symmetrical plan, with proportioned beds on either side of a central walkway. Considered to be excellent vegetable growers, the New York gardeners also quickly established fine fruit orchards and planted their favorite flowers from home. In 1655, Adrian Van der Donck wrote that the settlers from the Netherlands had planted various kinds of apple and pear trees along with white and red roses of different kinds, numerous bulbs—including tulips, crown imperials (*Fritillaria imperialis*), and lilies—and native flowers such as sunflowers and red and yellow lilies. The earliest gardens were a mix of vegetables, flowers, and fruit. From 1700 on, the wealthier Dutch and Huguenots established spacious estates with formal gardens and carefully laid-out orchards and flowerbeds.

MID-ATLANTIC GARDENS

Like their New England counterparts, early Pennsylvanians brought with them seeds of the vegetable crops they had grown in the old country. The early settlers established home orchards as soon as they cleared their farmsteads. Large orchards were planted for cider production, dried apples, and hog food. Hard cider was one of the most common drinks because poor sanitation often meant that while water was not safe to drink, fermented beverages were. 'Newtown Pippin' and 'Esopus Spitzenburg' apples were favorite varieties in the mid-1700s. The

New York Formal Gardens

Both the Dutch and the French Huguenots, working from their traditions, used raised beds as the New Englanders did, but designed their gardens in a formal manner. Well-to-do Dutch merchants were very proud of their gardens, and they featured topiary creations of animals and birds from clipped boxwood. To make an authentic New York garden, make sure your garden has:

* Symmetry, with balanced beds carefully laid out on either side of a central walkway.
* A sundial or decorative statue or vase highlighting the center of the garden.

You can fill the open spaces of a knot garden with colored gravel, flowers, or herbs.

settlers dried large quantities of apples, peaches, and pears for winter use or stored the fruit in root cellars.

Pennsylvania had a large influx of German settlers in the 1700s. Noted for their industry and neatness, they were also skilled gardeners. They organized their garden in a bed design with orderly rows, unlike the New England mixed plantings. They grew root vegetables and greens along with Native American crops and hop vines, which they used for making bread and beer.

By the late 1700s, gardeners were raising a greater variety of vegetables. Celery, spinach, lettuce, eggplant, peppers, sweet potatoes, and tomatoes were part of Pennsylvania German gardens. Herbs—including sage, rue, wormwood, tansy, peppermint, spearmint, thyme, horehound, chamomile, and dill—were grown largely for medicinal purposes.

Pennsylvania Germans used wood ashes to control insects, shaking the ashes from a loosely woven burlap bag onto their plants before the dew had evaporated in the morning. Ducks and geese helped with weed and insect control. Insects were hand-picked off plants and destroyed. Some diseases, such as peach yellows, did cause crop damage, but a number of the problems we face today—including pear psylla (a serious pear pest introduced from Europe in the 1830s) and Japanese beetles (those shiny metallic beetles that chew raspberry and rose foliage every July, first found in the United States in 1916)—had not yet migrated to the New World.

SOUTHERN GARDENS

Southern gardens have many cultural influences as part of their gardening history. Native Americans, Spanish explorers, French missionary priests, African-Americans, and British settlers have all made contributions to Southern gardening.

The Cherokees of the Carolinas and Georgia were excellent gardeners. Along with corn, beans, squash, gourds, and sunflowers, they grew marsh mallow (*Althaea officinalis*) for its edible root. Mulberry was a popular fruit. Mayapples (*Podophyllum peltatum*) were used for medicinal purposes, and passionflower (*Passiflora* spp.) fruit was considered a cooling summer delicacy.

Early Spanish colonists contributed many vegetables that later became Southern heirlooms, including heat-tolerant kinds of asparagus, beets, cabbages, carrots, celery, cress, cucumbers, eggplants, endive, lettuces, mustards, radishes, spinach, okra, and turnips.

The French influence on Southern gardening is most obvious in the formal parterre style, where low-clipped shrubs are laid out in beds of decorative geometric patterns. Also called knot gardens, the enclosed beds could contain either flowers or vegetables. You can see a good example of this gardening style at the Ballroom Garden in Colonial Williamsburg.

African-Americans, arriving in America under the harshest of conditions, have made major contributions to American cuisine and gardening—after all, they were the cooks and

Raised beds surrounded by pathways give these gardens a neat and tidy look and make planting and harvesting easy.

Pennsylvania German Gardens

Pennsylvania Germans also gardened in the European raised-bed tradition, but their gardens had several distinctive features you might want to reproduce in your own garden:

* Four raised beds with a small circular bed in the center and pathways around all of the beds.

* A wooden fence or stone wall around the garden. The space between the fence and the pathway was planted with small fruits, herbs, and flowers.

* A center circular bed, which had a large plant such as a yucca (called the Adam and Eve plant) or rosemary (in remembrance of Mary, the mother of Jesus). Small flowers or herbs were planted around this center bed.

THE SHAKER SEED INDUSTRY

Unlike modern gardeners, gardeners in the past didn't always have the luxury of buying their seeds in neat little packets. In fact, it wasn't until the late eighteenth century that they could begin to rely on commercial seed companies. The first American seedsman was David Landreth, who established a seed business in Philadelphia in 1784. But it was the Shakers, a religious community that established settlements throughout the Northeast, Kentucky, and the Midwest, who were responsible for developing the seed industry in America.

Unlike others who imported seeds from Europe, the Shakers raised their own seeds for sale. By the early 1800s, the Shakers had developed the innovative idea of selling individual seed packets instead of bulk seed lots. They distributed their seeds by horse-drawn wagon, in late winter or early spring, to stores where the seeds were sold on commission. At the end of the summer, they would return to collect the unsold packets and their earnings. Herb seeds were a specialty of the Shakers. They also published several garden manuals.

After the mid-1800s, competition increased from commercial seed companies. The colorfully printed packets of the commercial seed companies became popular and eclipsed the Shakers' plain brown packets. (Colorful seed packets from that time are still prized by collectors today.) Seed production also began to move to the western United States, where it was easier to produce seed crops than in the humid East.

gardening staff on the antebellum plantations. Cooked greens, such as celosia cultivars that were related to spinach, were a staple in African cooking, according to Skip Kauffman, vice president and director of the National Colonial Farm: Ecosystem Farm in Accokeek, Maryland, which depicts a Revolutionary-period tobacco farm and contemporary sustainable agriculture. In America, African-Americans adapted their dishes to the colder

Romantic Southern Gardens

Southern gardens are noted for lush plantings of fragrant shrubs and blooming vines. An old-time southern garden should include:

* A border of flowering shrubs, wrought-iron fencing, or brick walls, to provide a sense of enclosure.
* Garden beds anchored with shrubs to provide a sense of informal symmetry.
* Spring bulbs, annuals, and perennials, combined with flowering shrubs, citrus trees, fig trees, and climbing vines, for a slightly overgrown, romantic effect.
* A latticework summerhouse for outdoor entertaining.

A latticework enclosure provides a shady spot to sit and enjoy a Southern garden.

climate, using cooked cool-season greens like turnips and mustard greens. Black-eyed peas, millet, okra, peanuts, rice, and yams are all African foods that became part of Southern cooking.

Some of the greatest gardeners of the eighteenth century lived in the South, including Presidents Washington and Jefferson. Many of these great gardeners enjoyed using wildflowers from the woodlands and plains in their gardens.

WESTERN DRYLAND GARDENS

Western gardens were influenced by the hot, dry growing conditions of the region. The Native Americans' understanding of the land and knowledge of native plants produced foods and a culture that thrived for centuries in this demanding environment. Later on, the Spanish contributed tree fruits, herbs, and flowers, and pioneer women brought their kitchen gardens and hardy self-sufficiency.

Early Spanish missions established in the mid-1600s and early 1700s influenced the gardening tradition in California. Spanish gardens, with their water fountains, represented a haven from the harsh, dry environment. The walled gardens of the missions in the Southwest followed this tradition and had beautiful orchard groves with a wide range of fruits, including apples, pears, peaches, apricots, plums, cherries, figs, olives, oranges, and pomegranates. Their flower gardens featured roses, lilies, pinks (*Dianthus* spp.), sweet peas (*Lathyrus odoratus*),

Mission Gardens

The structures of the Southwest missions had their roots in walled medieval monasteries. Housing, workshops, and the church building were arranged around a central plaza garden. The plaza garden sometimes had a water fountain in the center, but it typically had very few plants other than some trees for shade. The productive gardens, called *huertas,* adjoined the mission buildings and were enclosed by high walls or hedges of prickly pear cactus (*Opuntia* spp.). To recreate a *huerta,* include:

* Rectangular gardens divided into quadrants.
* Groves of fruit trees and mixed plantings of herbs, vegetables, and flowers in the quadrants.
* A water fountain in the center of the quadrants.

Native plants are the perfect accompaniment for a walled Southwestern garden.

hollyhocks (*Alcea rosea*), and nasturtiums (*Tropaeolum majus*), while their vegetable gardens contained peas, beans, beets, lentils, onions, carrots, red peppers, corn, potatoes, squash, cucumbers, and melons.

The mission gardens of the far West were beautiful and productive, but pioneers trekking across the Plains had little time or energy to garden for beauty. Their first priority was growing enough food to sustain their families through long, rough winters. Women also grew traditional herbs like feverfew and chamomile, and they began to learn which native plants had medicinal value. Even in these rugged conditions, though, gardeners grew a few of their favorite flowers, including hollyhocks (*Alcea rosea*), larkspur (*Consolida ambigua*), and Oriental poppies (*Papaver orientale*). Some even grew sunflowers on the "roofs" of their sod dugouts! Settlers often requested seeds and slips of plants in letters home, and women like Philena Pickett in 1860 packed their rose bushes between clothes and provisions for the journey westward.

CREATING YOUR OWN HEIRLOOM GARDEN

Now that your appetite's been whetted by all the possibilities, it's time to think about what type of garden you'd like. You'll find many heirloom plants to choose from in "Yesterday's Plants for Today's Gardens," starting on page 47. But first, let yourself become inspired by the possibilities in "A Sampler of Heirloom Garden Designs" on page 17.

Even in dry climates, you can reap a bountiful harvest if you use plants adapted to low-rainfall conditions.

Southwestern Gardens

A traditional garden in the Southwest emphasizes drought-tolerant heirloom vegetables and herbs, as well as native shrubs and flowers that will tolerate extreme growing conditions. To re-create an old-fashioned Southwestern garden, use:

* Heirloom and native plants adapted to the site conditions. You can grow the "three sisters" combination of corn, beans, and squash, but choose drought-tolerant varieties.

* Dryland planting techniques, such as deep planting (Navajo and Hopi corn are planted 8 to 12 inches deep, to reach soil moisture), funneling water into growing areas with contours, and ridging beds to collect water.

* Native wildflowers. Most will bloom in late winter and spring, but there are a few summer- and fall-blooming species, as well. Check the bloom time of native plants to extend garden interest.

A Sampler of Heirloom Garden Designs

Choosing the type of heirloom country garden you want to create is almost as satisfying as growing it—and it's lots easier! (All dreaming, no digging.) To help you get inspired, I've included this sampler of garden designs based on five different themes. The designs in this chapter are just a starting point, though. You can use them as they are; modify them to suit your site and tastes; or design your own variation on these themes.

If your budget doesn't permit ordering dozens of plants from nurseries, remember that old-time country gardeners created charming gardens with "a little bit of this and a little bit of that," meaning cuttings, perennial divisions, and seeds from friends' gardens. Plant swaps are still an excellent way to get new plants without spending a lot of money. Share favorites with neighbors and friends, or see if local garden clubs have an organized plant swap.

Keep in mind that gardens are always works in progress. If you're starting a new garden, give it several years to mature and look as though it has always been there. Over time, you will find which plants thrive in a particular corner, which reseed happily, and which ones you just aren't satisfied with and want to replace. Finally, plan a spot for a garden bench so that you can relax in your garden with a glass of herbal tea and a good book.

OPPOSITE: *A well-thought-out mix of perennials and annuals provides season-long color and interest in any old-time country garden, no matter what the design.*

COUNTRY COTTAGE GARDEN

A cottage garden is the ultimate country dream come true, where flowers mix with herbs and vegetables in colorful abandon. You'll love cutting fresh flowers for bouquets, snipping herbs and lettuces for salad, and picking tender beans for dinner.

A rustic wooden gate frames a welcoming entrance into this country cottage garden filled with a mix of flowers and vegetables.

Romance Made Real

Mention the term "cottage garden," and what comes to mind? Often, it's the image of a thatch-roofed cottage surrounded by gardens planted in a colorful jumble of hollyhocks, columbines, peonies, roses, and other beautiful and fragrant old-fashioned flowers. The real-life cottage gardens of English history do not quite fit this romantic ideal, but instead were commonly mixed plantings of vegetables, fruits, and herbs, complete with honeybees, chickens, and perhaps a family pig. Cottage gardens date back to the sixteenth century and were planted by laborers who barely made enough money to survive.

The early cottage gardens planted by European settlers in North America were also subsistence gardens of vegetables, herbs, and a

few flowers. As time went on and living conditions became less harsh, more flowers were
added to cottage gardens. Gardeners traded
seeds and slips of favorite plants with each
other and perpetuated old favorites. By the
nineteenth century, well-to-do European and
American landowners began to plant mixed
borders that emulated cottage gardens, and the
romantic ideal of the cottage garden became a

*A mission-style bench provides a
relaxing spot to sit and sip a
refreshing glass of iced tea made
from your own mint patch.*

popular gardening theme. I like both the romantic and realistic versions of cottage gardens, and I think both have a place in our landscapes today.

ABOUT THIS GARDEN

It seems almost a contradiction to offer a cottage garden plan, since the joy of these gardens is their casual, informal appearance. But if you're looking for some inspiration, here's a place to start. I've designed this cottage garden as a set of six small beds, surrounded on three sides by a narrow border, with a bench in one corner. This allows for a network of paths for easy access to all sides of the beds, simplifying maintenance and giving you lots of options for strolling through your garden. A bamboo-stake teepee covered with scarlet runner beans in one corner adds height to the garden and also provides a fun hiding place for children.

I've gone for a more romantic version of the traditional cottage garden, based on a mix of annual and perennial flowers along with attractive, aromatic herbs. But this layout is so flexible that it would be simple to customize it to your particular needs. You could, for instance, devote all or part of the center beds to growing vegetables, and keep the herbs and flowers in the outer border, or vice versa. Or you could move all the perennials to the outer border, and sow the annuals in the center beds to create a cutting garden.

This layout is also flexible enough to fit practically any site with ample sun and well-drained soil. If your site is smaller than 13 × 19 feet, simply get rid of either a horizontal or a vertical row of beds, and shorten the back or arms of the outer border. To fill a larger site, add more beds in the middle, and lengthen the outer borders. The important thing is to make the most of the space you have to work with!

ENJOYING YOUR COTTAGE GARDEN

With a wealth of flowers and herbs for you to choose from, this cottage garden is productive as well as pretty. Harvest the borage, dill, sage, and thyme to add zest to your cooking. The flowers of borage and scarlet runner beans add flavor and color to salads, too. Or make yourself a refreshing hot or iced beverage from your mint patch, so you can sip while you sit in your garden and enjoy its beauty. And don't forget to snip a few flowers here and there to bring the glory of the garden indoors.

Once your cottage garden is established, you can share plants with other gardeners and enjoy adding "new" heirlooms to your own garden. A cottage garden should not be overly neat and tidy. Let some annual flowers and vegetables go to seed. However, you *will* need to keep vigorous perennials and reseeding annuals from overstepping their bounds. Thin your perennials every few years, and weed out abundant volunteer seedlings.

If local zoning regulations permit, think about adding a small chicken shelter and run to your cottage garden—you'll have delicious eggs, and the manure will be a source of nitrogen for your garden!

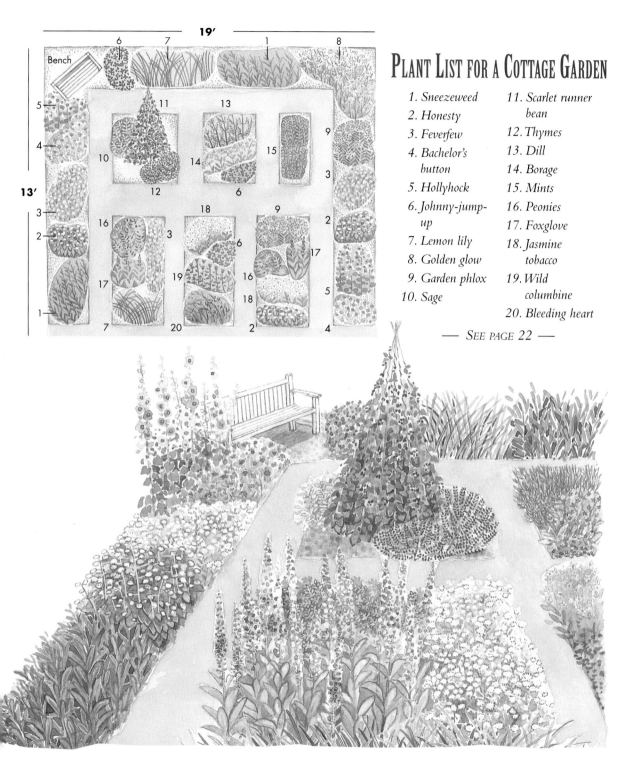

PLANT LIST FOR A COTTAGE GARDEN

1. Sneezeweed
2. Honesty
3. Feverfew
4. Bachelor's button
5. Hollyhock
6. Johnny-jump-up
7. Lemon lily
8. Golden glow
9. Garden phlox
10. Sage
11. Scarlet runner bean
12. Thymes
13. Dill
14. Borage
15. Mints
16. Peonies
17. Foxglove
18. Jasmine tobacco
19. Wild columbine
20. Bleeding heart

— SEE PAGE 22 —

Number	Plant Name	Quantity	Notes
1	Sneezeweed (*Helenium autumnale*)	6 plants	Space plants 2 to 3 feet apart. Pinch stem tips once or twice in spring to promote compact, sturdy plants.
2	Honesty (*Lunaria annua*)	1 seed pack or 8 plants	Thin seedlings or space plants 12 to 18 inches apart. Start with purchased plants to get flowers right away; otherwise, sow seed outdoors in early summer for flowers the second year.
3	Feverfew (*Tanacetum parthenium*)	1 seed pack or 12 plants	Thin seedlings or space plants 12 to 15 inches apart. After bloom, cut flowering stems to the ground to promote a flush of new growth and more flowers.
4	Bachelor's button (*Centaurea cyanus*)	2 seed packs	Thin seedlings to stand 8 to 12 inches apart. For earliest bloom, sow seed of this annual outdoors in fall; otherwise, sow in early spring.
5	Hollyhock (*Alcea rosea*)	1 seed pack or 5 plants	Thin seedlings or space plants 2 to 3 feet apart. Heirloom hollyhocks are available in both single- and double-flowered forms. Plants often self-sow.
6	Johnny-jump-up (*Viola tricolor*)	2 seed packs or 24 plants	Thin seedlings or space plants 6 to 9 inches apart. Cut plants back by half in summer to encourage fall bloom.
7	Lemon lily (*Hemerocallis lilioasphodelus*)	8 plants	Space plants 12 to 18 inches apart. Lemon lily adds yellow flowers and a light, sweet fragrance to the early-summer garden.
8	Golden glow (*Rudbeckia laciniata* 'Hortensia')	4 plants	Space plants 2 to 3 feet apart. This sturdy, summer-blooming perennial is a traditional favorite for country gardens.
9	Garden phlox (*Phlox paniculata*)	4 plants	Space plants 2 to 4 feet apart. Sweetly fragrant garden phlox comes in a wide range of colors to fit any preference.
10	Sage (*Salvia officinalis*)	2 plants	Space plants 12 to 18 inches apart. For extra interest, try purple-leaved 'Purpurea' or yellow-and-green 'Icterina'.
11	Scarlet runner bean (*Phaseolus coccineus*)	1 seed pack	Thin seedlings 6 to 8 inches apart. Pinch off the developing beans to encourage more flowers, or pick them as snap or shell beans.
12	Thymes (*Thymus* spp.)	2 plants	Space plants 8 to 12 inches apart. Thymes come in a range of sizes, scents, and flower colors; choose your favorites.
13	Dill (*Anethum graveolens*)	1 seed pack	Thin seedlings 10 to 12 inches apart. Dill flowers attract a wide range of beneficial insects to your garden, and they look great in bouquets, too.

Number	Plant Name	Quantity	Notes
14	Borage (*Borago officinalis*)	1 seed pack or 5 plants	Thin seedlings or space plants 12 inches apart. Sow seed outdoors as soon as the danger of frost is past. Borage will often self-sow.
15	Mints (*Mentha* spp.)	6 plants	Space plants 12 to 15 inches apart. Mints come in many heights and fragrances; plant a selection of your favorites.
16	Peonies (*Paeonia* spp.)	2 plants	Space plants 3 feet apart. Besides their beautiful, fragrant blooms, peonies offer shrubby clumps of handsome foliage that look great throughout the season. Double-flowered selections may need staking.
17	Foxglove (*Digitalis purpurea*)	1 seed pack or 6 plants	Thin seedlings or space plants 12 to 15 inches apart. Remove spent blossoms, but leave a few stalks to set seed so plants can self-sow.
18	Jasmine tobacco (*Nicotiana alata*)	1 seed pack or 8 plants	Thin seedlings or space plants 18 to 24 inches apart The fragrant white or pink flowers of jasmine tobacco open in the evening. Plants often self-sow.
19	Wild columbine (*Aquilegia canadensis*)	1 seed pack or 16 plants	Thin seedlings or space plants 8 inches apart. Wild columbine's red-and-yellow flowers are a welcome sight in early spring. Individual plants may be short-lived but will be replaced by self-sown seedlings.
20	Bleeding heart (*Dicentra spectabilis*)	2 plants	Space plants 2 feet apart. In warm climates or dry soil, bleeding hearts may go dormant by midsummer.

Cottage Garden Considerations

Cottage gardens are as individual as the gardeners who create them. Whether you want practical herbs and vegetables or pretty old-time ornamentals, here are a few pointers:

* Make the most of your available space. Leave some room for paths and perhaps a bench, then fill the rest of the space with whatever plants you find pleasing.

* Use native and "found" materials for trellises and walkways. An old metal gate, for instance, will probably fit your garden better than something new from the garden center.

* Don't be afraid to plant combinations that don't fit the rules of attractive garden borders. Cottage gardens should be an expression of your individuality!

MEDIEVAL HERB GARDEN

Seek out this serene garden for quiet and contemplation, pick roses and lavender for your knight errant, or relax to the soothing hum of bees in the flowers. Or, like your medieval forebears, harvest leaves and flowers to cure what ails you.

A Fragrant Retreat

You may be surprised to learn that backyard herb gardens are a fairly recent gardening trend, but it's true! In bygone days, gardeners traditionally grew their herbs in cottage or kitchen gardens, not in gardens of herbs alone. Many herbs, especially medicinal ones, were also gathered from the wild. The monastery gardens of the medieval period were an exception to this rule. These monasteries did have medicinal herb gardens, or "physic" gardens, that supplied the monks with the herbs they needed to treat the sick and infirm.

A ninth-century garden plan designed for the Benedictine monastery at St. Gall, Switzerland, includes a physic garden. The monastery gardens, which were adapted from the layout of ancient Roman villa gardens, are a simple design of 16 raised beds that we can readily adapt for our heirloom gardens.

Recreating medieval garden design is not really that much of a stretch for heirloom country gardeners. The first European settlers in North America were still basically following medieval gardening techniques, although their gardens were generally less formal than the very structured gardens of the monastery.

About This Garden

Each bed in the St. Gall design contained a single medicinal plant, to reduce the chances of harvesting the wrong plant for a medicinal cure. But since we are not distilling and preparing all of our own medicinal preparations, we can be more flexible about growing different plants together. We can also omit some of the medicinal herbs and include culinary herbs and beautiful flowers, as well.

The great advantage of this layout is the network of pathways, which allows easy access

Look for garden additions, like this rustic container, at flea markets and auctions.

to all sides of the beds when it is time for maintenance and harvesting. In the original design, the monks edged the beds with boards or low fences of woven willow branches. These edgings are still practical today for holding the soil in place and preventing the herbs from sprawling into the pathways. But if you'd prefer not to have edgings, plain, soil-sided raised beds will work fine, too.

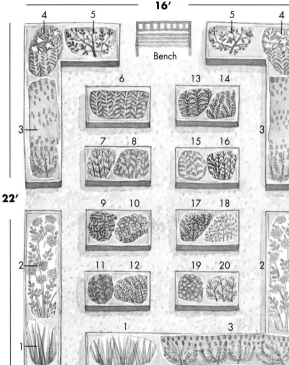

Plant List for a Medieval Herb Garden

1. Flag iris
2. Angelica
3. Lavender
4. Madonna lily
5. Apothecary's rose
6. Mints
7. Dill
8. Borage
9. Parsley
10. German chamomile
11. Basil
12. Summer savory
13. Bee balm
14. Tansy
15. Sage
16. Rosemary
17. Thymes
18. Chervil
19. Nasturtium
20. Fennel

— See page 28 —

Give this planting a spot with full sun and well-drained soil. Don't have room for the whole garden? It's easy to modify this plan to fit just about any size site—split it in half in either direction, or shorten the outer borders and remove a row of beds. For a larger site, add more inner beds and lengthen the outer borders—it's that easy!

Enjoying Your Medieval Herb Garden

In medieval times, healers used a wide range of plants in their work, including plants we now consider to be mainly ornamental, such as flag irises, Madonna lilies, and roses. You can still grow these plants in an herb garden for their historic interest, since they are so beautiful. (Note that the bench in this garden is placed close to the roses and lilies, so you'll have a comfortable spot to rest and enjoy their fragrance.) You'll certainly have plenty of herbs to harvest and enjoy in this garden! Pick some bee balm or mint to brew a cup of herbal tea, or liven up your meals with the flavor and aroma of basil, dill, fennel, rosemary, sage, and other culinary herbs. Borage and nasturtium leaves and flowers are great for garnishing salads. And if you enjoy crafts, you could harvest and dry rose petals, mint leaves, tansy flowers, and lavender shoots and flowers to create attractive, aromatic potpourris.

Don't hesitate to harvest your herbs—regular picking will encourage plants to produce bushier growth. If you want your annual herbs to self-sow (and most of them will), allow a few flowers on each plant to mature and drop seed. If the resulting seedlings are too close together, thin them out to the recommended spacing. If they come up in the wrong place (such as in the path or in another bed), transplant them to the desired spot while they are still small. Divide clumps of perennial herbs if the beds look crowded, or if they start to spread out of bounds. In many parts of the country, rosemary is not winter-hardy outdoors. Unless you live in a frost-free zone (Zone 8 or warmer), you'll want to dig up and pot the clump each fall and grow it indoors for the winter. (Growing your rosemary as a container plant year-round makes moving it indoors easier.) If space is limited, you could take cuttings in summer and overwinter them indoors for planting out after the last spring frost.

The Cloisters, a branch of the Metropolitan Museum of Art, features a medieval herb garden.

Number	Plant Name	Quantity	Notes
1	Flag iris (*Iris pseudacorus*)	6 plants	Space plants 18 inches apart. This dependable perennial likes boggy soil, but also adjusts to average garden soil.
2	Angelica (*Angelica archangelica*)	6 plants	Space plants 3 feet apart. Remove spent flower heads to help plants live longer, or let them self-sow; seedlings will replace the parent plants.
3	Lavender (*Lavandula angustifolia*)	1 seed pack or 20 plants	Thin seedlings or space plants 15 to 18 inches apart. 'Lady' is a selection that blooms the first year from seed.
4	Madonna lily (*Lilium candidum*)	8 bulbs	Plant bulbs 1 inch deep and 12 to 24 inches apart. The pure white, fragrant flowers of Madonna lilies light up the early-summer garden. For ornamental use only.
5	Apothecary's rose (*Rosa gallica* var. *officinalis*)	2 plants	Apothecary's rose blooms once a year in early summer, with fragrant, 3- to 4-inch-wide pink flowers. These shrubby plants tend to spread by suckers.
6	Mints (*Mentha* spp.)	3 plants	Space plants 12 to 15 inches apart. Mints come in a variety of heights and flavors; choose a selection of your favorites.
7	Dill (*Anethum graveolens*)	1 seed pack	Thin seedlings 10 to 12 inches apart. Dill flowers attract a wide range of beneficial insects, and they make wonderful fillers in flower arrangements.
8	Borage (*Borago officinalis*)	1 seed pack	Thin seedlings 12 inches apart. Sow seed outdoors as soon as the danger of frost is past. Borage will often self-sow.
9	Parsley (*Petroselinum crispum*)	1 seed pack or 4 plants	Thin seedlings or space plants 6 to 12 inches apart. Choose curly parsley for its crimped foliage or flat-leaved Italian parsley for its flavor.
10	German chamomile (*Matricaria recutita*)	1 seed pack	Thin seedlings 6 inches apart. This annual form of chamomile produces daisylike blooms on bushy clumps to 2 feet tall. Sow seed outdoors in spring.
11	Basil (*Ocimum basilicum*)	1 seed pack or 4 plants	Thin seedlings or space plants 12 inches apart. Basil comes in both green- and purple-leaved forms, as well as a variety of flavors, including lemon and cinnamon.
12	Summer savory (*Satureja hortensis*)	1 seed pack	Thin seedlings 6 inches apart. Sow this easy-to-grow herb in your garden after your last frost date. Plants often self-sow.
13	Bee balm (*Monarda didyma*)	1 plant	If powdery mildew is a problem in your area, look for mildew-resistant cultivars such as red 'Jacob Cline' or pink 'Marshall's Delight'.

Number	Plant Name	Quantity	Notes
14	Tansy (*Tanacetum vulgare*)	1 seed pack or 2 plants	Thin seedlings or space plants 18 inches apart. Cut plants back by half in midsummer to promote a flush of new growth.
15	Sage (*Salvia officinalis*)	2 plants	Space plants 12 to 18 inches apart. Choose the regular gray-green culinary sage, or try purple-leaved 'Purpurea' or yellow-and-green 'Icterina'.
16	Rosemary (*Rosmarinus officinalis*)	2 plants	Space plants 18 to 24 inches apart. Snip leaves at any time for cooking or enriching potpourri; regular harvesting will keep your plants full and bushy.
17	Thymes (*Thymus* spp.)	2 plants	Space plants 15 to 18 inches apart. Thymes come in a range of sizes, scents, and flower colors; choose your favorites.
18	Chervil (*Anthriscus cerefolium*)	1 seed pack	Thin seedlings 6 to 9 inches apart. For a steady harvest, sow seeds every two weeks until late spring and then again in fall. Chervil often self-sows.
19	Nasturtium (*Tropaeolum majus*)	1 seed pack	Thin seedlings 12 to 20 inches apart. Nasturtiums come in a range of colors and may have bushy or trailing stems. Sow seeds outdoors after danger of frost is past.
20	Fennel (*Foeniculum vulgare*)	1 seed pack	Thin seedlings 18 inches apart. Regular fennel has feathery green foliage; 'Purpureum' has chocolate-brown foliage.

Herb Garden Guidelines

Here are some pointers to help you make the most of your Medieval herb garden, or any other herb planting!

* When planning your planting, look for herbs that you can use, as well as admire. If you like to cook, concentrate on culinary herbs. If potpourri and herbal soaps are more interesting to you, grow aromatic herbs.

* To get the most flavor from culinary herbs, pinch off the flower buds regularly through the summer.

* Herbs that spread rapidly via their root systems—including bee balm, mint, and tansy—can quickly crowd out less-vigorous herbs. To keep these spreaders under control, give them their own bed or growing area.

BOUNTIFUL KITCHEN GARDEN

Try companion planting, heirloom style, when you mix herbs among your vegetables in a kitchen garden. As our ancestors knew, the herbs will repel or confuse insect pests. And you can harvest your seasonings as you harvest your supper!

A Historic Harvest

Kitchen gardens are probably the oldest type of garden. They used to be relegated to the back of the yard and hidden from view, grown in truck-patch fashion with long, straight rows. But kitchen gardens are now recognized as attractive and productive plantings. The forms, colors, and textures of vegetable plants can be as attractive as an ornamental border— plus, they add taste and appeal to mealtimes! Kitchen gardens are certainly a natural choice for an old-time country gardener interested in heirloom varieties. The traditional vegetable garden of raised beds can be found in many cultures and time periods, and it lends itself to a garden of any scale.

Perhaps the most well-known traditional kitchen gardens are the French "potagers." Two of the most magnificent and formal French kitchen gardens are the Chateau de Villandry in the Loire Valley and the Potager du Roi at Versailles. The Potager du Roi, the royal fruit and vegetable garden begun in 1677 for King Louis XIV, is 20 acres in size and contains 29 separate walled enclosures. Villandry was restored by Joachim and Ann Carvallo in the early twentieth century and is an inspired reconstruction of a formal sixteenth-century garden done in vegetables. Individual garden beds are edged in low-cut boxwood and surrounded by white gravel paths that form the geometric patterns in this 2½-acre garden. Two famous American kitchen gardens are at George Washington's Mount Vernon and Thomas Jefferson's Monticello, which are both located in Virginia. (These gardens are open to the public. See "Historical Gardens" on page 226 for contact information.)

LEFT: *Kitchen gardens can be both bountiful and beautiful, with the colors and textures of vegetable plants as attractive as any ornamental border.*

BELOW: *Include vertical accents such as these bean teepees for visual interest.*

About This Garden

Of course, kitchen gardens don't have to be the size of Versailles or Mount Vernon! Many of the same ideas can be used at any scale. The size of your kitchen garden will depend on how much time you can reasonably devote to gardening and how much produce you want to grow. The garden featured here will yield enough fresh produce to supplement an average family's meals throughout the growing season. For a single gardener, there would be enough harvest to put some by for winter or to share with friends.

The kitchen garden featured here has a simple pattern of uniformly shaped beds in the fashion of a Pennsylvania German kitchen garden. The beds are about 5 feet square, so you can reach the middle from all sides for planting, weeding, and harvesting, all without having to step onto the loosened soil. The circular bed in the center of the plan provides an ideal spot for a few culinary herbs, while also providing a decorative accent to the garden.

This simple layout is easy to tuck into just about any sunny spot with well-drained soil. Want to expand your planting? Once you have this basic kitchen garden installed, you could add perimeter beds or borders around the four square beds. The perimeter planting could include small fruits, such as currants, as well as herbs and flowers.

Enjoying Your Kitchen Garden

In the plan I've suggested here, the variety of crops will give you something to harvest from late spring through frost. To get even greater harvests from the available space, you can use a trick called succession planting. On the teepee trellis, for instance, you can plant a crop

of peas, then pull out the finished vines and plant a crop of pole beans for a later summer harvest. Succession planting also works well with crops that mature quickly, such as lettuce and radishes. Rather than planting all the seeds at once, sow a small patch in early to mid-spring, then another two weeks later, and so on. That way, you'll always have a patch ready for harvest at the peak of flavor, rather than being overwhelmed by an abundance of lettuce or radishes all at once.

Most of the plants in this plan are annual crops, so you'll need to replant them every year. To keep the soil healthy, rotate the crops to a new bed each year. (With this four-bed layout, rotation is as simple as moving the crops as a group a quarter-turn every year.) The rosemary in the center isn't winter-hardy in cold climates, so you'll need to either bring it indoors for the winter or buy a new plant each year. To overwinter it, take cuttings in summer and keep those small plants on a sunny windowsill for the winter. Or, if you have the room, dig and pot up the whole plant. (Keeping your rosemary in a portable pot year-round makes bringing it indoors for winter a snap!)

Consider keeping a few chickens along with your kitchen garden. Their appetite for insects will help control bugs in your garden—and you'll have fresh eggs, to boot.

PLANT LIST FOR A KITCHEN GARDEN

1. Salsify
2. 'Early Yellow Globe' onion
3. 'Oxheart' carrot
4. 'Mammoth Melting Sugar' peas
5. 'Genuine Cornfield' pole bean
6. 'Green Deer Tongue', 'Lolla Rossa', and 'Oakleaf' lettuces
7. 'French Breakfast' radish
8. Corn salad
9. 'Norfolk' spinach
10. Basil
11. 'Amish Paste' and 'Pruden's Purple' tomatoes
12. 'Sweet Banana' pepper
13. Thyme
14. Rosemary
15. Parsley

— SEE PAGE 34 —

A SAMPLER OF HEIRLOOM GARDEN DESIGNS

Number	Plant Name	Quantity	Notes
1	Salsify	1 seed pack	Thin seedlings 2 to 4 inches apart. Sow seed outdoors in spring four to six weeks before your last frost date. This root vegetable has a unique flavor that has been compared to oysters.
2	'Early Yellow Globe' onion	1 seed pack or ½ lb. onion sets	Thin seedlings or space sets 4 inches apart. Direct-sow seed of this cooking and storage onion if your soil temperatures are around 40°F in March; otherwise, start seed indoors in February or March.
3	'Oxheart' carrot	2 seed packs	Thin seedlings 3 to 4 inches apart. This heirloom produces broad, heart-shaped roots. Sow seed outdoors starting three weeks before your last frost date. To extend your harvest, plant additional rows every two to three weeks.
4	'Mammoth Melting Sugar' peas	1 seed pack	Thin seedlings 1 inch apart. This wilt-resistant variety has edible pods. Direct-sow seed four to six weeks before the your last frost date, when the soil is around 40°F.
5	'Genuine Cornfield' pole bean	1 seed pack	Thin seedlings 4 to 6 inches apart. Direct-sow seeds around your pea vines one to two weeks after the last spring frost. Pick pods before they fill out for snap beans, or harvest when dry.
6	'Green Deer Tongue', 'Lolla Rossa', and 'Oakleaf' lettuces	1 seed pack per variety	Thin seedlings 6 to 9 inches apart. Sow seed directly into the garden two to four weeks before your last frost date. These three varieties will provide an ample supply of tasty green and red looseleaf lettuce for a long salad season.
7	'French Breakfast' radish	1 seed pack	Thin seedlings 2 inches apart. Make small sowings every other week through spring to spread out your harvest. This mildly pungent, scarlet-and-white radish grows well from either spring or fall plantings.
8	Corn salad	1 seed pack	Thin seedlings 4 inches apart. A very hardy green that forms small rosettes of spoon-shaped leaves. Direct-sow in very early spring and in late summer through fall.
9	'Norfolk' spinach	1 seed pack	Thin seedlings 6 inches apart. 'Norfolk' is a very hardy variety with wrinkled leaves. Direct-sow seed starting in early spring, then every two weeks until early summer.
10	Basil	1 seed pack	Thin seedlings 12 inches apart. Direct-sow seed after all danger of frost is past. Pinch off the tops of the plants once they are established, to encourage branching.

Number	Plant Name	Quantity	Notes
11	'Amish Paste' and 'Pruden's Purple' tomatoes	2 plants of each variety	Set plants 2 feet apart, and provide sturdy support stakes. These two tasty heirlooms provide ample fruits for fresh eating and preserving; you could also substitute your personal favorites.
12	'Sweet Banana' pepper	3 plants	Set plants 18 inches apart after your last frost date. This productive heirloom yields pointed fruits that turn from green to yellow to crimson red as they ripen.
13	Thyme	3 plants	Space plants 8 to 12 inches apart. Thymes come in a range of sizes, scents, and flower colors; choose your favorites.
14	Rosemary	1 plant	Snip leaves at any time for cooking; regular harvesting will keep your plant full and bushy.
15	Parsley	1 seed pack or 3 plants	Thin seedlings or space plants 6 to 12 inches apart. Choose curly parsley for its crimped foliage or flat-leaved Italian parsley for its flavor.

Kitchen Garden Tips

Kitchen gardens may be practical as well as productive, but that doesn't mean they can't be pretty and fun, too! Here are some things to keep in mind to get the most enjoyment from your kitchen garden.

* Think of color and texture when you choose your crops. Heirloom vegetable varieties such as 'Rouge d'Hiver' lettuce, 'Scarlet Runner' bean, and 'Corno di Toro' pepper are good color accents, while vegetables like carrots and broccoli add different textures and forms to the garden.

Remember that creative plant combinations can be as much a part of a kitchen garden as they are a beautiful cottage garden.

* Vertical accents, such as pea and bean trellises, will also add interest to the garden. If you plant a large kitchen garden, you may want to train grapes or fruit trees on archways in the garden.

* Experiment with saving seeds from some of your heirlooms for next year's garden and for unique gifts for your gardening friends!

OLD-FASHIONED PARLOR GARDEN

If you want a front-yard garden that really struts its stuff, try a Victorian parlor garden. It's packed with bloom from spring to frost.

Highlight a nineteenth-century parlor garden with a picket fence and rose arbor for old-fashioned charm.

A Colorful Showplace

If you have a colonial- or Victorian-style house, a parlor garden can be a pretty complement to your home. Old-fashioned parlor gardens, traditionally the domain of women gardeners, were adjacent to the house, and unlike earlier, more utilitarian, gardens, they featured ornamentals and herbs. Garden historians are not certain whether parlor gardens existed in the early eighteenth century, but we know they were part of late-eighteenth-century gardening and remained a popular garden style in the nineteenth century, as well. Enclosed to keep wandering livestock from eating shrubs and prized flowers, parlor gardens were a cozy, pleasant place to walk or relax with visitors. The interior plantings were an informal mix of whatever the owner liked and was able to obtain for her garden,

Victorians prized ferns and lush greenery, such as shrubs, which are ideal for a relaxing shady nook in the garden.

including spring bulbs, climbing roses, annuals, and perennials. In the nineteenth century, arbors with vining plants and flowering shrubs became part of parlor gardens.

As the nineteenth century progressed, garden trends such as carpet bedding, water gardens, rock gardens, and tropical plants each took their turn. Parlor gardens hung on, though, as "grandmother's gardens," where gardeners grew collections of "old-fashioned" plants such as hollyhocks, poppies, pansies, and sunflowers. In an 1890s periodical, Victorian garden writer Margaret Sangster recommended that "I am taking for granted…that you have at least a little patch of ground before your door, which you may plant with hardy flowers, or in which from year to year you may have a brave show of the bright little flowers which come in spring, or the beautiful and brilliant things which delight our eyes in the fall." Bring the beauty and pleasure of these plants to your door by adding a parlor planting to your heirloom country garden!

About This Garden

This simple plan includes a wealth of bulbs, annuals, perennials, and flowering shrubs to provide color from early spring well into fall. With the broad paths, there's plenty of room for you to stroll through the bounty of blooms, and the bench provides a welcome resting spot. Besides including a variety of plants for a long season of bloom, I've also tucked in a number of flowers and herbs with fragrant blooms and foliage to add an extra element of enjoyment. All of these plants will do fine in a sunny site with well-drained soil.

If you don't have enough room to plant this whole plan, adjust the length and width of the beds and borders as needed, or plant just half of the garden. Don't skimp on the paths too much, though—parlor gardens are meant to be walked through, not viewed from a

distance, and narrow paths can be uncomfortable to navigate. In a larger site, of course, it's a simple matter to expand the width or length of the plantings.

Enjoying Your Parlor Garden

A parlor garden is primarily for the indulgence of your senses: It offers bright colors to look at, sweet scents to sniff, and aromatic foliage to rub. It's a show-off garden, a place where you can bring guests and share the best your garden has to offer with them. If you have the room, you might want to plan for a bench or even a picnic area in your garden, where you can serve a Victorian high tea when your garden is in full bloom—the ultimate treat! With such a wealth of blooms to choose from, don't hesitate to snip some for indoor enjoyment, as well.

Many of the annual flowers and herbs planted in this garden will self-sow, meaning that they'll return year after year from just one planting. If they pop up in the wrong spot (in a path, for example), simply weed them out or transplant them to the desired location while they are still small and manageable. Most of the perennials will only need division every three to five years, but gooseneck loosestrife can spread quickly, so divide it as often as is needed to keep it inbounds. To keep your bridal wreath spireas looking their best, prune out one-third of the oldest branches to a few inches above the ground after bloom time.

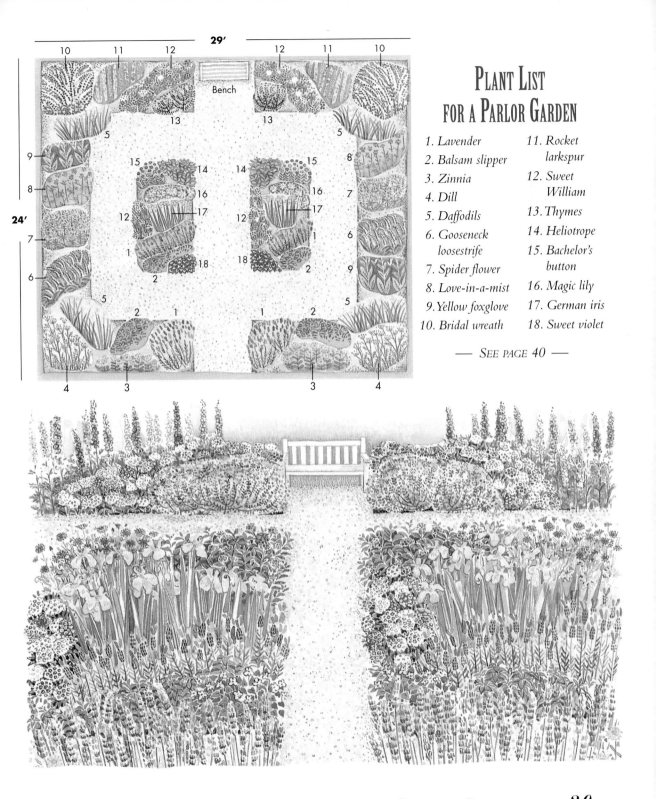

29'

10   11   12   12   11   10

Bench

13   13

5   5

9   8

15   14   14   15

8   7

16   16

12   12

17   17

7   6

1   1

6   18   18   9

2   2

5   15   15   5

2   2
2   1   1   2

4   3   3   4

24'

PLANT LIST FOR A PARLOR GARDEN

1. *Lavender*
2. *Balsam slipper*
3. *Zinnia*
4. *Dill*
5. *Daffodils*
6. *Gooseneck loosestrife*
7. *Spider flower*
8. *Love-in-a-mist*
9. *Yellow foxglove*
10. *Bridal wreath*
11. *Rocket larkspur*
12. *Sweet William*
13. *Thymes*
14. *Heliotrope*
15. *Bachelor's button*
16. *Magic lily*
17. *German iris*
18. *Sweet violet*

— SEE PAGE 40 —

Number	Plant Name	Quantity	Notes
1	Lavender (*Lavandula angustifolia*)	8 plants	Space plants 6 to 12 inches apart. Trim plants back by one-third in mid- to late spring to promote bushy growth.
2	Balsam slipper (*Impatiens balsamina*)	1 seed pack	Thin seedlings 10 to 12 inches apart. Direct-sow seed when danger of frost is past. This easy-care heirloom often self-sows.
3	Zinnia (*Zinnia elegans*)	1 seed pack	Thin seedlings 12 to 24 inches apart (use smaller spacing for dwarf varieties, larger spacing for full-size varieties). Direct-sow after last frost.
4	Dill (*Anethum graveolens*)	1 seed pack	Thin seedlings 10 to 12 inches apart. Direct-sow in spring. Dill flowers look great in bouquets.
5	Daffodils (*Narcissus* spp.)	24 bulbs	Plant bulbs 6 inches apart. Trim off the developing seedheads after bloom, but let the foliage yellow and die back before cutting it off.
6	Gooseneck loosestrife (*Lysimachia clethroides*)	6 plants	Space plants 15 to 20 inches apart. This white-flowered, summer-blooming perennial is beautiful and tough. Plants spread quickly, so divide every year or two for control.
7	Spider flower (*Cleome hasslerana*)	1 seed pack	Thin seedlings 18 to 24 inches apart. Direct-sow seeds in mid- to late spring. Spider flower's pink or white blooms attract butterflies and moths to the garden. Plants often self-sow.
8	Love-in-a-mist (*Nigella damascena*)	2 seed packs	Thin seedlings 18 to 24 inches apart. Direct-sow every three to four weeks from early spring to summer for continued bloom. This fast-growing annual is great for filling gaps left by dormant spring bulbs.
9	Yellow foxglove (*Digitalis grandiflora*)	6 plants	Space plants 18 to 24 inches apart. Remove spent blossoms, but leave a few stalks to set seed if you want plants to self-sow.
10	Bridal wreath spirea (*Spiraea prunifolia*)	2 plants	This upright, rounded shrub offers a profusion of pure white, double flowers in spring. It also has a soft orange-red fall color.
11	Rocket larkspur (*Consolida orientalis*)	1 seed pack	Thin seedlings 18 to 24 inches apart. In the North, sow seed four weeks before the last spring frost; in the South, sow in fall (seeds need cool temperatures to germinate).
12	Sweet William (*Dianthus barbatus*)	1 seed pack	Thin seedlings 9 inches apart. Direct-sow seed of this biennial from April to July for blooms the following year. Plants will often self-sow.

Number	Plant Name	Quantity	Notes
13	Thymes (*Thymus* spp.)	4 plants	Space plants 8 to 12 inches apart. Thymes come in a range of sizes, scents, and flower colors; choose your favorites.
14	Heliotrope (*Heliotropium arborescens*)	6 plants	Space plants 12 to 24 inches apart. While usually grown as an annual, heliotrope is actually a tender perennial, so take cuttings or bring it indoors for the winter.
15	Bachelor's button (*Centaurea cyanus*)	2 seed packs	Thin seedlings 8 to 12 inches apart. For earliest bloom, sow seed of this annual outdoors in fall; otherwise, sow in early spring.
16	Magic lily (*Lycoris squamigera*)	6 bulbs	Plant bulbs 12 to 18 inches apart in summer. Magic lily produces its leaves in spring and then dies back; the lavender-pink flowers bloom in late summer.
17	German iris (*Iris germanica*)	6 plants	Space plants 12 to 18 inches apart. Plant iris rhizomes just below the soil surface in spring or fall.
18	Sweet violet (*Viola odorata*)	8 plants	Space plants 6 to 8 inches apart. The spring blooms of this heirloom favorite are deliciously fragrant.

Parlor Garden Pointers

Here are some tips to help you make the most of your parlor garden:

* Plan for "people-friendly" paths, wide enough for two people to walk comfortably side by side. The main path should be 5 to 6 feet wide; the side paths should be no less than 4 feet wide. Gravel or oyster shell paths were preferred over grass in the old days because they didn't stain women's long skirts!

* Try to plan for a combination of flowering shrubs, bulbs, perennials, biennials, and annuals, so you'll always have something in bloom—and an excuse to go out to the garden!

* For more inspiration and ideas, read some of the garden writers of bygone eras, such as Gertrude Jekyll, Helen Rutherford Ely, Bernard McMahon, and Louise Beebe Wilder. (See "Recommended Reading" on page 232.)

OLD-FASHIONED FRUIT GARDEN

If you love the flavor of fresh-picked fruits and berries but don't have time or space for an orchard, try this charming little garden. Enjoy a delightful grape arbor, your own apple trees, and a host of berries at their best.

A Family-Size Fruit Plot

Fruit crops have always been an important part of old-time country gardens. European kitchen gardens always included fruit. Early-American country dwellers maintained large orchards, and even early city planners included fruit gardens in small lot designs. Andrew Jackson Downing, author of *Victorian Cottage Residences*, recommended a "small orchard" for a residence on a 4-acre lot. He wrote "...a select collection of fruit is planted in the small orchard. This little orchard...if planted with the selection of fruit trees, seventy four in number...will furnish a moderate supply to the family, for a greater part of the year."

Most of us are not up to that Victorian standard—Mr. Downing probably assumed some paid gardening assistance—and many of us today's gardeners have much less land to work with. Still, a small-scale fruit garden is an attractive addition to any backyard.

About This Garden

Given a spot with full sun and well-drained soil, the garden design shown here will provide a generous amount of fruit that you can harvest and enjoy at the peak of its flavor. The apple and pear trees in this design are freestanding semidwarf trees. If you have never trained and pruned fruit trees, semidwarf apples are an easy and forgiving place to start. Standard full-size trees are handsome, but they take more room and agility to prune and harvest. Sometimes the romance of a beautiful, 30-foot tree fades when one is perched clumsily across a branch trying to reach high enough to prune the top!

Tree fruits require time and effort, but the harvest is well worth it!

Of course, you can substitute different varieties for the ones I've suggested—just make sure the two apple varieties that you choose will effectively cross-pollinate, so you end up with fruit. You could also choose full-dwarf trees instead and espalier them if you want to fit more trees into the same amount of space. Remember that espaliered trees require support: You'll need to attach them to a fence, trellis them along wires, or provide a sturdy support post for each one.

Enjoying Your Fruit Garden

While the primary function of this garden is practical, there's no reason your fruit garden shouldn't be pleasant, as well! The grass paths feel soft and cool underfoot, and the bench provides a spot for you to sit and enjoy some of your just-picked harvest with a friend. Want to add some flowers to the scenery? English gardeners have a pretty tradition of planting drifts of daffodils and bluebells in their orchards. These bulbs will naturalize well as long as you let the foliage turn brown and die back before mowing.

Regular pruning, as described in the individual plant entries in "Flavorful Old-Time Fruits and Berries," starting on page 149, will keep your fruiting plants healthy and productive. I recommend weeding the soil around the base of the trees and shrubs to reduce competition from weeds for moisture and nutrients. Mulch is beneficial, but be sure to remove it in fall so that rodents will not be encouraged to overwinter there and feed on tree roots and bark. And be sure to read "Favorite Fruits from Monticello" on page 154 for some very historic advice on fruit gardens.

PLANTS FOR AN OLD-FASHIONED FRUIT GARDEN

Number	Plant Name	Quantity	Notes
1	'Concord' grape	2 plants	Space plants 8 feet apart. 'Concord' is a classic heirloom variety, but you can substitute a variety appropriate for your region.
2	'Poorman' gooseberry	4 plants	Space plants 6 feet apart. This mildew-resistant variety is considered one of the finest American gooseberries.
3	'Blakemore' strawberry	12 plants	Provide 1 square foot of space for each plant. Try this proven heirloom variety or substitute your favorite.
4	'Red Lake' currant	4 plants	Space plants 6 feet apart. 'Red Lake' is a red currant variety from the 1930s. Mulch with organic matter to keep roots cool.
5	'Latham' red raspberry	4 plants	Space plants 4 feet apart. This vigorous, flavorful heirloom has long been a favorite.
6	Elderberry	2 plants	Space plants 5 feet apart. Plant two different varieties or two seed-grown plants to produce better yields.
7	'Golden Pearmain' and 'Fallawater' apples	1 tree of each variety	Space trees 20 feet apart. These are two varieties I enjoy, but you can substitute your favorites; just make sure they are compatible pollinators.

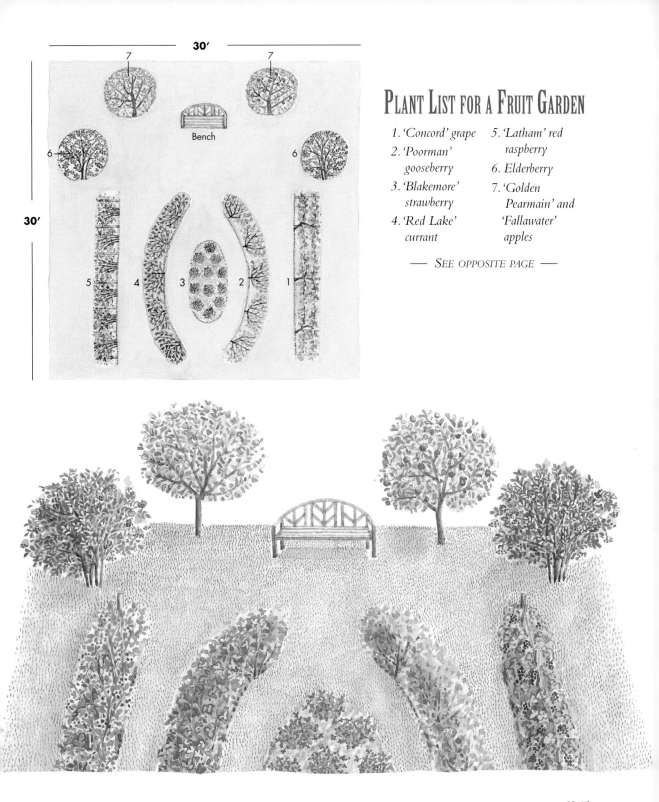

30'

30'

Bench

7

7

6

6

5   4   3   2   1

Plant List for a Fruit Garden

1. 'Concord' grape
2. 'Poorman' gooseberry
3. 'Blakemore' strawberry
4. 'Red Lake' currant

5. 'Latham' red raspberry
6. Elderberry
7. 'Golden Pearmain' and 'Fallawater' apples

— *See opposite page* —

Part Two

YESTERDAY'S PLANTS
for
TODAY'S GARDENS

In this section, you'll learn about the wide range of plants that you can use to create your own heirloom country garden. The chapters on vegetables, flowers, herbs, and fruits have directories of many heirloom varieties to choose from. With so many wonderful plants available, you'll have a hard time deciding what to grow!

Heirloom Vegetables:
A Gardener's Guide

The more I learn about heirloom vegetables, the more they enrich my own gardening and cooking experiences. I'm not sure if it's the uniqueness of the varieties, the promise of a particularly flavorful vegetable that can't be purchased at the grocery store, or the wonderful stories behind each variety—but whatever it is, I'm hooked. I hope this chapter encourages you to search out heirloom vegetables for your own garden.

The most challenging part of growing heirloom vegetables is actually finding the seeds and plants to start with. In my quest to track down heirloom vegetables and the seed companies that carry them, I've found the *Garden Seed Inventory*, published by the Seed Savers Exchange (SSE), to be an invaluable resource. (See "Seed-Saving Organizations," starting on page 227, for SSE's address.) The *Inventory* contains an extensive listing of heirloom, open-pollinated vegetables with a brief description of each variety and the seed companies that carry it, plus a full listing of the seed companies' addresses.

Other sources of heirloom vegetables are mail-order plant and seed companies and other seed-saver organizations (see "Resources for Heirloom Country Gardens" on page 226). Some historical museums, such as Monticello, also carry interesting heirloom varieties.

OPPOSITE: *Growing heirloom vegetables will provide you with incredible diversity of colors and flavors.*

Selected Heirloom Vegetables

This directory will give you a taste of the heirloom vegetable varieties that are available. The varieties featured here are all available from mail-order seed catalogs. (See "Resources for Heirloom Country Gardens" on page 226 for a list of companies that feature heirloom varieties.) You may also be interested in searching out the rare heirloom varieties that are only available from various seed-saver organizations. (They're listed in the resources, too.) Bear in mind that planting-to-maturity dates are averages; they will vary with location and growing conditions.

BEANS

Phaseolus vulgaris
Fabaceae

ORIGIN

Beans are native to the Americas and were domesticated in Mexico around 5000 B.C. The nutritious trio of beans, corn, and squash were the primary foods of Native Americans for hundreds of years.

CLASSIFICATIONS

Gardeners divide beans into categories relating to how the crops grow or how they're used. *Pole beans* are varieties that have long vines and require support. *Bush beans* do not need any poles or trellising. *Snap beans* are eaten in the green-pod stage. Older varieties of snap beans were often *string beans,* which have a "string" where the two halves of the pod come together. *Wax beans* are yellow snap beans. *Shell beans* are picked in the green shell stage, when the pods are grown past the snap stage but before the bean seeds have begun to dry. Many heirloom beans are *dried beans,* which are left in the pod to dry and then harvested and saved for winter soups (an important quality if you were a settler trying to put enough food away for the winter). Some of the beans have good eating qualities in all stages: snap, shell, and dried.

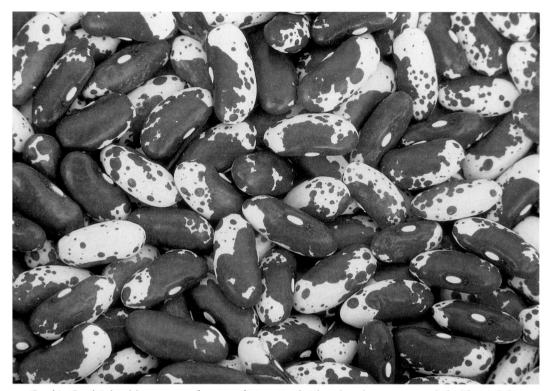

'Jacob's Cattle' dried beans are a favorite of New England cooks when preparing baked bean dishes.

GROWING BEANS

Beans prefer full sun and well-drained soil. Sow seeds directly in the garden one to two weeks after the last spring frost, and keep the soil evenly moist while the seeds germinate. You can extend your bean harvest by planting additional rows every two weeks until the middle of summer. Be sure to provide support for pole beans, and rotate crops to reduce the buildup of disease and insect problems. If you can keep out of the bean patch when the plants are wet, this will also help to lessen the incidence of disease.

SAVING SEED

Beans are a favorite with seed savers because they are relatively easy to grow as a seed-saving project. Beans are self-pollinating, and pollination usually occurs before the blossom opens. Occasional cross-pollination can occur, though, so if you are trying to perpetuate rare heirloom varieties, separate them by at least 100 feet. William Woys Weaver, author of *Heirloom Vegetable Gardening*, also plants flowers around his heirloom bean varieties to reduce the chance of cross-pollination by attracting insects to the ornamental blooms instead of the beans. After you've collected and threshed the mature bean seeds, you may want to freeze them for several days to destroy any pests, such as weevils, that are present in the seed.

Heirloom Selections

There are literally thousands of colorful and beautiful dried beans with great names and stories to go with them. Here are a few of these beans.

Dry or Snap Pole Beans

'BLUE COCO' (59 days from sowing to snap bean.) Introduced by the French in 1775, this early producing pole bean is good as a snap, shell, or dry bean. This heirloom got its name from the bluish purple, curved pods that are 5 to 6 inches long with cocoa-brown seeds. It is heat- and drought-tolerant.

'CHEROKEE TRAIL OF TEARS' (80 to 90 days from sowing to dry bean stage.) The Cherokee ancestors of Dr. John Wyche, a dentist in Hugo, Oklahoma, carried this bean over the Trail of Tears, the infamous winter death march that began in Georgia in October 1838 and ended March 26, 1839, in Indian Territory (now Oklahoma), leaving a trail of 4,000 Cherokee graves. The prolific, 8-inch plants produce green, 6-inch pods with a purple overlay. They are good for snap beans, and the small, shiny black seeds have fairly good flavor as dry beans.

'GENUINE CORNFIELD' (70 to 85 days from sowing to snap bean.) Believed to be an old Iroquois variety, this heirloom is the best pole bean for growing in a corn patch. To use it at the snap stage, pick the straight, 5- to 7-inch-long, medium green pods before the seeds fill out the pods. Most gardeners prefer this variety as a dry bean and harvest when the pods are already dry.

Dry or Snap Bush Beans

'BLACK VALENTINE' (50 days from sowing to snap bean.) Dating back to the 1850s and available since 1933 as a stringless variety, this productive bush bean is hardy in cold-weather conditions and resistant to bean mosaic. It's good as a snap bean and also as a dry bean.

'DRAGON LANGARIE' OR 'DRAGON'S TONGUE' (57 to 65 days from sowing to snap bean.) An heirloom Dutch wax bean, this bush bean has 6-inch-long, stringless yellow pods. For snap beans, pick when the pods develop thin purple stripes. For shell beans, wait until the stripes turn red, if you prefer. These beans are both productive and quite flavorful.

'JACOB'S CATTLE' (80 to 100 days from sowing to dry bean.) A very old and popular heirloom vegetable from New England, this is a good short-season dried bean. Its name is derived from the biblical account of Jacob and the spotted cattle, as the dark red speckles on the white seeds look like cattle markings.

Sweet-flavored 'Red Drumhead' cabbage is a dramatic purplish red.

CABBAGES

Brassica oleracea Capitata Group
Brassicaceae

ORIGIN

Cabbage is a very old vegetable that was probably developed from a wild perennial cabbage that grew along the coastal regions of Northwestern Europe. Described in Greek and Roman literature, cabbage and its relatives (such as kale and cauliflower) have been important food staples for centuries.

The early European settlers always grew this easy-to-store, versatile vegetable in their kitchen gardens.

CLASSIFICATIONS

Cabbage varieties are divided into four different groups by their shape and leaf texture. Cabbages with pointy heads are called *Wakefield* cabbages, while cabbages shaped like round balls are included in the *Copenhagen* group. There are also the *drumhead* cabbages, with broad, flat heads, and the *savoy* cabbages, which have puckered leaves.

GROWING CABBAGES

This cool-weather crop requires rich, evenly moist soil and full sun to produce nice heads. Plant early-maturing varieties for spring use and later-maturing varieties for a fall harvest. Start seed inside around eight weeks before your last frost date and transplant into the garden four to six weeks later, or direct-sow seed of fall cabbage in the garden in early summer. Cabbage worms and cabbage loopers can be damaging insect pests. Hand-pick the larvae off the plants and destroy or spray with *Bacillus thuringiensis* (BT), a naturally occurring bacterium that will control caterpillars without harming plants or people.

SAVING SEED

Saving cabbage seed is a challenge. Cabbage is cross-pollinated by insects and will cross with any other *Brassica oleracea,* such as broccoli, brussels sprouts, kale, kohlrabi, or cauliflower. Save seeds from only one of these at a time (don't let the others flower), or separate these brassicas by at least 200 feet (a mile is preferred).

Also, cabbages are biennial, so you will need to store them indoors through the winter if you live where temperatures drop below 28°F. Dig the plants up carefully in the fall and trim the root systems to around 12 inches long. Place the roots in damp sand and wrap the heads in newspaper. Store in a cold root cellar or basement at 32° to 40°F and 80 to 90 percent humidity. Replant outdoors in spring, and cut a shallow X across the top of the cabbage head to allow the emerging seed stalk to push up through the leaves.

HEIRLOOM SELECTIONS

Cabbage was a mainstay in the old days because it's relatively easy to grow and store over winter—plus, it's nutritious!

'CHIEFTAIN SAVOY' (80 to 105 days from transplanting to harvest.) Chosen as an All-American Selection in 1938, this pretty cabbage has a flattened, round head that is wrapped with finely curled blue-green leaves. Weighing around 6 to 8 pounds, it can withstand light fall frosts.

'JERSEY WAKEFIELD' (60 to 75 days from transplanting to harvest.) Still a standard early variety today, this cabbage was introduced around 1840. It weighs 2 to 4 pounds and has a very solid, conical head. This variety is resistant to cabbage yellows, a root disease.

'LATE FLAT DUTCH' (100 to 110 days from transplanting to harvest.) Introduced by early European settlers, this heirloom cabbage has a large, firm, flattened head and is one of the best late-fall and winter cabbages available.

'RED DRUMHEAD' (74 to 90 days from transplanting to harvest.) This beautiful, deep purplish red cabbage was introduced around 1860 and forms a large, flat head. It is an excellent winter-keeper and has a delicious sweet flavor.

The oldest cultivated carrots were purple, red, and white. Orange carrots weren't developed until the 1600s.

CARROTS

Daucus carota var. *sativus*
Apiaceae

ORIGIN

Carrots were mentioned in Roman literature, but they weren't often found in European kitchens until the 1600s. By 1620, Dutch vegetable breeders had developed the 'Long Orange' carrot, which was a good winter-keeper, and 'Horn', a sweet, flavorful variety. Carrots were important vegetables in early New England and Pennsylvania gardens.

CLASSIFICATIONS

Carrots are loosely grouped into long and slender or round and short varieties. All are botanically the same.

GROWING CARROTS

Carrots need deep, loose, well-aerated soil and full sun. Direct-sow seeds in the garden in spring, starting three weeks before your last frost date. To extend your harvest, plant additional rows every two to three weeks, up to two months before the average date of your first fall frost. Remember to thin your carrot seedlings to 1 inch apart when the foliage is 2 inches tall. Two weeks later, thin to 3 to 4 inches apart. I sometimes put off this chore and wind up with beautiful carrot foliage but cramped, tiny roots.

SAVING SEED

Saving carrot seed ranks as one of the more challenging projects for heirloom vegetable gardeners. Carrots are biennial and will flower the second season. Mulch your carrot bed heavily in late fall or, if winter is severe in your area, dig the carrots out before a killing frost, cut the foliage back to 1 inch, and store the trimmed roots in sand in a damp root cellar or an evenly cool but frost-free garage. Plant them out in spring. Carrots are pollinated by insects and will cross with one another and also with Queen-Anne's-lace, which is a wild carrot. Keep carrots separated by at least 200 feet (preferably 1,000 feet, for unique heirloom varieties), and mow down any Queen-Anne's-lace near your garden.

HEIRLOOM SELECTIONS

Carrots were popular in early-American gardens because they were relatively easy to store for winter meals, when other vegetables were scarce.

'BELGIUM WHITE' (60 to 75 days from sowing to harvest.) Rare and delicious, this white carrot is attractive in salads and also good in soups. It is difficult to locate from a commercial source, but is currently available from the Seed Savers Exchange.

'CHANTENAY RED CORE' (65 days from sowing to maturity.) Introduced to America from France in the late 1800s, this carrot grows successfully in heavier soils. The cone-shaped root grows about 5½ inches long and has a sweet flavor.

'DANVERS HALF LONG' (75 days from sowing to maturity.) Originating in 1871 from the Danvers, Massachusetts, area, this is a tapered variety that's about 6 inches long. Still commonly grown, it is widely adaptable and a good winter-keeper.

'EARLY SCARLET HORN' (55 to 68 days from sowing to maturity.) A 300-year-old heirloom from England, this is one of the earliest cultivated varieties still available. The short, stump-rooted, 2- to 6-inch baby carrots have excellent flavor.

'LONG ORANGE IMPROVED' (85 days from sowing to maturity.) This 1850 variety is an improved version of the seventeenth-century Dutch carrot 'Long Orange'. The roots grow best in loose soil, reaching 11 to 12 inches long.

'OXHEART' OR 'GUERANDE' (72 to 80 days from sowing to maturity.) Introduced in 1884, this unique heirloom has stubby, heart-shaped, 5- to 6-inch-long roots that weigh up to 1 pound each. It is a tender carrot with good flavor.

'PURPLE DRAGON' (75 to 80 days from sowing to harvest.) This unique carrot is the best of the rare purple carrots, since it does not have the bitter, wild-carrot taste that the others do. It is beautiful grated in salads or used in stir-fries.

ODDS AND ENDS

The earliest carrots were white, yellow, red, or violet. Orange varieties were first introduced by Dutch breeders in the 1620s. Today, white and violet carrots are quite rare, but are listed in the Seed Savers Exchange's annual yearbook.

For high yields, try 'Country Gentleman', a late-season white heirloom sweet corn with excellent flavor.

CORN

Zea mays
Poaceae

ORIGIN

Corn is descended from a wild grass—teosinte—from southern Mexico. By the time the Conquistadors arrived in the Americas, Native American farmers had already developed five classes of corn by selecting plants with different traits.

CLASSIFICATIONS

Corn comes in five major types: *flour, dent, flint, pop,* and *sweet*. Flour corn is mostly starchy when ripe. Dent corn (*Zea mays* var. *indenta*)—so called because each kernel has a dent in it—is mainly used as field corn for livestock. Also known as Indian corn, flint corn (*Z. mays* var. *indurata*) has very hard kernels. Still a favorite for snacking, popcorn (*Z. mays* var. *praecox*) is one of the earliest cultivated types of corn. Sweet corn (*Z. mays* var. *rugosa*) is the stuff we anxiously await in midsummer.

GROWING CORN

Corn needs full sun and rich, well-drained soil. Plant about two weeks after the last frost date in the spring, when your soil has warmed to 55° to 65°F. Plant open-pollinated heirloom corn varieties in blocks of five rows for good cross-pollination. Plant seeds 3 to 4 inches apart and 1 inch deep in a 4-inch-deep furrow. That way, you can mound soil around the stalks to help support them as they grow. Thin seedlings to leave 8 to 10 inches between plants. Corn is a heavy nitrogen feeder, so it's a good idea to rotate it with other vegetables in your garden every year. Harvest sweet corn when it reaches the milky stage (when milky liquid spurts from a kernel when it's pierced.) Harvest dent, flint, flour, and popcorn varieties when the green husks begin to turn tan.

SAVING SEED

Saving corn seed is a challenge even for advanced seed savers. Corn is wind-pollinated, and corn pollen can travel up to 1,000 feet. Most experts agree, however, that if you keep 200 feet between varieties, you'll have a minimum of crossing. Planting a tall crop such as sunflowers between varieties will help control unwanted crosses.

You will need to plant a minimum of 100 plants for healthy genetic diversity because corn is sensitive to genetic inbreeding. Choose 35 to 50 ears for seed saving. Mark the ears you want to save with brightly colored yarn so that helpful corn pickers will not harvest those ears for eating. Let the corn ripen on the plant about a month more than you would have for fresh eating. Peel the husks back and hang up the cobs in a well-ventilated building. (Make sure they are out of reach of mice.) You can shell the corn when both the cob and the kernels are hard and dry. Discard any kernels that are small or not completely formed.

HEIRLOOM SELECTIONS

Here's a brief overview of heirlooms that are worth growing as sweet corn.

'BLACK MEXICAN' OR 'BLACK AZTEC' (75 to 80 days from sowing to harvest as sweet corn.) Develops 6- to 8-inch ears on 6-foot-tall stalks. The kernels are white if you harvest the ears as a sweet corn but turn a beautiful blue-black if dried. 'Black Mexican' can be used as a flour corn and is reported to make a great cornbread. It was introduced in 1864 by James Gregory of Massachusetts.

'COUNTRY GENTLEMAN' (93 days from sowing to harvest as sweet corn.) White, 7- to 8-inch ears on 7- to 8-foot stalks. It is described as a "shoe-peg type" sweet corn because of its deep and narrow kernels arranged irregularly on the cob. It's good for fresh eating, and it's still grown commercially for freezing and canning. 'Country Gentleman' was introduced in 1891 by Peter Henderson of New York.

'GOLDEN BANTAM' (70 to 85 days from sowing to harvest as sweet corn.) A very popular yellow sweet corn with a classic corn taste, this variety produces 5- to 7-inch ears on 5- to 6-foot stalks. 'Golden Bantam' was introduced in 1902 by W. Atlee Burpee.

'STOWELL'S EVERGREEN' (92 days from sowing to harvest as sweet corn.) White, 7½- to 8-inch ears on 7- to 8-foot stalks. Developed in 1848 by Nathan Stowell in Burlington, New Jersey, this is a cross between a Northern Iroquois sweet corn and 'Menomony', a soft field corn. 'Stowell's Evergreen' holds its eating quality a long time in the garden.

'Boothby's Blonde', an unusual creamy white cucumber, is a good choice for northern gardeners.

CUCUMBERS

Cucumis sativus
Cucurbitaceae

ORIGIN

Cucumbers are believed to have originated in India more than 3,000 years ago and were popular with the Egyptians, Greeks, and Romans. The Romans spread cucumber-growing throughout Europe. Cucumbers came to the New World with Columbus and were adopted by Native Americans. Today, many of the heirloom varieties are commercial varieties from the 1800s. In the past several years, Seed Savers International has collected interesting Eastern European varieties and offered them in their catalog.

CLASSIFICATIONS

Home gardeners tend to prefer either fresh-slicing or pickling varieties. Most varieties are suitable for either purpose, however.

GROWING CUCUMBERS

Cucumbers like full sun, well-drained soil, and ample water during dry spells. They are a warm-season crop, so wait three to four weeks after the last frost to sow seed directly in the garden. Most varieties are disease-susceptible, so wait three years after growing cukes (or other squash-family plants) before you try planting cucumbers in that spot again.

SAVING SEED

Different varieties of cucumbers will cross with each other but not with other cucurbits, such as melons and squash. Separate varieties by at least 200 feet, or a half-mile or more for absolute seed purity for rare heirlooms. If you grow several varieties, try covering them with floating row cover and hand-pollinating the flowers. Let cucumbers ripen past the edible stage, until they turn orange, and use the fresh-processing method to save seed. (For more information, see "Wet Processing" on page 189).

HEIRLOOM SELECTIONS

Sure, it's easier to buy a jar of pickles at the grocery store, but you just haven't lived until you've experienced the satisfying crunch of a flavorful, home-canned dill pickle!

'BOOTHBY'S BLONDE' (63 days from sowing to maturity.) This is a short, oval, creamy colored cucumber that food historian and master gardener William Woys Weaver recommends picking at about 3 inches long. A productive cucumber for northern gardeners, this heirloom variety was preserved by the Boothby family from Maine for several generations.

'BOSTON PICKLING' (50 to 60 days from sowing to maturity.) A high-yielding, reliable cucumber for pickling, this variety was introduced before 1880 and is still widely available today. The 5- to 6-inch-long fruits are a smooth, bright green with black spines. The plant continues to bear if harvested regularly.

'EDMONSON' (70 days from sowing to maturity.) This cucumber produces whitish green, 4-inch fruits suitable for both pickling and slicing. Southern Exposure Seed Exchange considers this one of their hardiest cucumbers, with good resistance to disease, insects, and drought.

'STRAIGHT EIGHT' (52 to 75 days from sowing to maturity.) This is a productive, vigorous variety resistant to the mosaic virus that can attack cucumbers. The slender, dark green, 8- to 9-inch fruits are great for slicing.

'WHITE WONDER' (53 to 60 days from sowing to maturity.) Introduced in 1893, this variety's oval, 9-inch-long, ivory-white fruits have black spines and crisp, mild flesh that is good for slicing and pickling.

ODDS AND ENDS

English market gardeners in the 1800s went to great pains to produce straight cucumbers. According to the 1885 classic *The Vegetable Garden* by M. M. Vilmorin-Andrieux, these gardeners inserted young fruits into individual glass cylinders 1½ to 2 inches in diameter and 12 to 15 inches long because "one good and straight cucumber is worth nearly a dozen small and deformed ones."

Beautiful 'Rouge d'Hiver' lettuce is heat- and cold-tolerant, making it ideal for spring and fall plantings.

LETTUCES

Lactuca sativa
Asteraceae

ORIGIN

Cultivated lettuce is probably the offspring of a wild, inedible, prickly lettuce (*Lactuca serriola*) from the eastern Mediterranean area. Lettuce was popular with the Greeks and Romans and was used as a medicinal herb by medieval Europeans. Columbus probably brought lettuce to the New World. By the mid-1600s, American kitchen gardens always had lettuce.

CLASSIFICATIONS

Gardeners can grow a wonderful range of heirloom lettuces: *bibb* or *butterhead* lettuce, *cos* or *romaine* lettuce, *looseleaf* or *cutting* lettuce, and *crisphead* lettuce. Bibb or butterhead lettuce has green outer leaves and white or yellow hearts, while cos or romaine lettuce has crunchy, long leaves and cylindrical heads. Looseleaf lettuce, with its open, nonheading rosettes, is the easiest type to grow and tolerates a range of soil and weather conditions, while crispheads, like 'Iceberg', are the most difficult to grow because they need constant cool temperatures to form tight heads.

Growing Lettuce

Lettuce is an easy-to-grow spring crop that thrives in well-drained, moderately rich garden soil. Sow seed directly in the garden two to four weeks before your last frost date. Lettuce does best in moderate temperatures (60° to 65°F). Water during dry periods.

Saving Seed

Lettuce is generally self-pollinating and ranks as one of the easiest crops for seed saving. Some crossing may occur, though, so try to separate varieties by at least 10 feet. Lettuce also crosses with the weedy wild lettuce (*Lactuca serriola*), so cut down any wild lettuce within 200 feet of your garden. Collect seed from the plants that are among the last to bolt (flower and set seed). Lettuce seed matures irregularly, so make several trips to the garden with a paper bag to harvest seed.

Heirloom Selections

Heirloom lettuce varieties are beautiful, easy to grow, and a wonderful taste treat.

'Green Deer Tongue' or 'Matchless' (45 to 65 days from sowing to maturity.) Seed Savers Exchange lists this as a popular lettuce with pioneer families because of its hardiness and reliability. This looseleaf lettuce dates back to around 1740 and has thick green leaves in a rosette 7 to 9 inches in diameter.

'Lolla Rossa' (55 to 65 days from sowing to maturity.) An Italian heirloom, 'Lolla Rossa' is a beautiful looseleaf lettuce with frilly, light red leaves that are green at the base. It performs well as a cut-and-come-again lettuce and is much in demand by gourmet restaurants.

'Oakleaf' (50 to 55 days from sowing to maturity.) A looseleaf lettuce that forms nice rosette heads, this variety was popular in the 1880s and is still a favorite with gardeners today. It tolerates hot weather without becoming bitter.

'Merveille des Quatre Saisons' or 'Marvel of the Four Seasons' (55 to 70 days from sowing to maturity.) A French heirloom from the 1880s, this beautiful head lettuce has a pale green heart, magenta-red outer leaves, and a wonderful flavor. It does best in cool weather and will bolt when temperatures turn hot.

'Rouge d'Hiver' or 'Red Winter' (55 to 60 days from sowing to maturity.) A delicious French heirloom from the 1840s, this romaine lettuce has dark bronze-red outer leaves. The 10- to 12-inch heads are very cold tolerant and do well as an early-spring crop.

'Schweitzer's Mescher Bibb' (50 days from sowing to maturity.) An Austrian variety dating back to the 1700s, it is an extremely cold-hardy head lettuce with small, tight heads of green leaves edged with red.

'Tennis Ball' (45 to 55 days from sowing to maturity.) Grown by Thomas Jefferson at Monticello, this butterhead lettuce forms small, tight rosettes of light green leaves. It is best as an early spring lettuce.

Satisfy your sweet tooth with the fruit of turban-shaped 'Jenny Lind' melon.

MELONS

Cucumis melo and *Citrullus lanatus*
Cucurbitaceae

ORIGIN

Watermelon hails from the African tropics; other melons are thought to have come from West Africa and Persia. Spanish explorers brought both to the New World, where they were widely grown by Native Americans. European settlers grew several Native American varieties and imported seeds from Europe, but it wasn't until 1880 to 1900 that breeders developed many of the heirloom varieties available today.

CLASSIFICATIONS

There are several subgroups within *Cucumis melo,* but most of the melons grown in the United States are either in the Indorus group (with green or white flesh) or the Reticulus group (which includes musk-melons and Persian melons). Watermelons are not categorized into any botanical groups but come in a variety of flesh colors with varied rind colors and patterns.

GROWING MELONS

Melons and watermelons like a long growing season with three to four months of warm, sunny conditions. Give them a site with rich, well-drained soil, and add compost to your planting hills or rows. Northern gardeners should start seedlings indoors two weeks before their last spring frost date. Southern growers can direct-seed melons in the garden when soil temperatures reach 75°F. Cucumber beetles can infect melons with bacterial wilt, so use row covers until bloom time to protect plants.

SAVING SEED

Melons are a bit tricky for seed savers. They are pollinated by insects and will cross with one another, although they do not cross with cucumbers or pumpkins (as is sometimes believed). The best suggestion is to either grow only one variety per year or to separate varieties by at least 200 feet (¼ mile for rare heirlooms). Melon seed remains viable for at least four years; the same planting and viability guidelines apply to watermelons. Harvest seeds when the fruit is ripe for eating.

HEIRLOOM SELECTIONS

To me, a ripe heirloom melon represents summer at its fullest and sweetest.

Melons

'BANANA' (80 to 100 days from sowing to maturity.) Introduced in 1883, this long, banana-shaped melon weighs 5 to 8 pounds and has salmon-orange flesh with smooth, yellow skin. The flavor is sweet and spicy.
'HONEY ROCK' (74 to 88 days from sowing to maturity.) An All-American Selection in 1933, this vigorous variety is a good choice for northern gardeners. Each plant of 'Honey Rock' produces five to seven melons weighing 3 to 4 pounds each with thick, sweet, salmon-color flesh. This variety is resistant to fusarium wilt.
'JENNY LIND' (70 to 85 days from sowing to maturity.) Introduced in 1846, this heirloom was named for Jenny Lind, a popular Swedish singer. It is an early-maturing variety that performs well for northern gardeners. The fruits are turban-shaped and weigh 1 to 2 pounds. The melon skin is brownish green, and the flesh is light green and sweet-tasting.
'OLD TIME TENNESSEE' (90 to 110 days from sowing to maturity.) Famous for its flavor and texture, this thin-skinned muskmelon is large (up to 12 pounds) and should be harvested exactly at peak ripeness for best flavor. Southern Exposure Seed Exchange reported that one gardener could find the melons in the dark because of their fragrance!

Watermelon

'CREAM OF SASKATCHEWAN' (80 to 85 days from sowing to maturity.) This variety is one of the best heirloom watermelons for short-season areas. The round, 5- to 12-pound melons have white flesh and a pale green skin that's striped with dark green.
'GEORGIA RATTLESNAKE' (90 days from sowing to maturity.) An old southern favorite from Georgia that is becoming rare

(D. Landreth Seed Co. is one of the few remaining commercial sources), this variety is noted for its size, productivity, and flavor. The long, 25- to 30-pound fruits have light green skins with dark green stripes and bright red flesh.

'ICE CREAM' (75 to 90 days from sowing to maturity.) A pre-1885 heirloom, this watermelon produces oval fruit with a pale green, veined rind, bright red flesh, and white seeds. Too thin-skinned to be a good market variety, this is a high-yielding, juicy, sweet melon for the home gardener. A black-seeded strain is also available.

'MOON AND STARS' (90 days from sowing to maturity.) The medium-size, oval, dark green fruits are covered with pea-size bright-yellow "stars" and usually one larger yellow "moon." The fruit have sweet pink flesh and brown seeds. This now-famous heirloom has come to symbolize efforts to preserve our heirloom varieties.

'NAVAJO SWEET' (85 to 90 days from sowing to maturity.) This heirloom produces round, 10- to 20-pound fruits with red flesh and a pale green rind striped with dark green. 'Navajo Sweet' is considered to have an unusually sweet flavor and a good storage life.

ONIONS

Allium cepa
Liliaceae

ORIGIN

Onions are an ancient vegetable. The Chinese enjoyed them as far back as 3000 B.C., and the ancient Egyptians, Romans, and Greeks also cooked with them. Onions were an important food and medicinal plant in medieval Europe. Christopher Columbus is believed to have been responsible for bringing onions to the New World.

CLASSIFICATIONS

The *common* or *globe* onion is the most widely grown onion, but there is a huge range of onions that are both easy to grow and wonderful to cook with. *Topset* or *Egyptian* onions and *multiplier* onions are also included in *Allium cepa.* Topset onions form small bulbs below ground and set small bulbils at the top of their flower stalks. *Bunching* onions (*A. fistulosum*) are hardy perennial onions that divide and multiply at their bases. They do not form single, large underground bulbs but are used as scallions. *Shallots* or *multiplier* onions (*A. cepa* var. *aggregatum*), leeks (*A. ampeloprasum*), and garlic (*A. sativum*) are also closely related to globe onions, and there are good heirloom varieties for each of these; check the *Garden Seed Inventory* (refer to "Recommended Reading" on page 234) for selections.

Globe-shaped 'Red Wethersfield' onion has pink-tinged white flesh with red circles.

GROWING ONIONS

Onions appreciate rich, well-drained soil; they will not tolerate soggy conditions. Many heirloom globe varieties are available as seed. If you live in the North, choose a "long-day" variety like 'Red Wethersfield' or 'Yellow Globe Danvers'. Southern gardeners do best with "short-day" varieties, such as 'White Portugal'. You can direct-sow seed outdoors if your soil temperatures are around 40°F in March. Otherwise, start the seed indoors early in the season, in February or March. Onions do not like drought, so water during dry spells. Harvest globe onions when the tops are yellow and withered.

SAVING SEED

Globe onions are biennial. If you live where the ground freezes in winter, store your largest, sound bulbs over winter at 32° to 45°F and 60 to 70 percent humidity. Replant bulbs in the spring after danger of a hard frost. Harvest seeds as soon as seedpods in the flower head begin to dry. If you grow more than one variety, separate them by at least 100 feet; one mile is required for seed purity.

HEIRLOOM SELECTIONS

The following varieties are all heirloom globe onion selections. I also have Egyptian onions in my garden (passed down from my grandfather) because they are great in early spring and require so little attention. I am eager to try bunching onions to round out the selection in my garden.

'RED WETHERSFIELD' (100 to 115 days from sowing to maturity.) Originating from Wethersfield, Connecticut, around 1800, this dark-red-skinned onion is still widely available from seed companies today. Best suited for northern gardens, this strong-flavored onion is medium in terms of storage abilities. (Yellow globe onion varieties are usually the best keepers, staying firm in storage.)

'SOUTHPORT WHITE GLOBE' (110 to 120 days from sowing to maturity.) A good choice for northern and mid-Atlantic gardeners, this perfectly round, medium-size, white-skinned globe onion was introduced in 1906 and is still a popular commercial variety.

'WHITE PORTUGAL' (96 to 150 days from sowing to maturity.) Introduced from Portugal in the 1780s, this medium-size, silver-white-skinned globe onion is a short-day variety that's well suited for growing in the South. It has a mild, sweet flavor and medium storage qualities.

'EARLY YELLOW GLOBE' (90 to 110 days from sowing to maturity.) This yellow-skinned onion is a good storage and cooking onion. Introduced around 1930, it is a good choice for both mid-Atlantic and northern gardeners.

PEAS

Pisum sativum
Fabaceae

ORIGIN

One of the world's oldest vegetables, peas were grown around the eastern Mediterranean area possibly as early as 8000 B.C. For centuries, peas were dried and then cooked into porridge. (Remember the nursery rhyme "Pease porridge hot, pease porridge cold, pease porridge in the pot nine days old"?) Columbus is thought to have brought peas to the New World, where Native Americans adopted peas as a garden crop.

CLASSIFICATIONS

Garden peas are classified by their use. *Sugar* or *snow* peas are harvested before the pods fill out; the whole pod is edible. *Snap* peas, a more recent version of snow peas, also have edible pods but should be picked when the pods have filled out. *Shell* peas are harvested when the pods have filled out, and they're then shelled for fresh peas; the pod is not edible.

GROWING PEAS

A cool-weather crop that prefers air temperatures between 60° and 65°F, peas prefer full sun but will grow in partial shade, and they thrive in well-drained soil that contains lots of organic matter. Peas produce best as a

'Lincoln' shelling pea, dating to the early 1900s, has always been a favorite with gardeners because of its great flavor.

spring crop, so plant seed directly in the garden four to six weeks before your last frost, when the soil is around 40°F. Unlike dwarf varieties, tall (climbing) varieties need staking or trellising. An old-time staking technique was to stick brushy prunings from fruit trees or shrubs in the soil near young pea plants for support.

SAVING SEED

Peas have perfect flowers and are usually self-pollinating, making them a good choice for beginning seed-savers. Bees may occasionally cause cross-pollination, though, so it's a good idea to plant different varieties 5 to 10 feet apart. (If you are preserving a rare heirloom, separate varieties by 50 feet.) Allow the peas you want to save for seed to turn yellow and dry on the vine; then simply harvest and shell them.

HEIRLOOM SELECTIONS

Peas with edible pods were culinary favorites in France in the 1800s, and they're once again popular with gardeners. I also like to grow shelling peas for freezing.

Shelling Peas

'LANCASHIRE LAD' (65 days from sowing to harvest.) This heirloom is a productive and tasty bush shell pea; constant picking prolongs harvest. Will Woys Weaver enjoys these peas raw and adds them to salads. This variety is available from the Seed Savers Exchange.

'Lincoln' or 'Homesteader' (64 to 67 days from sowing to maturity.) Still available from numerous seed companies, this dwarf shelling pea is very productive. The 18- to 30-inch vines produce 3- to 4-inch pods that are easy to shell. 'Lincoln' has excellent flavor and is a good choice for northern gardeners.

'Tall Telephone' or 'Alderman' (68 to 78 days from sowing to maturity.) Introduced in 1891 and named in honor of Alexander Graham Bell's invention, this heirloom has 6- to 7-foot vines that need strong support. The 5-inch pods yield sweet-tasting peas that are good for freezing and canning.

Edible-Podded Peas

'Golden Sweet Edible-Podded' (55 to 65 days from sowing to maturity.) An unusual, light gold pea, this variety was introduced from India. They are best eaten as young snow peas, though you can also dry the seeds and use them in soup. The 6-foot vines have two-tone purple flowers that contrast beautifully with the striking golden pods.

'Mammoth Melting Sugar' (65 to 75 days from sowing to maturity.) This wilt-resistant variety has 4- to 5-foot vines that need to be staked. Introduced in the early 1900s, it has high yields of stringless, 4-inch, sweet-flavored pods.

PEPPERS

Capsicum annum
Solanaceae

ORIGIN

Botanists believe that peppers originated around southern Brazil and Bolivia and that birds carried them across South and Central America. (Unlike people, birds are immune to the burning sensation caused by peppers' capsaicin content. Attracted by the colorful red pods, birds eat the peppers; the seeds pass through their digestive system intact and are deposited on the ground, where they sprout.) Peppers became an important cooking ingredient of the Aztecs and Incas. Columbus brought pepper seeds back to Spain, and from there they eventually spread throughout Europe, Africa, India, and the Far East.

CLASSIFICATIONS

There are hundreds of different kinds of peppers—both wild and cultivated species. *Capsicum annuum* includes most of our garden varieties: *sweet, wax, cayenne,* and *jalapeño.* The species *C. baccatum* consists mainly of South American pepper varieties that are large-leaved plants with unusually shaped fruit. *C. chinense* includes the extremely hot *habaneros,* while the

Add a little spice to your dishes with bright red 'Cyklon', a hot pepper from Poland.

C. frutescens varieties are the *tabasco* in Tabasco hot sauce. Finally, *C. pubescens*, the oldest known cultivated pepper (about 6,000 years old), grows up to 6 feet tall, with 8-inch-diameter trunks. Varieties of *C. pubescens* are usually not listed in seed catalogs but are available from seed-saver exchanges.

GROWING PEPPERS

Peppers prefer full sun and well-drained, evenly moist soil. Most books recommend sowing pepper seeds indoors 6 to 8 weeks before the last frost date. However, I have found Nancy Bubel's recommendation of seeding early (12 to 14 weeks before the last frost date) in *The New Seed-Starters Handbook* to be helpful. Peppers are much slower starts than tomatoes, especially under the less-than-ideal seed-starting conditions that most of us work with, so an early sowing will give you bigger transplants and an earlier harvest. Pepper seeds germinate best between 70° to 80°F. Harden off transplants before planting out after your last frost date.

SAVING SEED

Although peppers are usually self-pollinating, cross-pollination by insects can be a problem if you are growing several varieties of peppers for seed saving, especially if you plant both sweet and hot varieties side by side. The "hot" gene in peppers is dominant, and you may wind up with fiery-tasting bell peppers!

To minimize the chance of crossing, keep varieties at least 50 feet apart and grow tall "barrier" plants in between different varieties. If you have rare heirloom varieties, separate different sweet pepper varieties by 150 feet; allow 600 feet between sweet and hot peppers or between different hot pepper varieties. If that isn't possible, you can cage different varieties or cover individual pepper flowers with small bags.

HEIRLOOM SELECTIONS

Sweet peppers have the best flavor if you wait until they turn from green to red or yellow before harvesting. When handling the fruits or seeds of your hot peppers, be sure to wear gloves to protect your hands.

Hot Peppers

'CHIMAYO' (95 days from transplanting to maturity.) From the Mexican farming town of the same name, 'Chimayo' produces 4- to 5-inch-long fruit. They have a mild flavor when green and turn mildly hot when red. The pepper is traditionally strung into ristras (beautiful dried-pepper ropes) that you can hang in your kitchen and use as needed during the winter.

'CYKLON' (80 days from transplanting to maturity.) This heirloom hot pepper from Poland is offered in the Seed Savers Heirloom Seeds and Garden Gifts catalog. The bright red, tapered fruits are 2 inches wide and 4 inches long. The spice industry in Poland uses this pepper for drying because of its thin flesh.

'CZECHOSLOVAKIAN BLACK' (65 days from transplanting to maturity.) An heirloom variety from Czechoslovakia, this mildly hot pepper is an attractive 3-foot-tall plant. Its dark green leaves have purple veins and its purple flowers are streaked with white. The 2-inch-long fruits start as a dark green color that appears black, and they ripen to red.

'LONG RED CAYENNE' (72 days from transplanting to maturity.) Introduced around 1827, this is the heirloom variety that is used for dried cayenne pepper. The plants are 20 to 30 inches tall with 4- to 6-inch fruits.

Sweet Peppers

'BULL NOSE' (60 days from transplanting to maturity.) Described by Fearing Burr Jr. in his classic 1865 book *The Field and Garden Vegetables of America*, this heirloom offers 4-inch-long, blocky-shaped, four-lobed fruits. The flesh of the pepper is sweet, while the ribs are slightly hot.

'CHERRY SWEET' (70 to 80 days from transplanting to maturity.) Dating to before 1860, this variety has 20-inch plants that produce 1-inch-long, cherry-shaped fruits that are great for pickling or stuffing.

'CORNO DI TORO' OR 'HORN OF THE BULL' (75 to 90 days from transplanting to maturity.) This Italian heirloom sweet pepper is both productive and flavorful. The 20-inch plants bear 6-inch-long, tapered red fruits that are curved like a bull's horn.

'SWEET BANANA' (65 to 70 days from transplanting to maturity.) This popular and reliable sweet pepper produces lots of fruit— sometimes more than 20 peppers per plant! The pretty, 6-inch-long, pointed fruit turn from green to yellow to crimson red as they ripen. 'Sweet Banana' is considered an excellent pepper for the mid-Atlantic region.

ODDS AND ENDS

The pungency or "heat" of peppers can actually be measured with scientific instruments in what is termed "Scoville heat units." A sweet bell pepper measures 0, while the hottest *C. chinense* variety ever tested measured 577,000 Scoville heat units. Habanero measurements are typically 50 times greater than jalapeños.

POTATOES

Solanum tuberosum
Solanaceae

ORIGIN

Potatoes are native to the Andes Mountains of South America, where they were cultivated 4,000 years ago. The Spanish explorer Pizarro took potatoes back to Europe in the early 1500s. At first, Europeans considered potatoes (and tomatoes) inedible and poisonous because they were related to the deadly nightshade weed. By the 1600s, however, potatoes were deemed an edible and nutritious food and were recommended by scientists as a good food supplement for the poor, particularly when grain crops failed. After a blight disease destroyed the Irish potato crop and caused a devastating famine in the 1840s, botanists looked for disease-resistant wild potatoes to breed with the domestic potato. Hundreds of potato varieties were developed during this time period.

CLASSIFICATIONS

Gardeners loosely divide potatoes into *early-, mid-,* and *late-season* varieties, based on harvest times. *Fingerling* potatoes, a fourth category, are longer and thinner than other potatoes, and have interesting skin and flesh colors.

GROWING POTATOES

Potatoes do best in full sun and well-drained soil with lots of organic matter. You can plant them early: one to four weeks before

Potatoes are easy vegetables to grow, so try several colorful heirloom varieties—then compare their baking and eating qualities to discover your favorite.

your last frost date, when the soil temperature is around 40°F. Be sure to hill soil around the growing plants to cover the developing potatoes; exposed tubers will turn green from sunlight and will be inedible. Rogue out plants that have yellow or diseased leaves, and destroy them to prevent blight diseases from spreading. After the potato plants have completely died back, you can dig out your potatoes. New potatoes are one of the best taste treats that a gardener can anticipate each year. "Cure" your potatoes for storage by spreading them in a

single layer in a dark area at 50° to 60°F for several weeks to allow scratches and bruises to heal; then store them in a dark basement at 38° to 40°F.

SAVING SEED

Potatoes are usually propagated by "seed potatoes," tubers saved from last year's harvest. Seed potatoes should be free of potato scab (scabby, russetted patches on the skin of the potato) and any other disease symptoms. Store seed potatoes in a cool (40°F), damp, dark place over winter. At planting time—

two to three weeks before your last frost date—cut the seed potatoes into pieces that have two "eyes" (small depressions in the surface of the potato that will produce sprouts and roots).

Potatoes do form seed balls, which look like small green tomatoes on the stalk. Potatoes raised from seed will not be "true to type" and will be a mixed lot of sizes, colors, and shapes. If you want to experiment, pick the seed ball when it is completely mature, about two months after it forms. Dry the seeds and sow them indoors six to eight weeks before your last frost date. Plant outdoors after all danger of frost is past.

HEIRLOOM SELECTIONS

Today, there is a resurgence of interest in uniquely colored and flavored potato varieties. You can impress your friends at the Labor Day cookout with an incredibly flavorful potato salad made from layered yellow, pink, and blue potatoes!

'ALL BLUE' (Midseason; 70 to 90 days from planting to maturity.) This heirloom produces dark-blue-skinned, oblong, moderate-size potatoes. It keeps its color when baked or steamed and has good flavor and yield.

'ANNA CHEEKA'S OZETTE' (Late-season; more than 90 days from planting to maturity.) A late-season fingerling potato, this is a very old heirloom that's said to have been brought from Peru in the late 1700s by Spanish explorers who traded it with the Makah-Ozette tribe of northwest Washington State. It is a 2- to 8-inch-long, slender potato with yellow flesh.

'BINTJE' (Late-season; more than 90 days from planting to maturity.) Introduced in 1911 from the Netherlands, this heavy-yielding, yellow-fleshed potato is very flavorful and a good keeper. It is one of the most popular yellow potatoes.

'COW HORN' (Late-season; more than 90 days from planting to maturity.) An heirloom fingerling potato from New Hampshire, this blue-skinned potato is shaped like a cow's horn. It is a productive late-season potato that is a good keeper.

'GARNET CHILE' (Late-season; more than 90 days from planting to maturity.) A parent of many of the potatoes grown in the United States, this light-pink-skinned, white-fleshed, oval potato was introduced in 1853 and is descended from 'Rough Purple Chile', which was collected in a port in Panama. It is a vigorous and productive potato.

'GREEN MOUNTAIN' (Late-season; more than 90 days from planting to maturity.) Introduced in 1885, this Vermont potato is buff-color, large, and oblong, with excellent flavor. 'Green Mountain' adapts to a wide variety of soil types and is considered to be a good yielder, but it's susceptible to some viruses.

'RUSSIAN BANANA' OR **'BANANA'** (Late-season; more than 90 days from planting to maturity.) This yellow-fleshed, yellow-skinned fingerling potato is probably from Russia. A good keeper that is resistant to scab and late blight, this is one of the more popular heirloom potato varieties because of its wonderful flavor and waxy texture. You won't need to put butter on this fingerling!

ODDS AND ENDS

Viral diseases are a serious problem for heirloom potato growers. These diseases can overwinter on seed potatoes and infect the next year's crop. After several seasons, a diseased potato variety will degenerate into a low-yielding, stunted crop. Seed Savers Exchange is tackling this problem with a tissue culture project that will enable them to keep their collection of 400 heirloom varieties free of viruses. If you are buying seed potatoes, only buy "certified" seed potatoes, which have been inspected and proven to be free of disease.

RADISHES

Raphanus sativus
Brassicaceae

ORIGIN

Radishes were probably first grown in China and were a favorite food of the early Greeks and Romans. The Greek and Roman radishes were huge winter-keeper radishes that could weigh up to 40 pounds! American colonists grew a wide variety of radishes in their gardens.

CLASSIFICATIONS

Short-season spring or fall radishes are the small, round, or slender varieties and are typically eaten raw. Long-season radishes include the long (up to 20 inches) daikon type and the European winter-storage varieties. The unusual heirloom called "rattail radish" is grown not for its root but for its edible, foot-long seedpods. Radish sprouts are also edible and taste much like the roots.

GROWING RADISHES

Short-season radishes are one of the earliest spring crops, maturing in as little as three weeks' time. Sow the seed directly in the garden four to six weeks before your last frost date in spring, and again in fall. (Since radishes pass their prime quickly, make small sowings every other week through spring to spread out your harvest.) Thin seedlings to stand 2 inches apart. Plant seed of winter radishes in midsummer in loose, deeply worked soil. Thin seedlings to 4 inches apart.

SAVING SEED

Radishes are insect-pollinated and may cross with other radish varieties within a ¼-mile radius, so only allow one variety to flower at a time in your garden. Short-season radishes planted in the spring will produce seedpods

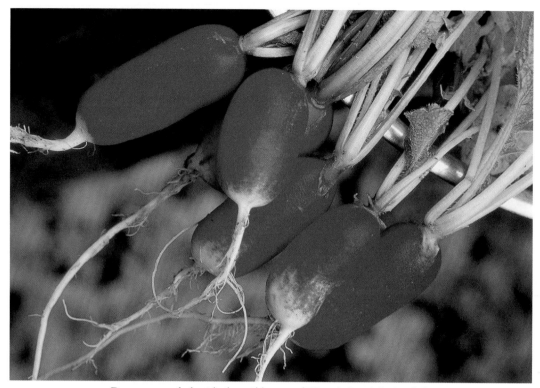

Dress up a salad with the mild taste of 'French Breakfast' radish.

by midsummer. You'll need to store winter-keeper radishes over winter. Cut the greens back to 1 inch and bury the trimmed roots in containers filled with damp sand; store in a damp, cold basement or root cellar. Plant them out the following spring to flower and set seed.

HEIRLOOM SELECTIONS

Heirloom radishes are easy to grow and will add zip to your salad mixes. The winter-keeper radishes are a good addition to the fall vegetable garden.

'CHINA ROSE' (52 days from sowing to maturity.) Jesuit missionaries brought this winter-keeper radish back from China. It has been grown in the United States since 1850. The 5-inch-long roots have white flesh and rose-colored skin.

'FRENCH BREAKFAST' (20 to 30 days from sowing to maturity.) This classic oblong radish grows about 2 inches long and is a pretty scarlet color with a white tip. Introduced in 1879, it is a mildly pungent radish that grows well from either spring or fall plantings.

'LONG BLACK SPANISH' (55 to 60 days from sowing to maturity.) This keeper radish reaches 7 to 10 inches long and 2 inches in diameter. 'Long Black Spanish' was offered by the Shaker seed industry in the 1820s and was known as an existing variety since the 1600s.

'WHITE ICICLE' (30 days from sowing to maturity.) This heat-tolerant, mild-flavored white variety is a favorite of the Southern Exposure Seed Exchange. For best flavor, harvest 'White Icicle' when it is 4 to 5 inches long.

ODDS AND ENDS

Both the roots and greens of radishes are good sources of Vitamin C and were eaten to prevent scurvy in the Middle Ages.

SQUASH AND PUMPKINS

Cucurbita spp.
Cucurbitaceae

ORIGIN

Squash and pumpkins are native to the New World, and some squash remains dating from 5000 to 9000 B.C. have been found in South America and Mexico. The early wild species were small and bitter-tasting, but by the time the first Europeans arrived in North America, squashes were an important part of the Native American's diet. 'Connecticut Field', a pumpkin variety now grown mainly for jack-o'-lanterns, was being grown by North American tribes when the Pilgrims arrived in 1620. Squash became a lifesaving food source for the Pilgrims during their first grim years when food was extremely scarce.

CLASSIFICATIONS

Gardeners divide the vast array of squash into *summer squash, winter squash,* and *pumpkins.* Summer squash are harvested when the fruit is young and tender (unless you go on vacation and return to baseball-bat-size squash!), while winter squash are harvested when the fruit has hardened. Pumpkins are really winter squash that just have the traditional pumpkin shape. Some pumpkin varieties are not as rich and flavorful as winter squash and are better used for decorating.

Botanically speaking, squash are divided into four species. *Cucurbita maxima,* with its long vines and large leaves, includes the winter-keeper squash and large pumpkins. Native to South America, this group of cucurbits tolerates the cold, wet weather of the Northeast, but in general is susceptible to wilts and vine borers. *C. pepo* includes acorn squash, summer squash, gourds, and the traditional orange

'Rouge Vif d'Etampes' pumpkin, grown in French gardens since the early 1800s, was introduced in North America in 1883.

pumpkins. These crops have prickly leaves and stems that can cause a skin rash on some people; they are also susceptible to vine borers. *C. mixta* includes the drought-tolerant cushaws that are the traditional winter squash grown in the South. These crops have good resistance to vine borers and cucumber beetles. Members of *C. moschata,* such as 'Butternut Squash', are good winter-keepers and can be used for pies and cakes. These squash have good resistance to vine borers and cucumber borers once they are past the seedling stage.

GROWING SQUASH

Squash like full sun and rich, well-drained soil. Plant seeds in the garden after your last frost date, when soil temperatures have reached around 60°F. Some gardeners sow seeds in old compost piles and allow the vines to run rampant. (Be sure to check the space requirements of your variety before you plant; some vines can take up a lot of room! Vining types have vines that can reach 10 feet long, while bush and semi-bush squash are more compact.) If cucumber beetles, squash bugs, or squash vine borers are a problem in your area, protect plants with floating row covers. Remove the covers when the female blossoms begin to open to allow for insect pollination, or keep plants covered and pollinate the flowers by hand.

SAVING SEED

Squash and pumpkins are tricky crops for beginning seed-savers. These crops are pollinated by bees, and different varieties within the same squash species will cross-pollinate. Varieties from the four different species will generally not cross-pollinate (cushaws, for example, usually don't cross with zucchini), although field research studies show there may be occasional crossing. For your own seed-saving purposes, growing only one variety of each species per season should provide acceptable results. To ensure the purity of very rare heirloom varieties, seed-saving experts recommend growing only one squash variety (total) each year. Another option is to cage your plants with floating row covers so they don't cross-pollinate. If you choose this route, you'll need to pollinate the flowers by hand. Be sure to save squash seed from healthy plants with no disease symptoms.

HEIRLOOM SELECTIONS

Summer squash are a familiar part of the summer vegetable garden. While not as widely grown, heirloom winter squash offer a beautiful array of sizes, shapes, and colors.

Summer Squash

'BENNING'S GREEN TINT SCALLOP' (47 to 56 days from sowing to maturity.) Introduced in 1911, this is a very pretty pale green, oval-shaped, slightly flattened squash with scalloped edges. For best flavor, harvest when fruit reaches 3 to 4 inches wide. The semibush plants offer a high yield.

'COCOZELLE' (53 to 65 days from sowing to maturity.) This heirloom bush zucchini, introduced in the late 1800s, is still a classic. Its long, cylindrical fruits are dark green with white stripes. As with most zucchini, harvest young for best flavor.

'DELICATA' (95 to 100 days from sowing to maturity.) Noted for its rich, sweet flesh, this variety was introduced before 1900 and is popular again. The fruits are oblong with a cream-color skin that is striped with green. 'Delicata' is considered a summer squash, but it can be stored for up to four months after harvest.

'YELLOW CROOKNECK' (42 to 60 days from sowing to maturity.) This standard yellow summer squash variety was introduced around the 1700s and is still widely available. For best flavor, pick the fruits when they are 5 to 6 inches long; if you miss this stage, they will turn orange and develop a warty skin.

Winter Squash and Pumpkins

'AMISH PIE' (90 to 105 days from sowing to maturity.) This heirloom squash was obtained from an Amish gardener in the

Maryland mountains. The moist orange flesh measures up to 5 inches thick and is excellent for making pies. The plants have long vines and large stems, and the pinkish, heart-shaped fruit weighs 60 to 80 pounds.

'**BOSTON MARROW**' (90 to 110 days from sowing to maturity.) Grown by Native Americans in the Northeast, this was introduced as a variety in 1831. The bright orange fruits weigh 10 to 20 pounds and are a hubbard shape. (Hubbard squash are large, rounded, warty winter squash that are great keepers.) The flesh of 'Boston Marrow' is fine-grained, thick, and flavorful.

'**CONNECTICUT FIELD**' (100 to 120 days from sowing to maturity.) One of the oldest Native American pumpkins, this variety dates back to before 1700 and is still carried by many seed companies. It is a classic jack-o'-lantern-shaped pumpkin weighing in at around 20 pounds. It is passable for cooking but pretty for fall decorating.

'**GREEN HUBBARD**' (95 to 120 days from sowing to maturity.) Originating in Massachusetts from the West Indies in the late 1700s, 'Green Hubbard' was introduced as a variety in the 1840s. An excellent winter-keeper, the dark green, 10- to 15-pound fruit has golden yellow flesh with a sweet flavor.

'**ROUGE VIF D'ETAMPES**' (105 to 130 days from sowing to maturity.) An old French heirloom, this is the classic pumpkin that is used to illustrate the Cinderella fairy tale. If I were the fairy godmother, I also would have chosen this variety for its slightly flattened shape with deep ribs and beautiful red-orange color. Weighing an impressive 25 to 35 pounds, the mild-flavored fruits are rather fibrous for cooking but very pretty for decorating.

'**SEMINOLE**' (95 days from sowing to maturity.) Cultivated in the 1500s by the Seminole Indians in Florida, this variety is a good choice for hot, humid, disease-prone areas. It is also resistant to vine borers. The large vines bear bell-shaped, buff-color fruits that average 7 inches in diameter and have sweet, firm, deep orange flesh. The fruit will keep up to one year at room temperature!

'**THELMA SANDERS' SWEET POTATO**' (96 days from sowing to maturity.) This acorn-shaped squash is a family heirloom from the Sanders family from Missouri. It was introduced in 1988 by the Seed Savers Exchange and is now offered by the Southern Exposure Seed Exchange. The acorn-shaped fruits are fine-textured and have an excellent flavor.

ODDS AND ENDS

Women of the Huron tribe would gather rotted wood from old stumps in the woods, powder it, and put it in a large bark box. They planted squash seeds in the box and suspended it over a gentle wood fire that would warm the box. After the seeds germinated and reached the proper size, the women planted out the seedlings.

Like many favorite heirloom tomatoes, 'Radiator Charlie's Mortgage Lifter' was developed by a home gardener. You may want to try your hand at plant breeding, too.

TOMATOES

Lycopersicon esculentum
Solanaceae

ORIGIN

Tomatoes originated in the South American Andes, where they grow as a perennial. Spanish explorers took the tomato back to Europe, where it was slow to gain acceptance. (It was grown as an ornamental and was thought to be poisonous or an aphrodisiac if consumed.) George Washington and Thomas Jefferson both grew tomatoes in their vegetable gardens—probably out of curiosity. Tomatoes did not become popular with American kitchen gardeners until the mid–1800s.

CLASSIFICATIONS

With so many tomatoes to choose from, there are several ways to categorize tomato types. The appearance of the fruit is an easy and obvious place to start. The Seed Savers Exchange, for instance, groups tomato varieties by color: "orange to yellow," "pink to purple," "red," and "other." Fruits can also be grouped into *cherry* tomatoes, which are the small, bite-size ones; *paste* tomatoes, which have the thick, meaty flesh that is best for sauce-making; and *slicing* tomatoes, which are the classic round beauties.

Tomatoes are also described by how they grow. *Determinate* tomatoes will stop growing at a certain point, do not usually need to be staked, and will bear most of their crop at one time. *Indeterminate* tomatoes bear over a longer period of time on vining plants that need either a lot of room to sprawl on the ground or support from cages or stakes.

Yet another way to classify tomatoes is by their foliage. *Regular* is the type of foliage we are most familiar with. *Potato-leaf* plants have foliage that resembles that of their tuberous cousins, while tomato plants described as *ferny* have distinctive carrot-type foliage.

GROWING TOMATOES

Tomatoes need full sun and moderately fertile soil with good drainage. Excessive nitrogen will produce lots of foliage but fewer fruit. Start seeds indoors six to eight weeks before your last frost date. Set transplants into your garden when soil temperatures are above 60°F. To reduce the chances of disease problems, avoid planting tomatoes in the same place for at least a year after growing tomatoes or their relatives (including potatoes, peppers, and eggplants).

SAVING SEED

Tomatoes are self-pollinated, making them one of the simpler seed-saving projects. Try to keep tomato varieties at least 20 feet apart, though, to prevent accidental crosses made by insects in search of pollen. Choose good-size fruit from healthy plants over the course of the growing season. Use the wet-processing method for seed saving. (See "Saving Seeds" on page 188.)

HEIRLOOM SELECTIONS

There are literally hundreds of heirloom tomato varieties to choose from! The listing below is just an introduction.

'AMISH PASTE' (80 to 85 days from transplanting to maturity.) One of my personal favorites, this large (6- to 8-ounce) paste tomato has solid, meaty flesh with few seeds. Originally from Wisconsin, this indeterminate heirloom is also tasty for fresh eating.

'BIG RAINBOW' (90 days from transplanting to maturity.) An heirloom from Polk County, Minnesota, this variety bears fruits that resemble a rainbow as they ripen: green on the shoulder, yellow in the middle, and red on the blossom end. When fully ripe, the fruits are gold on the stem end and red on the blossom end. The earliest fruits are the largest and can weigh over 2 pounds. This is a productive variety with good resistance to foliar diseases.

'BRANDYWINE' (80 to 90 days from transplanting to maturity.) This indeterminate variety first appeared in the 1889 catalog of Johnson & Stokes of Philadelphia, and by

1902 it was also being offered by four additional seed companies, but it soon disappeared from all catalogs. This pink-fruited variety is thought by many to have the most incredible taste of any tomato.

'CHEROKEE PURPLE' (75 to 85 days from transplanting to maturity.) This indeterminate variety from Tennessee was originally cultivated by the Cherokee tribe. The globe-shaped, 8- to 12-ounce fruit have a dusty rose color with dark green shoulders. The flavor is rated highly by Seed Savers Exchange members.

'MULE TEAM' (86 days from transplanting to maturity.) This heirloom earned its name by being a workhorse of a tomato that is productive long into the season. 'Mule Team' produces disease-resistant, indeterminate plants bearing slightly oval, 8- to 12-ounce fruits continuously until frost.

'PRUDEN'S PURPLE' (65 to 72 days from transplanting to maturity.) An indeterminate, potato-leaved heirloom variety that bears deep pink, 1-pound, globe-shaped fruit that resist cracking. It has a delicious flavor similar to the very popular 'Brandywine', but it bears earlier.

'RADIATOR CHARLIE'S MORTGAGE LIFTER' (79 days from transplanting to maturity.) This legendary heirloom was developed in the 1930s by a radiator repairman, M. C. Byles, from Logan, West Virginia. "Radiator Charlie" selected this tomato after years of crossing four varieties and saving seed. The huge (up to 4 pounds!) beefsteak-

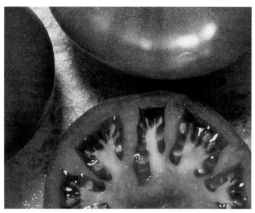

Although 'Cherokee Purple' is a thin-skinned tomato that wouldn't hold up in commercial shipping, the unusual color and rich flavor make this a great tomato for home gardeners.

type fruits made this variety a big success. The disease-resistant, indeterminate plants sold for the extravagant price of $1 each, and Radiator Charlie paid off his mortgage in six years with the profits.

'STRIPED GERMAN' (78 days from transplanting to maturity.) This indeterminate variety bears rib-shouldered fruits in shades of yellow and red. They are beautiful for slicing and highly rated for flavor. Johnny's Selected Seeds found it ripened in late August and early September in Maine and considers it a better selection for more southern gardens.

'YELLOW PEAR' (70 to 80 days from transplanting to maturity.) The productive, indeterminate plants bear clusters of pear-shaped, 1-ounce, yellow fruits all season long. This disease-resistant heirloom may date back to the 1600s.

Antique Flowers: Lore and Romance

In recent years, gardeners have developed a greater appreciation of the beauty of heirloom flowers. For many, it's the connection to the past—either to personal memories or favorite historical periods. Jean Stahl, an heirloom gardener who re-creates a Pennsylvania German garden each year for the Goschenhoppen Historians Folk Festival in eastern Pennsylvania, remembers her mother's flower garden fondly:

"In my own reflections, one thing stands out in my mind as making the house a more pleasant place," says Jean. "My mother always had a flower garden, separate from the vegetables. From springtime until frost, there were always flowers on the large, oak kitchen table. The blossoms were often shared with neighbors who had little or no yard space and those in whose homes there was illness." It's wonderful memories like these that make the lure of heirloom flowers such a strong one!

There are many wonderful heirloom flowers for today's gardeners to choose from. Since my space is limited, I'll stick to some of the most well-loved favorites—annuals, bulbs, perennials, and flowering vines—plus some old-time selections that are unfamiliar today but deserve more attention. To learn more about the heirloom flowers available, check out "Seed and Plant Sources" on page 228.

OPPOSITE: *Matching heirloom flowers to the time period of older homes adds authenticity to the garden.*

Selected Heirloom Annuals

Annuals are flowers that grow from seed, flower, set seed, and die, all in one growing season. Heirloom annuals are open-pollinated, so you can save their seed each year and usually end up with plants that resemble the parents they came from. (This is an advantage you don't get with fancy modern hybrids!) Just make sure you don't grow two varieties of a particular heirloom annual next to each other, or they may cross. To keep your seeds pure, it's best to grow only one variety of each flower each year.

LOVE-LIES-BLEEDING

Amaranthus caudatus

SPECIAL FEATURES

Love-lies-bleeding bears unusual, 15-inch-long, tassel-like, crimson flower heads that dangle from a 3-foot-tall plant. They are interesting cut flowers and also dry well for winter bouquets.

A BIT OF HISTORY

The Aztecs grew amaranths as a food crop—the small seeds are very nutritious—and some species are still raised as specialty grain crops. Other species are strikingly beautiful. Victorian gardeners liked this colorful annual and also grew Joseph's coat (*Amaranthus tricolor*) for its tropical-looking green foliage splashed with maroon, red, and yellow.

GROWING LOVE-LIES-BLEEDING

It's easy to grow this showy annual in full sun and average, well-drained soil. You can direct-sow love-lies-bleeding outdoors after the soil has warmed to 75°F, but the seeds are tiny and give more dependable results if you start them indoors four weeks before the last frost date. Set transplants outside after all danger of frost has passed.

Bachelor's buttons are easy to grow by planting the seed directly in the garden in fall or early spring.

BACHELOR'S BUTTON

Centaurea cyanus

SPECIAL FEATURES

This 2- to 3-foot annual has silvery green foliage. The blue, pink, maroon, or white summer flowers are 1 to 2 inches wide.

A BIT OF HISTORY

Bachelor's button, also known as cornflower, is native to England. It was considered a problem weed in English fields, but gardeners enjoyed this bright annual and have included it in their flower gardens since Tudor times. It traveled to North America with the earliest European colonists. Victorians used it for a boutonniere, hence the name "bachelor's button." 'Jubilee Gem' (an All-American Selection), 'Emperor William', 'Red Boy' (1942), and 'Black Boy' (1942) are old cultivars that are still available.

GROWING BACHELOR'S BUTTON

This flower likes full sun and average, well-drained soil. It's easy to grow and often self-sows once established. Sow outdoors in fall or early spring. You can extend bloom time by successive sowings (sowing small amounts of seed every few weeks through spring) and by deadheading spent flowers. If you wish to dry the flowers for winter bouquets, Jo Ann Gardener, author of *The Heirloom Garden*, suggests cutting them just as the flowers begin to open.

SPIDER FLOWER

Cleome hasslerana

SPECIAL FEATURES

In *A Little Book of Annuals,* Alfred Hottes described cleome as "a most interesting garden subject" that is given "a peculiar, airy appearance by the long stemmed stamens and pistils which protrude from the flowers for several inches." Worth growing for its beauty alone, this fast-growing 4-foot-tall annual also attracts moths and butterflies to the garden.

A BIT OF HISTORY

Native to South and Central America, cleome was introduced to the United States around 1810. 'Rose Queen', a cultivar with light pink blossoms, was offered in an 1836 catalog and is still available.

GROWING SPIDER FLOWER

Ideal for the back of the border, spider flower is easy to grow and prefers full sun to light shade and average, well-drained soil. Direct-sow it in your garden in mid- to late spring, or start it indoors about four weeks before your last frost. It self-sows readily.

LARKSPURS

Consolida ambigua and *C. orientalis*

SPECIAL FEATURES

Both species of larkspur can reach 2 to 4 feet tall, depending on the variety you choose to plant, and both bear spikes of blue, purple, pink, and white blooms. Larkspurs are wonderful in the garden border and as cut flowers, and they're much easier to grow than delphiniums.

A BIT OF HISTORY

Branching larkspur (*Consolida ambigua*) has been a favorite of English cottage gardeners since the late 1500s, and it is native to the Mediterranean region. It was valued as a

Larkspurs work well as cut or dried flowers, and the single flowers press beautifully.

healing medicinal herb—the juice of the flower was thought to improve eyesight—as well as for its beauty. Rocket larkspur (*C. orientalis*) was introduced to England shortly after branching larkspur, and it also became a favorite of gardeners. Both rocket and branching larkspur are still available for use in today's heirloom flower gardens, as is a named variety of branching larkspur, 'White King', a 1937 All-American Selection.

GROWING LARKSPURS

These showy annuals prefer full sun and average, well-drained soil with lots of organic matter. They grow best if you sow them ¼ inch deep directly in your garden. If you live in the North, sow seed four weeks before the last spring frost. In the South, it's best to sow in the fall, because the seeds need cool temperatures to germinate. After the first year, you may not need to replant, as larkspurs will often reseed in the garden.

HELIOTROPE
Heliotropium arborescens

SPECIAL FEATURES

Heliotrope bears clusters of ¼-inch-wide deep purple blooms atop 2- to 2½-foot-tall stems from summer through to frost. While this heirloom is noted for its fragrant flowers, individual plants can vary in scent, so be sure you've sniffed out your favorite before making a purchase.

A BIT OF HISTORY

A favorite of the sentimental Victorians, heliotrope was introduced to France in 1757 from its native Peru. It was very popular with European gardeners, who called it "cherry pie" because of its fragrance (some varieties have a vanillalike scent). Thomas Jefferson sent seeds home to America from France, and Presidents George Washington and Andrew Jackson also grew it in their gardens.

GROWING HELIOTROPE

Give heliotrope a site in rich, well-drained soil in full sunlight (or afternoon shade, where the summers are hot). Start seed indoors 10 to 12 weeks before your last frost date. The seeds will take several weeks to germinate, but the plant is well worth the wait! Set your plants out two or three weeks after your last frost, spacing seedlings about 12 inches apart. While it is usually grown as an annual, heliotrope is actually a tender perennial, so you can take cuttings or grow it in a container and bring it indoors for the winter. (This is a great way to keep plants that are exceptionally fragrant!)

Balsam Lady's Slipper

Impatiens balsamina

Special Features

Balsam lady's slipper will grow to around 2 feet tall, with a thick, succulent stem and pretty doubled flowers in various shades of red, pink, and violet from midsummer through frost. It acquired the name "touch me not" because of its seedpods, which pop open at a slight touch when ripe. (I can remember pinching them open when I was a kid—just in the interest of reseeding them, of course.)

Balsam lady's slipper is a little-known but easy-to-grow "grandmother's garden" flower.

A Bit of History

A native of tropical Asia, balsam lady's slipper was introduced to England in about 1540. This heirloom was cultivated for centuries in English gardens. It has been grown in American gardens since colonial times and was a very popular garden plant during the Victorian era, when the colorful flowers worked well in the then-fashionable annual bedding-plant gardens. Balsam lady's slipper is also very pretty in a cottage garden setting. It fell out of favor in the 1900s, except in old-time country gardens where gardeners continued to enjoy the colorful blooms, which resemble little roses.

Growing Balsam Lady's Slipper

The 2-foot-tall plant grows well in full sun to light shade and well-drained soil. For the earliest bloom, start the seed indoors four to six weeks before your last frost date, or simply sow directly in your garden when the danger of frost has passed. This easy-care heirloom thrives with virtually no care, and it often self-sows.

SWEET PEA

Lathyrus odoratus

SPECIAL FEATURES

Seedsman Joseph Breck, author of *The Flower Garden,* described sweet pea as "one of the most beautiful and also one of the most fragrant of the species…and deservedly one of the most popular annuals which enrich the flower garden." The lovely, delicate flowers bloom in shades of pink, lavender, maroon, and white, with large upper petals, two side petals, and two small bottom petals. These vining plants climb by attaching their tendrils to supports.

A BIT OF HISTORY

The wonderful sweet pea cultivars from the nineteenth century originated with a Sicilian wildflower first described by a Father Franciscus Cupani in 1697. This sweet pea had short stems and irregular maroon-and-purple blooms, but it had an incredible fragrance. In 1700, Father Cupani sent seeds to England, where early gardeners depended on natural variation to increase the selection. In 1870, Henry Eckford, an estate gardener, realized the commercial possibilities of improved sweet pea cultivars and left his employment to begin an intensive breeding program in his own garden. He was so successful with his endeavors that by a flower exhibition in 1900, he had submitted 115 of the 264 varieties that existed at the time! The W. Atlee Burpee Seed Company in America also developed sweet pea varieties with salmon, orange, and scarlet shades. Sweet peas were the overwhelming cut-flower favorite during the Edwardian period, and they were used at both dinner parties and weddings. Although the fragrance was bred out of sweet peas in the first half of this century (because the breeding emphasis was on developing large flowers and a wide variety of colors), some of the older, fragrant cultivars, such as 'Captain of the Blues' (1891), 'Butterfly' (1878), and 'Janet Scott' (1903) are once again available to heirloom gardeners.

GROWING SWEET PEA

Sweet pea prefers evenly moist, alkaline soil and a sunny site with some afternoon shade. Start seed indoors six to eight weeks before your last frost date, or sow them outdoors very early in spring, as soon as the ground can be worked. (Preparing the planting site in fall is a great way to make sure you're ready for early spring sowing outdoors.) Support the vining tendrils with brush or a trellis of netting. Cutting blooms encourages plants to produce more flowers. Sweet peas will falter in hot weather—water if it gets very dry and apply mulch to help the plants stay cool and moist—but their beauty and fragrance certainly makes up for their somewhat limited bloom season.

FLOWERING TOBACCOS

Nicotiana spp.

SPECIAL FEATURES

Flowering tobaccos are actually short-lived tender perennials, but most gardeners grow them as annuals. Three different species will provide you with fragrance: sweet-scented tobacco (*Nicotiana suaveolens*), jasmine tobacco (*N. alata*), and the towering woodland tobacco (*N. sylvestris*). Sweet-scented tobacco and jasmine tobacco bloom in the evening; woodland tobacco's flowers stay open all day. Sweet-scented tobacco grows 2 to 3 feet tall with a profusion of 3-inch-long, fragrant white blooms. Woodland tobacco reaches 5 feet tall and has a dramatic presence with its 5-inch-long, slender white flowers atop branching stems. Jasmine tobacco bears 2-inch-long tubular flowers in white or shades of pink on 4-foot-tall plants.

A BIT OF HISTORY

While sweet-scented tobacco originated in Australia, jasmine tobacco and woodland tobacco are native to South America, and they were introduced to the United States from Brazil in the mid-nineteenth century. Flowering tobacco quickly became popular for its wonderful fragrance. Gertrude Jekyll, the famous English garden designer and writer, also enjoyed flowering tobacco, recommending it for its white flowers and strong, sweet scent.

GROWING FLOWERING TOBACCOS

These fragrant heirlooms thrive in full sun to light shade and average to moist, well-drained soil. Start seedlings indoors six to eight weeks before your last frost date and set them out after all danger of frost has passed, or sow seed in the garden after your last frost date. Flowering tobacco will often self-sow.

Jasmine tobacco was a favorite of Victorian gardeners for its fragrance.

LOVE-IN-A-MIST

Nigella damascena

SPECIAL FEATURES

Love-in-a-mist, also known as fennel flower, grows about 1½ to 2 feet tall, with blue, pink, or white flowers surrounded by lacy foliage. (The curious arrangement of flowers and foliage gave rise to many other common names, including devil-in-the-bush, lady-in-the-green, maiden-in-the-green, and Jack-in-the-bush.) The fresh-picked blooms make dainty cut flowers, and the 1-inch-tall, rounded seedpods are attractive in dried arrangements.

A BIT OF HISTORY

Love-in-a-mist appeared in England around 1570 and was illustrated in Gerard's *Herbal*. It was always a favorite of cottage gardeners, and a much-later British garden designer and writer, the famous Gertrude, loved it and used it in her garden designs. The sky-blue variety 'Miss Jekyll' was named for her.

GROWING LOVE-IN-A-MIST

Select a site with full sun to light shade and average, well-drained soil. Sow this fast-growing annual outdoors in early spring, and make successive plantings every three to four weeks until June for continued bloom.

NASTURTIUM

Tropaeolum majus

SPECIAL FEATURES

These colorful, easy-to-grow annuals produce bushy or trailing stems with unusual circular leaves and scarlet-, yellow-, or orange-spurred flowers. They grow best in cooler weather and are at their most glorious in late summer and early fall.

A BIT OF HISTORY

Nasturtiums reached Spain from their native Peru via the explorers and were favorites in Europe for ornamental and culinary purposes. English gardeners grew them against apple trees or between stones on the tops of walls. By the early 1800s, they grew in American gardens. More recently, the artist Monet used long, trailing varieties at his gardens in Giverny. 'Golden Gleam', loaded with yellow flowers, was discovered by a California nurseryman in 1928 and quickly became popular.

GROWING NASTURTIUM

After danger of frost, sow nasturtium seed directly in the garden where you want them to grow, as they are not fond of being transplanted. Don't overdo the nitrogen, or you'll have lots of leaves but few flowers. Aphids can be a problem; if you notice them on the undersides of leaves, treat plants with a strong spray of water to knock off the pests.

The cheerful Johnny-jump-up readily naturalizes in gardens.

JOHNNY-JUMP-UP

Viola tricolor

SPECIAL FEATURES

Parent to the larger garden pansy, Johnny-jump-up is a diminutive, cheerful annual that's found throughout the Northern Hemisphere. The plants are 4 to 8 inches tall and have small, five-petaled purple-and-yellow flowers. They love cool weather, so they bloom best in spring and fall. Besides enjoying the flowers in your garden, you can also press them for floral art or candy them for use as cake decorations.

A BIT OF HISTORY

Grown for centuries, this heirloom has been mentioned in British literature since Elizabethan times. Back then, it was commonly known as heart's-ease or wild pansy. Arriving in America in the seventeenth century, it was given the name Johnny-jump-up for its habit of scattering its seeds widely and producing new plants that pop up in the most unexpected places.

GROWING JOHNNY-JUMP-UP

Johnny-jump-up likes sun or partial shade and average, well-drained soil. Its seeds will take 8 to 12 weeks to germinate. In most areas of the country, start them indoors in midwinter and set plants out in early spring. In Zones 9 or 10, you can set plants out in fall for early-spring bloom. Cutting plants back by half in summer will help encourage fall bloom.

ZINNIAS

Zinnia spp.

SPECIAL FEATURES

Zinnias are always a summer garden favorite for their prolific, long-lasting flowers. Classic zinnia (*Zinnia angustifolia*), also called narrow-leaved zinnia, is a disease- and drought-resistant species that forms loose mounds of foliage with 1½-inch orange, daisylike blooms. Common zinnia (*Z. elegans*) is much larger, with single or double flowers in a veritable rainbow of colors on 3- to 4-foot stems. Peruvian zinnia (*Z. peruviana*) is a good choice for the cutting garden. Its richly colored red or yellow flowers have a double row of petals surrounding the center disk.

A BIT OF HISTORY

Peruvian zinnias grew in Montezuma's gardens at the time of the Spanish invasion of 1521. (The Aztecs were excellent horticulturists who also grew dahlias, sunflowers, and morning glories.) 'Red Peruvian' and 'Yellow Peruvian' are varieties dating back to 1753 that you can still grow in your garden. The more widely grown common zinnia, also a native of Mexico, was not introduced in Europe until 1796. With its drab row of scarlet petals around a dark central cone, it was not very popular until the mid-1800s, when French flower breeders developed the attractive large double blooms we know today.

GROWING ZINNIAS

These colorful annuals need full sun and average, well-drained soil. You can sow the seed directly in the garden after your last frost date or get an earlier start on the season by starting seeds indoors three to four weeks before your last frost date. Powdery mildew on common zinnias may make foliage look unsightly by the end of the growing season. To reduce the chances of disease problems, space smaller cultivars 8 to 12 inches apart and taller ones 18 to 24 inches apart, and remove some of the sideshoots to allow good air circulation around the leaves and stems. Also, avoid wetting the foliage when you water.

Bulbs

Perhaps the best-loved flowers over the centuries have been the bulbs. The ancient Greeks wrote poetry about the narcissus; the Madonna lily (Lilium candidum), a symbol of purity and reverence, is one of the world's oldest cultivated flowers; and the rage over tulips caused economic chaos in Europe during the seventeenth century. It is fascinating that a little botanical package like a bulb could represent centuries of history and provide such pleasure in spring after the dreariness of winter. Check "Seed and Plant Sources" on page 228 for nurseries that carry heirloom varieties of these hardy and fragrant bulb beauties.

CROCUSES

Crocus spp.
Zones 4 to 9

SPECIAL FEATURES

Crocus, one of the most welcome harbingers of spring, have long been a favorite of gardeners. The small white, purple, or yellow flowers bloom 2 to 6 inches above the ground and have slender, grasslike foliage.

A BIT OF HISTORY

The saffron crocus (*Crocus sativus*) is the oldest crocus species, grown by the Mongols, Arabs, and Greeks and introduced into England by the Romans. It was an important economic crop, prized for its small stigmas, which were collected, dried, and sold as a spice. It takes approximately 4,000 blooms to produce 1 ounce of saffron! Saffron-dyed threads were also a substitute for the gold threads in church vestments in the fifteenth century.

Numerous types of ornamental crocus were described in the writings of the early botanists John Gerard (1545–1612) and John Parkinson (1567–1650). By the eighteenth century, crocus bulbs were part of Holland's bulb industry. The Victorians enjoyed these small but colorful bulbs outdoors

You can tuck heirloom crocus varieties like 'Purple Giant' in the fronts of perennial borders.

in spring beds, and they also grew them in pots for indoor bloom. Heirloom varieties include *C. angustifolius* 'Cloth of Gold' (1587) and 'Purpureus Grandiflorus' (1870).

GROWING CROCUSES

Plant crocus in fall, in a site with full sun or light shade and average, well-drained soil. Mice love to snack on crocus bulbs, so if these critters are a problem in your garden, try interplanting crocus with daffodil bulbs. (Daffodil bulbs are toxic to mice, so when these pests find daffodil bulbs, they tend to look elsewhere for food.) If this doesn't help, you can "cage" your crocus by digging all the soil out of each planting area and lining the sides and bottoms of the holes with wire mesh. Refill with some of the soil you removed, plant the crocus as normal, add more soil and a top layer of wire, and then finish filling the hole with soil. Crocus look great planted in grassy areas, but you'll need to let their leaves turn yellow before your first spring mowing. Otherwise you'll interfere with their ability to store food, and they won't bloom as well the following year.

HYACINTH

Hyacinthus orientalis
Zones 4 to 8

SPECIAL FEATURES

Hyacinths have always been known for their fragrance, but they are usually thought of as one of those potted plants that you pick up at the greenhouse to take to someone as a gift at Easter time. Perhaps we should change our preconceptions about this pretty spring bulb and begin to give it a place in our flowerbeds.

A BIT OF HISTORY

Native to Turkey, hyacinths were introduced to Europe in the mid-sixteenth century through the Orto Botanica of Padua, the first botanical garden of Europe. Hyacinths quickly became very popular, and by 1725 it was estimated that Dutch growers grew approximately 2,000 varieties.

Hyacinths were very popular with Victorians for indoor bloom forcing and bedding designs; the 1896 D. M. Ferry catalog listed 135 varieties. Some of the heirloom hyacinths that are still available today include the double-flowered varieties 'Chestnut Flower' (1880), 'General Kohler' (1878), and 'Madame Sophie' (1929). Single-flowered heirloom hyacinths include 'Distinction' (1880), 'King of the Blues' (1863), 'Marie' (1860), and 'L'Innocence' (1863).

GROWING HYACINTH

Hyacinths like full sun and rich, well-drained soil. Plant the bulbs in fall. The plants will go dormant in early summer. You may need to replant every few years to maintain your outdoor display. It's also easy to "force" the bulbs for indoor bloom. Plant them in fall in containers of potting soil with the tips of the bulbs showing through the soil. Water thoroughly, and store in a cool, dark place (33° to 45°F), until shoots appear; then bring them into the house.

Try planting a drift of old-fashioned hyacinth bulbs for spring color and, of course, fragrance.

LILIES

Lilium spp.
Zones 4 to 8

SPECIAL FEATURES

A chapter on heirloom flowers would be incomplete without lilies! There are many species to choose from, with bloom times from early to late summer. Madonna lilies (*Lilium candidum*) produce pure white, fragrant blooms in June on 3- to 4-foot stems. Scarlet Turk's cap lily (*L. chalcedonicum*) is 3 feet tall, with scarlet flowers that have reflexed petals that resemble a Turk's cap. Tiger lilies (*L. lancifolium*), introduced from Asia, got their name from their bright orange coloring with black spots. Reaching 4 to 6 feet in height, tiger lilies are easy to grow and will last for many years in gardens. They often carry a virus that doesn't affect them but that can infect and weaken other lilies. (To reduce the chance of problems, plant tiger lilies 300 feet from other lily species.) The regal lily (*L. regale*) is very popular, with its fragrant, white, trumpet-shaped midsummer blooms that are shaded with burgundy on 4-foot stems.

A BIT OF HISTORY

The Madonna lily is probably one of the oldest cultivated flowering plants. Madonna lilies grew in monastery gardens and continued as favorites of cottage gardeners during the Elizabethan age. The scarlet Turk's cap lily is also very historic, dating back to 1600 B.C. Minoan wall paintings. It was very popular with English gardeners of the sixteenth and seventeenth centuries. Lily growing greatly expanded in the nineteenth century, which was called the Century of the Lily, when the tiger lily and other Asian lilies were imported to Europe.

GROWING LILIES

Most lilies will grow well in full sun or light shade and average, well-drained soil. Madonna lilies in particular require well-drained soil. Plant Madonna lilies 1 inch deep, and plant other lilies 4 to 8 inches deep, depending on the size of the bulb. Plant lily bulbs in spring or fall as soon as you purchase them. Mulch to keep the soil moist and cool, and cut off the spent flower heads at the top of the stem to keep seeds from forming. (This directs the plant's energy into maintaining a vigorous bulb, rather than into forming seeds.)

If you plan to cut lilies for bouquets, grow a bunch in a cut-flowerbed, separate from your flower garden. Cut half the bed one year and the other section the following year so that you don't deplete the bulb by cutting the stem and foliage every season. Lilies make beautiful cut flowers, but be warned: The pollen that drops from the flowers can be messy, so you may want to remove the anthers before carrying these flowers through your house.

Magic Lily

Lycoris squamigera
Zones 5 to 9

Special Features

A member of the Amaryllis family, magic lily produces its leaves in spring and then dies back completely in early summer. The flower stems sprout in late summer, grow to about 2 feet tall, and bear clusters of fragrant, lavender-pink, trumpet-shaped flowers in August.

A Bit of History

Native to Japan, magic lily was brought to America in 1889. This trouble-free heirloom was a favorite in old-time flower borders, and it should be more well-known today.

Growing Magic Lily

Magic lily thrives in full sun to partial shade with well-drained soil. Be sure to plant it where you won't dig into it by accident in midsummer, when there are neither flowers nor foliage to mark the site.

Daffodils

Narcissus spp.
Zones 4 to 8

Special Features

Few flowers have been so beloved as daffodils over the centuries. In addition to beauty and fragrance, they are remarkably long lasting. They'll grow for decades and, like peonies or old roses, often mark the site of an old homestead. Daffodils range from single- and double-flowered narcissus to the delicate and fragrant jonquil. Colors can range from yellow and orange to ivory and apricot.

'King Alfred' is a classic heirloom daffodil that's still widely available.

A Bit of History

Daffodils are native to the Mediterranean and were grown by the ancient Greeks and Egyptians, who used them in funeral wreaths. Several varieties appeared in sixteenth-century botanical literature, and the American colonists quickly introduced daffodils to the new country.

The 1800s were a Golden Age for daffodil breeding. About 1,000 varieties were introduced between 1860 and 1900, with another 6,000 by 1930. Only a few of these are available today. A few of these venerable heirlooms include 'King Alfred' (1899), a classic big yellow trumpet type; 'Grand Soleil D'Or' (1890), a fragrant yellow and orange "tazetta"; and 'Mrs. R. O. Backhouse' (1923), the first ivory and pink daffodil.

GROWING DAFFODILS

Plant daffodil bulbs in early fall, in average, well-drained soil with added compost in full sun or partial shade. Plant at a depth approximately twice the bulb's height. Daffodils look wonderful when planted in natural-looking drifts, rather than in straight lines or blocks. Cut off the developing seedheads after bloom, and let the foliage yellow and die back before cutting it off.

TULIPS

Tulipa spp.
Zones 3 to 8

SPECIAL FEATURES

Of all the bulbs, tulips have the most notorious history and the most brilliant colors and shapes. Tulips are divided into 15 groups by bloom time and form. Heirloom tulips include both single and double tulips in a wide range of colors, as well as the diminutive and unusual species tulips.

A BIT OF HISTORY

Native to Persia, tulips were introduced to Europe in the mid-1500s from Turkey. Clusius, a noted botanist of French origin, is considered responsible for founding the Dutch bulb-growing industry. By the 1630s, gardeners throughout Europe and in the Netherlands were growing tulips. By 1634, tulip bulbs were traded like wheat and soybean futures. A single bulb of a red-and-white-flowered tulip with a blue-tinged base was sold for the equivalent of roughly $1,000. In 1637, the tulip market crashed and hundreds went bankrupt.

Around the same time as these events, the tulip traveled to America with Dutch settlers. Of the old striped tulips, 'Keizerskroon' (1750) is still available, as are some of the species tulips that have long histories, such as *Tulipa schrenkii* (1585) and *T. florentina* (1597).

GROWING TULIPS

Tulips prefer full sun to partial shade and need average, well-drained soil. The soil must be dry in summer, when the bulbs are dormant; otherwise, they'll bloom poorly (if at all) in future years. Plant the bulbs 6 to 8 inches deep in fall. Remove spent blossoms so seedheads don't develop, and allow the foliage to die back before trimming it.

Perennials and Biennials

Perennials will grow, flower, overwinter, and grow again the following spring, season after season. Short-lived perennials (such as columbines and hollyhocks) will live for several seasons; other perennials (like peonies and oriental poppies) can thrive for close to 100 years. Biennials will grow a mound of foliage the first year, overwinter, bloom, set seed, and die the second year. Many biennials and short-lived perennials will reseed in your garden, so they act almost like long-lived perennials. Here's an overview of the most popular heirloom perennials and biennials.

HOLLYHOCK

Alcea rosea
Zones 3 to 10

SPECIAL FEATURES

A biennial or short-lived perennial, hollyhock's tall spires bloom in midsummer for up to two months. The 4- to 5-inch, saucer-shaped blossoms are shades of yellow, red, purple, pink, and white on 5- to 6-foot stems.

A BIT OF HISTORY

Hollyhocks are native to China and the Middle East, but they've long been associated with English cottage gardens, where they have been growing since at least the 1500s. Hollyhocks have been gracing American gardens since the 1600s. Early colonists did not grow the plants for their beauty alone: the Puritans thought hollyhocks had medicinal value because the mucilaginous juice was said to be soothing in cough syrups and to provide relief from lung diseases. By the 1800s, when gardeners planted flower gardens, hollyhocks became more popular. 'Outhouse' hollyhock (*Alcea rosea*) is a classic variety that's especially famous for disguising outhouses and eliminating the need for a visiting lady to ask where it could be found, since she could just look for the beautiful flowers! Thomas Hogg, an English nurseryman in the early 1800s, developed 80 named varieties of hollyhocks. Hollyhock rust (a fungal disease that causes orange spots on the foliage) appeared in the 1870s, and gardeners discontinued growing many of the older, more susceptible varieties.

GROWING HOLLYHOCK

Hollyhocks like rich, well-drained soil and full sun. They're fairly easy to grow from seed by sowing outdoors in early fall or late spring. Or start the seed indoors six to eight weeks before transplanting seedlings outdoors. Hollyhocks are susceptible to rust; to help limit damage, treat leaves with a sulfur-based dust or spray once a week early in the season, as soon as the first orange spots appear. The black hollyhock (*A. rosea* 'Nigra') is reportedly more resistant to rust.

Hollyhocks are nostalgic favorites for cottage and parlor gardens.

COLUMBINES

Aquilegia spp.
Zones 3 to 8

SPECIAL FEATURES

European columbine (*Aquilegia vulgaris*) is a must-have for cottage gardens. This spring-bloomer has short-spurred blooms in rose, purple, blue, and white on 3-foot stems. Wild columbine (*A. canadensis*) blooms in early spring and has delicate red-and-yellow flowers atop 2-foot-tall plants.

A BIT OF HISTORY

European columbine was mentioned in botanical writings as early as 1310. This classic perennial was also a literary favorite and appeared in the writings of Chaucer and Shakespeare. European columbine was also a favorite of cottage gardeners who nicknamed it "Granny-bonnets." Joseph Breck, plantsman and author in the mid-1800s, described European columbine as "too well known to require description." Wild columbine is native to the United States and was already grown by John Tradescant the

Elder, a famous English plant collector, in the mid-1600s. Popular in the 1800s, it is once again a favorite of native plant enthusiasts.

GROWING COLUMBINES

European columbine prefers rich, well-drained soil in sun to partial shade, while wild columbine does best in less-fertile soil. Set young plants out in spring or fall, or sow seed directly in the garden in either spring or fall. Both species of this heirloom readily self-sow. The larvae of leafminer, an insect pest, form winding tunnels between the upper and lower layers of leaves. Hand-pick and destroy the leaves as soon as you see the tunneling.

BELLFLOWERS

Campanula spp.
Zones 3 to 9

SPECIAL FEATURES

Bellflowers offer pretty blue, lavender, pink, or white bell-shaped flowers that are favorites in gardens and floral arrangements. Biennial Canterbury bells (*Campanula medium*) have the largest flowers of the bellflowers (they can be 1 inch or more across) and bloom in early summer on 2-foot-tall stems. Perennial peach-leaved bellflower (*C. persicifolia*) blooms in summer with a profusion of blue or white, open bell-shaped flowers on 1- to 3-foot stems. Clustered bellflower (*C. glomerata*), a perennial native to the British Isles, has deep purple clustered flowers in early to midseason on 3-foot stems. Harebells (*C. rotundifolia*), a low-growing perennial native of English pastures that is nice in rock gardens, has nodding blue flowers on a 6- to 18-inch-tall plant.

A BIT OF HISTORY

Bellflowers have long been associated with English cottage gardens, and American gardeners have grown several species since the seventeenth century. Peach-leaved bellflower has been a part of English gardens since the Tudor days in the sixteenth century and was also used medicinally for gargles and lotions. The biennial or short-lived perennial Canterbury bells, dating from the same period, were also called Coventry bells because they grew in the hedgerows near the city of Coventry.

GROWING BELLFLOWERS

Choose a planting site with full sun or light shade and average, well-drained soil enriched with organic matter. Bellflowers tend to be short-lived where summers are hot and dry. Start seed of Canterbury bells in midsummer and overwinter the young plants in a cold-frame before planting out the following spring. Start seed of perennial bellflowers eight to ten weeks before planting them out in early spring. Stake the tall varieties.

Biennial sweet William will reseed readily in your garden.

SWEET WILLIAM AND COTTAGE PINKS

Dianthus barbatus
and *D. plumarius*
Zones 3 to 9

SPECIAL FEATURES

Easy to grow and wonderful as a cut flower, sweet William reaches 10 to 18 inches tall. The rounded heads of many individual ½- to 1-inch pink, red, crimson, or white flowers bloom in June. Sweet William plants may act as either biennials or short-lived perennials. Cottage pinks have a clovelike scent and can range in color from white through lilac to deep pink. Grown in North America since the first half of the nineteenth century, cottage pinks grow 6 to 10 inches tall and are good for edging or rock gardens.

A BIT OF HISTORY

Native to southern Europe, sweet William was probably introduced to England by Carthusian monks in the twelfth century. In 1533, this bright flower was included in Henry the Eighth's new garden at Hampton Court. Sweet William was popular in Scotland, and florists' societies in the eighteenth and nineteenth centuries offered prizes for the best specimens. (Florists in those days were not floral designers who worked with cut flowers, but avid gardeners, mainly from the working class, who grew and developed cultivars of their favorite flowers for displaying at local shows. The winners at local shows went on to larger shows in the big cities and were rewarded with a market for cuttings of their prizewinners.) Two heirloom varieties still available include 'Nigricans' (1883) and 'Newport Pink' (1928).

GROWING SWEET WILLIAM AND COTTAGE PINKS

This old-time favorite likes full sun and rich, moist, well-drained soil. Start seed indoors six to eight weeks before your last frost date, and set plants out after danger of frost has passed. (They may flower the same year.) You can also direct-sow seed in the garden from April to July for blooms the following year. Sweet William will often self-sow in the garden.

OLD-FASHIONED BLEEDING HEART

Dicentra spectabile
Zones 4 to 9

SPECIAL FEATURES

Bleeding heart's claim to fame is its long, arching stems with sprays of delicate pink-and-white, heart-shaped blossoms. Growing to around 30 inches tall and wide, bleeding heart flowers in late spring to early summer. Where summers are hot, bleeding heart will go dormant until the following spring, so don't be alarmed if your plants seem to disappear after they flower! Another common name for this heirloom is "lady of the bath"—turn a flower upside down and gently pull the wings apart to see how it acquired that nickname.

A BIT OF HISTORY

Old-fashioned bleeding heart is native to China. Although it seems as though it's been part of cottage gardens for centuries, it was probably first introduced to England around 1810. It has always been popular with gardeners, although Shirley Hibberd, a Victorian British garden writer, described it as a "cheap, common, but very charming flower." Well, I beg to disagree: It's a lovely, graceful plant.

GROWING OLD-FASHIONED BLEEDING HEART

This perennial thrives in moist, humus-rich soil in partial shade (morning sun and afternoon shade are ideal). It is possible to grow bleeding heart from seed, but you will need patience because germination time can vary from 30 to 365 days! Sow seed outdoors in late autumn or early winter; it needs a cold treatment to germinate. You can also propagate clumps by dividing them in spring.

FOXGLOVES

Digitalis spp.
Zones 3 to 8

SPECIAL FEATURES

Purple foxglove (*Digitalis purpurea*) blooms in early summer, with purple or white bell-shaped flowers on 4- to 5-foot stalks. It is usually grown as a biennial. Yellow foxglove (*D. grandiflora*), a perennial variety, is 1 to 3 feet tall when it blooms in early summer, with soft-yellow bells.

A BIT OF HISTORY

Various foxglove species are native to parts of Europe, Northwest Africa, and Central Asia. Purple foxglove is native to England, and its long-stalked flowers have been a familiar sight in English country gardens since the 1400s. Yellow foxglove has also been a part of English gardens since the Elizabethan times. No one is quite sure how foxglove got its name. One of the best stories is that the individual flowers are finger gloves or "folks" gloves. ("Folks" refers to the "little people," or fairies.) Dr. William Withering, an English physician, experimented with purple foxglove as a heart medication in the late 1700s. He also sent seeds to an American doctor, which is how the plant appeared in this country. Digitalin is still manufactured as a medication today. Foxglove is considered toxic; do not ingest it.

GROWING FOXGLOVES

Both purple and yellow foxgloves grow well in moist, well-drained soil. They prefer partial shade but will tolerate full sun. Start seed indoors in midwinter, 10 to 12 weeks before your last frost date, and set the seedlings out two to three weeks before your last frost date. Remove spent blossoms but leave a few stalks to set seed so plants can self-sow. Biennial and hybrid varieties of foxglove will need a little extra maintenance in order to thrive: After the plants flower, lift them and replant the new rosettes for the following year's bloom.

Purple foxglove likes fertile, well-drained soil.

DAYLILIES

Hemerocallis spp.
Zones 5 to 9

SPECIAL FEATURES

Tawny daylily (*Hemerocallis fulva*) is the summer-flowering, orange daylily found along roadsides all over the Northeast. Its roots and flower buds are both edible. The lemon lily (*H. lilioasphodelus*), native to northern Europe, is less vigorous but is still trouble-free. Tawny daylily blooms in mid-summer on 3- to 4-foot-tall stems; lemon lily is slightly smaller and blooms in June.

A BIT OF HISTORY

The tawny daylily has been cultivated in China from the twelfth century, where it was called the "plant of forgetfulness" because it was thought to cure sorrow by causing memory loss. Colonists brought it along from England, where it was cultivated since the late 1500s. Lemon lily has grown in America since the eighteenth century and is still a favorite for its delicate fragrance.

GROWING DAYLILIES

Daylilies are long-lasting perennials that grow in almost any soil condition but bloom best in full sun or partial shade. Betsey Lyman of the Pennsylvania chapter of the Nature Conservancy warns that tawny daylily can actually be invasive and choke out less-vigorous native flowers, so choose its planting site carefully. Although some daylilies can be started from seed, it's easiest to begin with divisions or purchased plants in spring or fall. Tawny daylily and lemon lily will grow happily with little attention for years.

IRISES

Iris spp.
Zones 3 to 10

SPECIAL FEATURES

Irises are majestic flowers that are available in almost every color (except bright red). Rising on thick stems from long, flat leaves, the flowers have three inner petals (usually erect), called "standards," and three outer petals that curve downward, called "falls." Iris species range in height from 4 inches—such as dwarf crested iris (*Iris cristata*)—to 3 feet—as in Siberian iris (*I. sibirica*) and German iris (*I. germanica*).

A BIT OF HISTORY

The name Iris comes from Greek mythology, where it takes its name from the goddess of marriage. A flower long revered by gardeners, there are hundreds of iris species, among which are many very old and respected histories. The stinking iris

Plant Siberian iris for colorful early-summer blooms.

German iris was grown in Europe in the ninth century. Old forms of it are very common in old-country gardens in the United States. Members of the Historical Iris Preservation Society have chosen their favorite iris varieties dating before 1900. These include 'Honorabile' (1840), 'Mme. Chereau' (1844), 'Iris Florentina' (1844), 'Crimson King' (1893), 'Pumila Atroviolacea' (1856), 'Flavescens' (1813), and 'Pallida Dalmatica' (1600). (For information about the Historical Iris Preservation Society, see "Seed and Plant Sources" on page 228.)

GROWING IRISES

Most irises will thrive in a sunny site, though their soil needs vary. Yellow flag iris likes boggy conditions, while the sturdy Siberian iris prefers rich, moist soil. The German iris grows fine in average, well-drained soil. Plant iris rhizomes just below the soil surface in spring or fall. Divide Siberian and German iris after they flower in summer or early fall every few years to prevent overcrowding. German iris may be troubled by iris borers, whose larvae tunnel through the leaves and into the rhizomes. (They not only eat the rhizome, but also spread bacterial infections.) The leaves will look ragged and the plant will lose vigor. Cut leaves off in fall and destroy them to eliminate overwintering eggs. Inspect young leaves in spring and crush larvae at the base of infected leaves.

(*I. foetidissima*)—so named for the odor released when you crush its leaves—has been grown in Europe since the sixteenth century. Gertrude Jekyll, the famous English garden designer and writer, recommended using the dried seedpods, with their orange-red seeds, in winter arrangements. Siberian iris, a very hardy species, is native to Europe and was cultivated before the 1600s. The early-summer-blooming

HONESTY

Lunaria annua
Zones 5 to 9

SPECIAL FEATURES

This biennial produces a rosette of foliage in its first year, expanding to a 2½- to 3-foot-tall stalk bearing rose-violet or white flowers the following spring. The flowers are followed by circular, flat seedpods that look like translucent silvery disks once the outer layer is rubbed off. (Pick them when they turn yellow, then gently rub off the outer layers of each pod with your fingers.)

A BIT OF HISTORY

English gardeners have been growing honesty since at least the 1590s, when the roots were boiled as a vegetable or eaten in salads. Honesty traveled to America in the seventeenth century and was popular in Victorian times, when ladies enjoyed hand-painting the seedpods.

GROWING HONESTY

This biennial is not fussy about soil but needs light shade to thrive. Sow seed outdoors in early summer for flowers the following spring. Once established, honesty will happily self-sow.

BEE BALM

Monarda didyma
Zones 4 to 8

SPECIAL FEATURES

Bee balm grows 2 to 3 feet tall and in early summer has blooms of small, tubular flowers arranged in whorls. The red flowers of this North American native attract hummingbirds, butterflies, and bees.

A BIT OF HISTORY

The Oswego Indians of New York State used the leaves of this plant as a tea (hence one common name, "Oswego tea"), as did the colonists during the Revolutionary period.

In 1744, the American botanist John Bartram sent seeds to England, where bee balm soon became a popular garden plant. It was also called wild bergamot because its fragrance resembled the bergamot orange, an orange-lemon hybrid from Italy prized by perfumers for its aromatic oil.

GROWING BEE BALM

Choose a planting site in full sun or partial shade. Set out plants in spring or fall. Bee balm spreads vigorously, so you'll need to divide it every other year or so to prevent it from taking over your garden. Powdery mildew can cause gray patches on leaves and stems, followed by leaf drop, but most plants seem to be able to tolerate the damage.

Once established, peonies can grow for years without requiring division.

PEONIES

Paeonia spp.
Zones 2 to 9

SPECIAL FEATURES

Peonies are bushy perennials with huge, beautiful pink, red, white, or yellow blooms in May or June on 3- to 4-foot plants. The fragrant blossoms make excellent cut flowers.

A BIT OF HISTORY

There are numerous species of peonies, but *Paeonia lactiflora* is the common garden peony or Chinese peony. Several French breeders, as well as the Kelway nursery in England, created many beautiful varieties. Chinese peony was introduced to America in the early 1800s, and peonies became a part of many settlers' homesteads. Peonies were an important part of the cut-flower trade until after World War II, when tropical and greenhouse flowers replaced them in popularity. Today, peonies are once again becoming a popular cut flower. Heirloom cultivars available today include 'Sarah Bernhardt' (1906), 'Duchesse De Nemours' (1856), 'Duchesse De D'Orleans' (1846), 'Francois Ortegat' (1850), and 'M. Martin Cahuzac' (1899).

GROWING PEONIES

Peonies need humus-rich, well-drained soil and prefer a sunny site, though they will tolerate light shade. Dig a planting hole approximately 18 inches wide and deep, and work compost and bone meal into the bottom of the hole. Plant the fleshy roots in fall, setting them no deeper than 2 inches below the soil surface. Space clumps 3 feet apart to give them room to grow. Stake tall and double varieties to keep their flowers from drooping. Most peonies do not grow well south of Zone 8 because they require winter cold.

ORIENTAL POPPY

Papaver orientale
Zones 3 to 7

SPECIAL FEATURES

Oriental poppies bloom on 2- to 3-foot stems in late May to early June. The striking flowers are 3 to 5 inches across, with colorful, translucent petals in many shades ranging from bright orange or red to salmon pink or white.

A BIT OF HISTORY

Numerous species of poppies have been grown for centuries, but the flamboyant and sturdy Oriental poppy has been a favorite of mine since childhood. The Oriental poppy was discovered by a French botanist named Tournefort, who brought seeds back to Paris. From there it spread to Holland and England. It was introduced to North America around 1741. I also like several of the annual poppies, such as the corn poppy (*Papaver rhoeas*). I confess that I didn't know why the British royal family are photographed wearing artificial corn poppies in their lapels at certain commemorative occasions. The corn poppy is worn in honor of those who sacrificed their lives on the battlefield at Flanders in World War I. The ground lay desolate at Flanders from the fighting during the war, but when peace arrived, the field bloomed again in a wonderful profusion of poppies.

GROWING ORIENTAL POPPY

This carefree perennial likes full sun and rich, well-drained soil. Start Oriental poppy seed indoors 6 to 8 weeks before the last frost, or direct-sow in the garden in early spring, when light frost is still possible. After flowering, Oriental poppies will go dormant, then reappear with new foliage in the fall. Combine the plants with bushy perennials such as catmints (*Nepeta* spp.) to hide the bare spots left by dormant poppies in midsummer.

A native flower, garden phlox quickly became a summer favorite in country gardens.

GARDEN PHLOX

Phlox paniculata
Zones 3 to 8

SPECIAL FEATURES

A mainstay of the midsummer perennial border, easy-to-grow garden phlox bears clusters of sweetly scented 1-inch-wide magenta, pink, white, purple, or red flowers atop 3- to 4-foot-tall stems. The leaves are 2 to 5 inches long.

A BIT OF HISTORY

Garden phlox is native to the northeastern United States. It was first cultivated in England in the 1730s and soon became popular for its beauty and hardiness. Garden phlox returned to North America as a garden plant between 1850 and 1900. Plant breeders, both amateur and professional, developed new cultivars in the early 1900s. 'Bright Eyes' (1934), 'Leo P. Schlageter' (1934), 'Mia Ruys' (1949), 'Rijnstroom' (1910), and 'Wilhelm Kisselring' (1942) are still standards today. 'Old Cellarhole' is a delightful fragrant phlox reclaimed from an abandoned homestead by Perennial Pleasures Nursery.

GROWING GARDEN PHLOX

Plant in full sun and rich, well-drained soil. Garden phlox enjoys cool summers, and may bloom for several weeks. Powdery mildew can be a problem, causing unsightly gray patches on leaves and stems. Removing several stems from each clump will allow better air circulation around the plant, reducing mildew problems. If you live where summers are hot and humid, though, thinning may not be enough; consider planting a mildew-resistant cultivar, such as 'Old Cellarhole'.

PRIMROSES

Primula spp.
Zones 4 to 8

SPECIAL FEATURES

Primroses add vibrant color to the landscape early in spring, and they look great with bulbs and wildflowers in a shaded garden area. The five-petaled, open-faced flowers bloom atop broad, crinkled leaves. Colors range from the soft yellow of the English primrose (*Primula veris*) to the deep pinks and reds of the Japanese primrose (*P. japonica*).

A BIT OF HISTORY

The English primrose (*P. vulgaris*), native to Britain, was cultivated as a garden flower in Europe before the end of the sixteenth century. English gardeners delighted in breeding double versions and new colors, such as purple, red, and white, although the single, pale yellow flowers of the native are beautiful in their own right. The English cowslip (*P. veris*) is native to English meadows and was brought to North America by the seventeenth century. A double form of the cowslip called "hose-in-hose" was very common in the sixteenth century, but is rare today. A primrose that is beautiful for boggy areas is the Japanese primrose (*P. japonica*), which was discovered by the famous plantsman Robert Fortune on his last trip to Japan in 1860. This showy primrose, called a candelabra type, blooms in late spring and early summer and was very popular in the late 1800s. All these species, along with many others, are still prized by today's gardeners.

GROWING PRIMROSES

Most primroses will thrive in light shade and fertile, moist soil and do best under cool growing conditions. If the site is hot and sunny, they will go dormant over summer and leaf out again in fall. Japanese primroses prefer acid, damp, heavy soil. Start seed indoors in early spring, or direct-sow outdoors in fall. Divide crowded plants after flowering.

Golden Glow

Rudbeckia laciniata 'Hortensia'
Zones 4 to 8

Plant tall golden glow in the back of the flower border or along a fence.

Special Features

This tall (5- to 7-foot), trouble-free heirloom perennial was once very popular for its double yellow flowers. Because I am someone who prefers informal gardens of tough plants to orderly designs filled with fussy varieties, I don't mind that golden glow sprawls a bit, and I like this July bloomer for summer bouquets. It ought to be included in more gardens.

A Bit of History

Native to North America, golden glow was available from seed catalogs in the early nineteenth century, and you can still find it growing around old farmhouses.

Growing Golden Glow

Choose a planting site in full sun with moist, well-drained soil. If you don't want to work at staking golden glow, plant it along a fence or shed wall, or at the back of the border. This dependable perennial is not troubled by pests. Start seed indoors six to eight weeks before your last frost date, or direct-sow outdoors in spring two weeks before your last frost date.

Roses

Roses have been grown and cultivated around the world for centuries, so it's no wonder that when gardeners think of heirloom flowers, these fragrant blooms are the first that spring to mind. Available in a myriad of colors, sizes, fragrances, and growth habits, you can find roses to suit nearly any garden or climate. Make sure that they have fertile, well-drained soil and six to eight hours of sun daily, and you'll find that many of these hardy heirloom beauties require no more effort than your garden perennials do.

ALBA ROSES

Rosa alba
Zones 3 to 10

SPECIAL FEATURES

Noted for their pleasingly light fragrance and delicate white or pale pink semidouble blooms, albas bloom once in early summer. They reach 6 to 9 feet tall, have gray-green foliage, and are hardy and disease-resistant roses.

A BIT OF HISTORY

Alba roses are thought to have been brought to England by Caesar's army and were used by early Europeans for perfume and medicine. Albas were popular during the Renaissance and can be seen in Italian paintings from that period. Notable alba cultivars include 'White Rose of York' (pre-sixteenth century), 'Queen of Denmark' (1826), and 'Felicite de Parmentier' (1828).

GROWING ALBA ROSES

Alba roses have robust canes that can grow 4 to 8 feet in a season. They flower on short sideshoots on year-old and older canes. These roses are hardy, vigorous plants that need minimal care. Prune out wood over five years old and any diseased or damaged branches.

BOURBON ROSES

Rosa chinensis
Zones 5 to 9

SPECIAL FEATURES

Ranging in height from 2 to 10 feet tall, Bourbon rose varieties can be either climbing roses or hedges. They are repeat-bloomers, blooming in midsummer and then again in fall. They produce blooms on new wood from the same growing season. The large flowers are cup-shaped semi-double or double flowers in shades of pink, red, purple, and white, and they are wonderfully fragrant.

'Boule de Neige', a Bourbon rose, has rich, fragrant white blooms.

A BIT OF HISTORY

The Bourbon roses originated in 1817, when a French botanist on Reunion Island in the Indian Ocean noticed a seedling that was a natural cross between two hedge roses. Many cultivars were developed during the 1800s and were very popular throughout the nineteenth century.

A few of the best Bourbons still available are 'Boule de Neige' (1867); 'Souvenir de la Malmaison' ('Queen of Beauty and Fragrance', 1843); and 'La Reine Victoria' (1872); 'Madame Isaac Pereire' (1881); which has raspberry-scented blooms, 'Louise Odier' (1851); and 'Honorine de Brabant' (mid-nineteenth century).

GROWING BOURBON ROSES

Grow Bourbon roses in rich, moist soil and full sun. Many Bourbons are, unfortunately, susceptible to blackspot and mildew, so good air circulation is important. Mulch your rosebushes to keep fungal spores from splashing up onto the foliage during rains or watering. Cut the slim canes back by one-third in late winter and trim sideshoots back to two or three growth buds after blooming. As with all roses, prune out any dead or diseased canes and put them out in the trash.

CABBAGE ROSES

Rosa centifolia
Zones 5 to 10

SPECIAL FEATURES

Also known as centifolia roses (the name means "hundred leaves," but refers to the many-petalled blooms), cabbage roses are the largest and fullest of any rose. The blossoms are 2½ to 5 inches across. Colors range from white to pink and mauve. They bloom once a season on long, thorny canes that range from 3½ to 7 feet and need staking or support. You'll find these opulent roses on Victorian-era fabrics. They are beautiful in informal borders.

A BIT OF HISTORY

Dutch and French rose breeders introduced over 200 cabbage roses between 1600 and 1710. Only about 20 varieties are easy to find now. 'Blanchefleur' (1835), 'Fantin-Latour' (1800s), 'Petite de Hollande' (prior to 1800), and 'Village Maid' (1845) are notable.

GROWING CABBAGE ROSES

Most varieties are susceptible to powdery mildew and blackspot. They need full sun; rich, moist soil; and good air circulation. Prune lightly after flowering.

CHINA ROSES

Rosa chinesis
Zones 7 to 10

SPECIAL FEATURES

China roses bear small single or loosely double flowers in clusters. They bloom in shades of pink, red, white, apricot, and yellow. The blooms actually darken in color after they open, unlike other roses that fade in the glare of the sun. Growing 3 to 6 feet tall, China roses have an open, twiggy habit with light green foliage and few thorns. They are attractive as a hedge or back-of-the-border shrub.

A BIT OF HISTORY

Introduced from China to Europe in the late eighteenth century, China roses bloom in spring and rebloom throughout the summer. European roses of the time were one-time bloomers. Popular China roses include 'Mutabilis' (of ancient origin), 'Slater's Crimson China' (1792), and 'Old Blush' (1789).

GROWING CHINA ROSES

China roses prefer a fertile, moist, well-drained soil and should be fed and watered regularly. Site them in a sheltered location, out of wind. Prune China roses lightly to remove diseased or damaged wood.

Damask Roses

Rosa damascena
Zones 3 or 4 to 10

Special Features

Damask roses have sprays of medium-size pink or white double or semidouble flowers with golden stamens. Most of the damask roses are midsummer bloomers, but "Autumn Damask" usually has a repeat bloom in the fall. Damasks are excellent choices for northern gardens because of their hardiness (they can survive winter lows of -30° to -40°F), but they are also well-adapted to mild climates.

Damask petals hold their delightful fragrance well when dried, so they are ideal for potpourri. Because pale petals tend to brown when air-dried, conceal them among brighter petals or choose crimson-pink 'Rose de Rescht' for drying.

'Celsiana' is an easy-to-grow damask rose that reaches 4 feet tall.

A Bit of History

The damask probably originated in Persia and was brought to England by Crusaders returning from the Holy Land. Damask roses became popular in Europe for their sweet fragrance and were grown in the gardens of noblemen and wealthy merchants.

The petals of damask roses were used to make attar of roses, a costly essential oil used in perfume. One and a half *tons* of fresh rose petals are needed to make one pound of attar of roses! Notable damask roses include 'Madame Hardy' (1832), 'Autumn Damask' (ancient origins), 'Celsiana' (pre-1750), and 'Rose de Rescht' (Persian; introduced in the West in the 1940s).

Growing Damask Roses

Damask roses prefer rich, moist soil. Prune out dead wood and cut long canes back by one-third to one-half during the dormant period. After bloom, trim back laterals (side shoots) by one-third. These durable plants only need a minimum of care.

Pick the buds of the gallica 'Rosa Mundi' for sweet-scented potpourri.

GALLICA ROSES

Rosa gallica
Zones 4 to 10

SPECIAL FEATURES

Gallicas bloom in early summer with fragrant 3- to 4-inch crimson, purple, or pink flowers. Blooms can be striped, speckled, blushed, or marbled. The plant forms a pest- and disease-resistant compact shrub (2 to 5 feet tall). Gallicas make good borders. If plants are grown on their own roots, they will sucker and spread.

A BIT OF HISTORY

Also known as the French or Provence rose, the gallica rose is most likely the oldest cultivated rose. Gallicas were grown by the ancient Greeks and Romans. During the Middle Ages, these roses were used as a medicinal herb and were included in monastery herb gardens. Gallicas were a very prominent part of the famous early nineteenth-century rose collection of the Empress Josephine at the Chateau Malmaison outside Paris. Some examples of well-loved gallicas are 'Cardinal Richelieu' (1840), 'Rosa Mundi' (of ancient origin), 'Ispilante' (1821), and 'Tuscany' (before 1500).

GROWING GALLICA ROSES

Easy-to-grow gallicas will tolerate poor soil. Allow them to become established for several years before doing any pruning. Then, prune out dead or weak old wood immediately after flowering.

HYBRID PERPETUALS

Hybrid origins
Zones 4 to 10

SPECIAL FEATURES

Hybrid perpetuals were the precursor to the modern hybrid rose. They bloom in early summer for several weeks and then again in fall (although the "perpetual" in their name is a stretch). Their large double flowers are up to 7 inches across and range from white to pink, maroon, and crimson. Plants are tall, narrow, and upright. Hybrid perpetuals can be planted as shrubs in a mixed border, but several are vigorous climbers.

A BIT OF HISTORY

Hybrid perpetuals were quite fashionable at garden shows during the Victorian era, when very industrious rose breeders developed literally thousands of different varieties. A few favorites of old rose fanciers include 'Baroness Rothschild' (1868), 'Baronne Prevost' (1842), 'Reine des Violettes' (1860), and 'Yolande d'Aragon' (1843).

GROWING HYBRID PERPETUALS

Plant these roses in fertile and moist but well-drained soil. Prune back canes by one-half to two-thirds of their length during the dormant period to promote flowering. Trim out any diseased or damaged wood.

MOSS ROSES

Hybrid origins
Zones 4 to 9

SPECIAL FEATURES

Moss roses acquired their name because of the fragrant, resiny mossy growth on their unopened buds and stems. The double 1- to 3-inch flowers occur in clusters on vigorous, upright plants and are shades of white, pink, and crimson. Most moss roses are one-time bloomers, but a few varieties are repeat bloomers.

A BIT OF HISTORY

Moss roses were discovered around 1700 and are sports (naturally occurring mutations) of the cabbage rose. A few favorites are 'Alfred de Dalmas/Mousseline' (1855), 'General Kleber' (1856), 'Old Pink Moss' (pre-1700), and 'Salet' (1854).

GROWING MOSS ROSES

These fast-growers hate hot weather. Arm them with rich, well-drained soil and mulch. Some are prone to blackspot. Prune repeat bloomers to two-thirds of their length; prune once-blooming varieties right after flowering.

NOISETTE ROSES

Hybrid origins
Zones 7 to 9

SPECIAL FEATURES

The charming noisettes are great roses for Southern growers and are both shrubs and climbers. These long-blooming roses have a spicy fragrance and bloom in elegant clusters of small flowers. They are repeat bloomers in shades of pink, cream, or yellow.

A BIT OF HISTORY

The one class of roses developed in North America, the first noisette was created by John Champneys of South Carolina in 1818.

He shared the seeds with a local nurseryman, Phillipe Noisette. Noisette was impressed with the new rose and sent plants to his brother Louis Noisette, who had a nursery in France and who developed numerous other varieties. 'Blush Noisette' (1825), 'Champneys' Pink Cluster' (1802), 'Alister Stella Gray' (1894), and 'Mme. Alfred Carriere' (1879) are some of the more famous noisette varieties.

GROWING NOISETTE ROSES

Noisettes are more drought-tolerant than other roses, and they need very little pruning. Remove a few of the oldest canes and shorten the sideshoots by two-thirds of their length during dormant pruning. Some of the noisettes are susceptible to blackspot and mildew.

PORTLAND ROSES

Hybrid origins
Zones 6 to 9

SPECIAL FEATURES

Portland roses are compact, rounded plants that reach about 4 feet tall with dark green foliage, and they are a good choice for smaller gardens. These repeat bloomers have fragrant, very double flowers.

A BIT OF HISTORY

Developed in the late 1700s from the China roses and the 'Autumn Damask' rose, Portland roses were popular in the early 1800s. Some of the best Portlands are 'Comte de Chambord' (1863), 'Duchess of Portland' (1790), and 'Pergolese' (1860).

GROWING PORTLAND ROSES

Plant Portland roses in fertile, well-drained soil. Prune back the canes by one-third and remove dead or damaged wood during dormant pruning.

SPECIES ROSES

Rosa spp.
All zones

SPECIAL FEATURES

Native to the Northern Hemisphere, species roses have single, five-petaled flowers and bloom once a season. They're hardy and often fragrant. Many have beautiful rose hips in fall, and some have colorful fall foliage and showy hips. Most work well as hedges.

A BIT OF HISTORY

Species roses are not really part of the old garden rose groups, but the old roses were bred from these roses, and many were grown in heirloom country gardens. *Rosa virginia, R. carolina,* and *R. nitida* are native North American roses and valuable garden plants.

GROWING SPECIES ROSES

These hardy roses naturalize well and require little or no pruning.

TEA ROSES

Hybrid origins
Zones 7 to 10

SPECIAL FEATURES

These easy-to-grow roses can be climbing or bushy plants with shiny, dark green, leathery foliage. The pastel blooms are single or double types with a spicy fragrance. These repeat bloomers thrive in the South and West.

A BIT OF HISTORY

Tea roses were introduced from China in the early nineteenth century and quickly became popular in Europe, where they thrived in the warmer countries. Some great climbing tea selections are 'Devoniensis' ('Magnolia Rose', 1838), 'Gloire de Dijon' ('Old Glory', 1853), and 'Sombreuil' (1850).

Tea roses bloom for a long time in early summer and again in fall.

GROWING TEA ROSES

Most tea roses are vigorous and disease-resistant. They do require fertile, well-drained soil. Do a minimum of pruning—just remove dead and diseased wood.

Vines

Vining plants can be annual or perennial, but they share one characteristic: They climb! Flowering vines are traditional favorites for summer color and fragrance on trellises, fences, and front porches.

CLEMATIS

Clematis spp.
Zones 5 to 9

SPECIAL FEATURES

Clematis offers adventurous heirloom gardeners a wide range of flower forms and bloom times to experiment with. In Victorian times, in fact, whole gardens were devoted to plantings of the many varieties of clematis for bloom from spring until fall. The most familiar of the clematis are those with the large, star-shaped flowers in purple, deep red, pink, and white, but the blooms of other clematis varieties can be double, single, small, large, or nodding bell shapes. Clematis climb by wrapping their leaf stems around a support, so you will need to provide a support or trellis if you train them against a flat wall.

A BIT OF HISTORY

Early-American colonists grew virgin's bower (*Clematis virginiana*), a rapid-growing native clematis with small white flowers and showy purple foliage in the fall. The large-flowered purple Jackman clematis (*C. × jackmanni*) was introduced by British clematis breeder George Jackman in the mid-1800s. Still very popular today, Jackman clematis was a huge success with Victorian gardeners and was the beginning of many clematis hybrids. 'Nelly Moser' (1867), another introduction from England, is a well-known selection with pink petals that have a rose-pink center. Lesser-known but also beautiful is the sweet autumn clematis (*C. paniculata*), an introduction from Japan that blooms in late summer with a rich fragrance. Used in Victorian times to disguise unsightly roofs, it quickly covers fences and trellises once it is established.

GROWING CLEMATIS

Clematis need rich, well-drained soil and full sun or light shade. They like to have their roots evenly moist in summer, but most don't tolerate soggy soil; a generous layer of organic mulch will help keep the soil conditions ideal for good growth. (Virgin's bower does tolerate wet soil and light shade.) Mulch in fall for winter protection. The species that bloom in spring or early summer (including *C. macropetala, C. montana,* and *C. patens*) can be pruned lightly after flowering; just prune off damaged wood. Those that flower in summer or fall, such as *C. × jackmanni* and *C. paniculata,* should be pruned at the end of winter, while the plants are dormant. Prune these back hard, leaving just the lowest set of buds on each stem to produce new growth. If you're not sure when your clematis blooms, err on the side of light pruning.

Jackman clematis sports large (4-inch), brilliant purple flowers.

MORNING GLORIES

Ipomoea spp.
Annual

SPECIAL FEATURES

American farmhouse porches and morning glories are a classic country garden combination. These easy-to-grow vines quickly scramble to 10 feet tall and will easily twine around a trellis, fence, mailbox post, or twine strung from the ground to a porch roof. (Grow them at one end of an open porch as a screen from the hot sun or strong winds.) The vines have heart-shaped leaves, and their trumpet-shaped flowers bloom in a variety of colors, including blue, pink, scarlet, white, and purple. Each flower lasts only one day, but the plants themselves will bloom from summer until frost; I think the flowers are the most luminous in early autumn.

The wine-red flowers of 'Crimson Rambler' are favorites of country gardeners.

A Bit of History

Morning glories have been favorite plants in several cultures for centuries because of their beautiful trumpet flowers and quick-growing vining ability. Common morning glories (*Ipomoea purpurea*) have been a favorite flower in Japan since they were introduced from their native Mexico in the 1830s. During that time period in Japan, a single seed of a prized variety would cost more than $10!

It's not known when the common morning glory was first introduced to Europe and grown in gardens there, but it was a popular flower with seventeenth-century Dutch and Flemish painters for its beautiful colors. Early colonists brought morning glories to North America, where they were widely grown in old-time gardens. Heirloom cultivars still available include 'Crimson Rambler' (1942), 'Heavenly Blue' (1930), 'Pearly Gates' (1942), and 'Grandpa Ott's', which was one of the original Bavarian varieties that started the Seed Savers Exchange. Cardinal climber (*I.* × *multifida*), an annual morning glory relative that has small, red, trumpet-shaped flowers and fernlike leaves, has been grown since the 1800s. Besides adding beauty to the landscape, cardinal climber has the added bonus of attracting hummingbirds to your garden.

Growing Morning Glories

Plant morning glory seed in full sun to partial shade in average, well-drained soil after temperatures have warmed up in the spring (three to four weeks after your last frost date, when all danger of frost is past). You can also start seeds indoors four weeks before your last frost date to get a jump on the season, but be careful when transplanting, because morning glories don't like their roots disturbed. It is helpful to nick the seed coats with a knife and soak the seeds overnight before sowing. Morning glories prefer cooler weather to sweltering hot summer days.

SCARLET RUNNER BEAN

Phaseolus coccineus
Annual

SPECIAL FEATURES

Scarlet runner beans are famed for their brilliantly colored red flowers. These bright blooms are followed by tasty broad beans that are best when cooked as a shell bean, though you can also prepare them as snap beans. Grow them on stakes or teepees in the garden (as you would pole beans), enjoy them as a front porch vine, or use them as a quick-growing screen on a trellis. These adaptable vines will even do well as decorative plants in window boxes. The vines will grow 6 to 8 feet tall, depending on the type of support.

The bright flowers of scarlet runner bean attract hummingbirds.

A BIT OF HISTORY

Truly old-time favorite, gardeners have been growing this pretty and productive vine since colonial times. Even Gertrude Jekyll, the grand dame of English horticulture and a garden designer and writer, recommended it, writing, "where the space devoted to flowers requires a screen from the vegetable ground, it may be well to remember that a hedge of Scarlet Runner beans, trained in the usual way, is beautiful as well as useful." This plant is still a great way to transition from your flower garden to your vegetable garden.

GROWING SCARLET RUNNER BEAN

Scarlet runner bean vines prefer a planting site with full sun and average, well-drained soil. You can sow the seed directly in your garden when all danger of frost is past. If you'll be growing the vines on a structure, be sure to put your trellis or supports in place when you plant the beans so that you won't disturb the vines' root systems later. Water during hot, dry periods.

Herbs with a History

Growing and using herbs is perennially popular with gardeners for a variety of reasons. There's the pleasure of cooking with flavor-packed fresh herbs. There's the fun of making herbal vinegars, herbal soaps, and other pretty herbal gifts, plus the fascinating history of herbs, which are as old as the human race itself. And finally, there's the fact that herbs look and smell so good!

While today we enjoy herbs primarily as a hobby, growing and preparing herbs were essential parts of people's lives up to the development of modern medicine in the late nineteenth century. For thousands of years before that, herbs were the primary treatment for ailments and diseases. Today we can have the best of both worlds. We have gained from the knowledge and technology that modern medicine offers, but we can still return to herbs if we want to explore alternative healing options.

Growing these versatile plants is as much of a pleasure as using them. While many people think that herbs need a special place set aside for them, you really don't have to have a separate "herb garden." As long as you give your herbs the light and soil conditions they need, there's no reason you can't grow them in either your vegetable garden or your flowerbeds—just as they did in colonial times. Herbs will even repel pests!

OPPOSITE: The varied textures, colors, and fragrances of herbs combine to create beautiful gardens of any scale—from a small, backdoor herb bed to a large, enclosed garden.

Selected Heirloom Herbs

This heirloom encyclopedia skims the surface of the hundreds of herbs that have been used over the centuries. Here you'll find information on how to grow and use annual herbs, such as basil and dill, and hardy perennials like sage, along with a bit of history about each herb.

ANGELICA

Angelica archangelica
Zones 3 to 9

SPECIAL FEATURES

Angelica is a striking herb that blooms with airy-looking clusters of small, white flowers atop thick stems that can reach 4 to 6 feet tall. The plants usually bloom in their second or third year and tend to die soon after flowering, so they are considered to be biennials or short-lived perennials. Angelica looks great planted at the back of a flower border or herb bed.

A BIT OF HISTORY

Native to Northern Europe and Lapland, angelica was popular in Europe from the sixteenth century as a medicinal herb for many illnesses and afflictions. It was thought to ward off evil spirits and witchcraft. In fact, legend has it that during the terrible time of the plague, a monk dreamed that an angel instructed him that the herb could ward off the disease; that's how angelica got its name. Sixteenth-century herbalists recommended it to cure coughs and colds, as well as to help with digestive disorders and flatulence. And in 1647, Reverend John Clay from Virginia wrote that a woodsman had observed a Native American attracting deer by rubbing angelica roots between his hands.

People still use angelica for colds and in the kitchen, adding young leaves to salads and candying the young stems. The dried leaves are a pleasant addition to potpourri, and angelica is used to flavor liquors such as gin, Benedictine, and vermouth.

Try adding angelica, a tall, imposing herb, to perennial beds as well as to your herb garden.

GROWING ANGELICA

This imposing herb prefers partial shade and rich, moist, well-drained soil. Angelica seeds don't stay viable long, so you need to start with fresh seed (not more than three months old). Sow the seed directly in your garden, or sow in pots in fall and leave outdoors through the winter for germination in spring. (Placing the sown seed pots in your refrigerator for six to eight weeks before moving them to a warm, bright place indoors can replace the outdoor chilling period.) You can prolong angelica's life by cutting off the flowers before seeds form. Or you can let it bloom and set seed to begin a new crop of plants. Allow the seed to drop around the base of the parent plant, or gather it and sow it where you want it to grow.

Basil is a must for so many favorite sauces that it should be a part of any herb planting.

BASIL

Ocimum basilicum
Annual

SPECIAL FEATURES

Basil grows into an attractive, bushy, 1- to 2-foot-tall plant with large, shiny green leaves, making it attractive enough to include in an ornamental border. Just brushing against the foliage produces the aromatic fragrance that makes one want to head into the kitchen and start cooking.

Left untended, the plants will produce clusters of small, white flowers along the tops of the stems. The blooms are not especially showy, however, so most gardeners pinch them off to encourage their plants to produce more sideshoots (and in turn, more of those flavor-packed leaves).

A BIT OF HISTORY

Native to India, Africa, and Asia, basil is thought to have made its way to the Mediterranean area via Alexander the Great, who collected it on a plant-and-animal expedition around 330 B.C. From Greece, it spread throughout Europe.

Basil has had a mixed reputation due to a misunderstanding of the meaning of its name. Part of its botanical name—*basilicum*—was derived from the Greek word *basilikos,* meaning king. That got confused with *basilcus*—the Latin name for a mythical monster that could kill you by looking at or breathing on you. Basil was thought to be able to produce a scorpion in two days if you placed the leaves under a rock in a moist place. By the seventeenth century, though, its culinary qualities were overcoming its bad reputation, and by 1706, Louis Liger, author of the *Retir'd Gardner,* reported that it was "a fine and delicate Plant and of very extraordinary Use in our Gardens." Since that time, basil has been very popular in both French and Italian cuisine.

Growing Basil

This aromatic herb thrives in full sun and rich, well-drained soil. Basil is easy to grow but very sensitive to frost. You can sow the seed directly in your garden when all danger of frost has passed or, for an earlier harvest, start seed indoors four to six weeks before your last frost date. You can make successive sowings through midsummer to extend your harvest. Encourage branching by pinching off the tops of the plants once they are established. Water during dry periods.

BORAGE

Borago officinalis
Annual

Special Features

This easy annual herb's claim to fame is its luminous blue to bluish pink, star-shaped flowers. They are gorgeous in the garden and look lovely floating in lemonade or when sprinkled over salads. They also are charming when candied and used as cake decorations.

The flowers bloom atop 1½- to 2-foot-tall, bushy plants with thick, hollow stems and wrinkled, hairy leaves. Borage tends to look a bit ungainly and sprawling by the end of the growing season, but those beautiful flowers you'll be rewarded with make it worth giving the plants a little extra space to grow.

A Bit of History

A very old herbal plant that is native to the Mediterranean, borage was thought by the Roman author Pliny (A.D. 23 to 79) to "make a man merry and joyful." Borage also developed a reputation for giving a person courage if drunk in a beverage: Crusaders who were leaving for battle in the Holy Land would drink wine laced with borage flowers. Medieval herbalists prescribed borage for fevers and bronchial infections and as a poultice to help heal sores and bruises. Borage was included in early kitchen gardens of the European settlers in North America and is still a beautiful addition to gardens today.

GROWING BORAGE

This annual will thrive in full sun and rich, well-drained soil. You can sow borage seeds directly in your garden as soon as the danger of frost is past, and mulching with compost will help promote vigorous growth. Thin seedlings to stand 1 foot apart. Borage will often self-sow.

ROMAN CHAMOMILE

Chamaemelum nobilis
Zones 3 to 8

SPECIAL FEATURES

This creeping perennial herb grows only 6 to 12 inches tall, with finely cut, bright green, apple-scented foliage and small, daisylike blooms. Besides making a great groundcover, chamomile is also handy to have around the house. You can use a rinse of chamomile tea to add highlights to blond hair. Just steep dried chamomile flowers in hot water, let cool, and strain out the flowers. This mild tea can also help calm upset stomachs or soothe frazzled nerves. (Note: If you're allergic to ragweed, chrysanthemums, or other plants in the daisy family, you may be allergic to chamomile.)

German chamomile (*Matricaria recutita*), an annual form of chamomile, is also reported to have healing properties.

A BIT OF HISTORY

Throughout time, chamomile tea has soothed upset stomachs. The ancient Egyptians valued it and dedicated the plant to their gods. The Greek botanist Dioscorides (A.D. 500) recommended it for headaches. Like lavender, it was used as a "strewing" herb in medieval homes, being scattered on the floor to repel insects and freshen air. In Elizabethan times, it was planted in lawns or as groundcover in between flagstones for its fragrance. American colonists included chamomile in their kitchen gardens for its medicinal qualities.

GROWING ROMAN CHAMOMILE

Roman chamomile grows in full sun or partial shade and light, well-drained soil. It prefers cool summers. Direct-sow in a well-prepared bed in early spring, when there is still a chance of light frost. You can also start it indoors at low temperatures (55° to 65°F) six to eight weeks before your last frost date. Harvesting the flowerheads regularly will help prolong bloom. Chamomile often self-sows.

CHERVIL

Anthriscus cerefolium
Annual

SPECIAL FEATURES

Chervil is a low-growing herb with clumps of fernlike, light green foliage. In summer, clusters of small, white flowers bloom atop 1-foot stems. (If you want the foliage for cooking, harvest leaves before the plant flowers.) This delicate-looking, pleasant-tasting herb deserves a place in more gardens.

A BIT OF HISTORY

Chervil is native to the Middle East and eastern and southern Europe. The Roman writer Pliny, who wrote the 37 volume *Natural History* in A.D. 77, believed that chervil was good for "warming" the stomach. Medieval users also valued chervil as a cleansing tonic for stomach upsets and as a poultice for aching joints. It is a traditional herb in French cuisine, and the foliage enhances soups, sauces, and vegetables, as well as egg, chicken, and fish dishes. For best flavor, use the foliage fresh; it loses most of its flavor when dried. Also, wait until the last few minutes of cooking to add it to the pot, since lengthy cooking will make it bitter.

GROWING CHERVIL

Sow chervil seed directly in your garden in early spring or fall, in a site with moist, rich soil and partial shade. It grows quickly and

Jazz up omelets with the fernlike foliage of chervil.

the young, fernlike leaves will be ready to pick in six to eight weeks. For a steady harvest, sow seeds every two weeks until late spring and then again in fall. If you allow a few plants to flower and self-sow each season, you can have a crop in spring and a second crop in fall without replanting every time. You can also grow chervil indoors on a windowsill for a taste treat during the winter doldrums.

DILL

Anethum graveolens
Annual

SPECIAL FEATURES

Dill grows to around 2 feet tall, with feathery foliage and small yellow flowers clustered together in umbels. The tiny but numerous flowers are rich in pollen and nectar, providing a haven for beneficial insects. By planting dill, you can have fresh herbs in your kitchen and biological control in your garden!

A BIT OF HISTORY

Dill is one of the oldest cultivated herbs and was grown by the ancient Mediterranean cultures. It was used by the Hebrew people and described in early Greek writings. The Roman epicure Apicius suggested using dill with pork, while Pliny, the ancient Roman writer, wrote that dill seeds would stop hiccoughs and dispel indigestion. During medieval times, dill was thought to have magical powers and was used in love potions and witches' spells. In the colonial days of the United States, Puritan parents would give children dill and fennel seeds to chew on to stave off hunger during long sermons on Sunday mornings. Other traditional uses for dill seeds include flavoring soups, sauces, dressings, and vinegars. The leaves, seeds, and stems have long been used to create flavorful dill pickles.

Dill does double-duty as a cut flower.

GROWING DILL

Dill is one of the easiest herbs to grow—simply direct-sow the seed in spring, after danger of frost, in a sunny, well-drained site. (If you're in a hurry for your harvest, you can start seed indoors in early spring, but make sure you transplant the seedlings carefully so you don't damage their taproots.) Thin seedlings or set transplants to stand 6 inches apart in rows 10 inches apart. For a continuous supply of dill foliage, sow a new crop every two to three weeks throughout the season. Dill will often self-sow in the garden.

FENNEL

Foeniculum vulgare
Zones 6 to 9

Fennel, an annual herb, grows best in full sun and cool weather.

SPECIAL FEATURES

Fennel forms showy clumps of feathery green foliage and 3- to 4-foot-tall stems topped with airy clusters of tiny, yellow flowers. Bronze fennel (*Foeniculum vulgare* var. *rubrum*), with its reddish brown foliage, is particularly attractive. Fennel is perennial in many areas but is often grown as a short-lived perennial. Florence fennel, a close relative, is characterized by its swollen leaf bases that create a bulblike structure at the base of the plant; it also has the finely cut green leaves of common fennel.

A BIT OF HISTORY

Thought by the Romans and the Greeks to give strength and courage, fennel is rich in folklore. William Turner (1508–68) wrote that "serpentes waxe yonge agayne by tastinge and eatynge of this herbe," and medieval villagers thought one could ward off evil spirits by stuffing fennel in a keyhole. Fennel was used traditionally to cure colic in babies, get rid of internal parasites, and cure obesity. Nowadays, we primarily enjoy fennel in the kitchen. It's great with meat and fish, and its aniselike flavor enhances salads, baked fruits, and pastries. The "bulbs" of Florence fennel make a tasty side dish, either raw or blanched.

GROWING FENNEL

Choose a planting site with full sun and average, well-drained soil. You can start seed indoors four to six weeks before your last frost date, but the seedlings may be stunted after transplanting if the roots are damaged in the process. The best way to get started is to direct-sow the seed in your garden as soon as the danger of frost has passed. Thin seedlings to stand 6 to 12 inches apart. You can harvest leaves once the plants are well established. Florence fennel will mature in about 80 days and prefers cool temperatures, so try planting in spring or fall. Harvest by cutting just below the "bulb" with a sharp knife.

HOREHOUND

Marrubium vulgare
Zones 4 to 10

SPECIAL FEATURES

This beautiful herb produces bushy clumps of woolly, silver-green leaves and whorls of tiny, white flowers on 2- to 3-foot stems. Horehound stems can get lanky in summer, so trim them back by about half to shape the plants and keep them more compact. Harvest the leaves anytime to make teas or cough drops. In the garden, the flowers attract bees and other beneficial insects.

Horehound is a classic remedy for sore throats.

A BIT OF HISTORY

Native to southern Europe, North Africa, and Asia, horehound has naturalized in many areas. This herb has been used to treat coughs and sore throats since the days of the ancient Egyptians, who took the plant's name from Horus, the god of the sun and sky. Horehound's botanical name is derived from the Hebrew *mara* or *marob*, meaning bitter juice. For many centuries, herbalists and doctors recommended horehound to soothe a variety of ills. It was also thought to break magical spells. The English herbalist Culpepper advised taking horehound in dried powder form for worms and boiling it in hog's grease to make an ointment to heal dog bites and "abate the swollen part and pains which comes by pricking thorns." North American settlers carried it with them to their new homes, and old timers in my area of Pennsylvania still make horehound cough drops. My mother used to make them occasionally, and I could never decide whether or not I liked the bittersweet taste that the herb and sugar created when they were mixed together.

GROWING HOREHOUND

Horehound likes full sun and dry, well-drained, sandy soil. It is easy to grow and, like mint, is vigorous, so give it a site where it won't out-compete other herbs. Start plants from seed indoors in spring, or increase existing plants by divisions or stem cuttings in late summer.

Once lavender plants are established, they'll tolerate dry spells without a lot of watering.

LAVENDER

Lavandula angustifolia
Zones 6 to 8

SPECIAL FEATURES

Think of lavender, and traditional associations come to mind—perhaps the fragrance emanating from a sweet old lady's dresser drawers, or the picturesque lavender fields of France. I also saw lavender used to great effect in an English manor garden as part of a floral depiction of the Union Jack along with red and white roses. It sounds like a bit much, but the garden in full bloom was beautiful. Lavender forms a small, 1- to 3-foot shrub with silvery, narrow foliage and long spikes of purple-blue flowers in early summer. Pick the flowers when the buds are just beginning to open; dry them on trays or hang them in small bunches.

A BIT OF HISTORY

Native to the Mediterranean region, this old-time perennial was probably introduced into England by the Romans. The Romans and Greeks added lavender to their bath water, and the botanical name *Lavandula* is derived from the Latin "to wash." In medieval times, lavender was used in a variety of ways—as a "strewing" herb scattered on floors to reduce odors and repel insects, and as a tonic for nervous and digestive disorders. Using lavender water was supposed to keep the wearer chaste. Lavender was also used to flavor jellies, vinegars, and stews. Commercial production of lavender oil began in the mid-1500s. An acre of lavender yields 15 to 20 pounds of essential oil. William Turner (1508–68), the Father of British Botany, recommended quilting the flowers into a cap for comforting the brain. Today, lavender is a prized plant in herb gardens and perennial beds, and it is very popular in perfumes, potpourris, soaps, and dried floral wreaths.

GROWING LAVENDER

Lavender needs full sun, alkaline soil, and good drainage. Allow the soil to dry between waterings to discourage root rot. Cover plants with pine boughs for winter protection. In areas where the foliage dies back in winter, prune back hard in early spring. Lavender grows slowly from seed, so it's best to propagate new plants by cuttings (in late spring) or layering.

MINTS

Mentha spp.
Zones 5 to 9

SPECIAL FEATURES

Mints come in an amazing array of heights, habits, and flavors, so don't limit your garden to just one type. Most mints are fast-spreading plants that grow 2 to 3 feet tall and have small white, pink, or purple flowers that grow in spikes in midsummer. Cutting your plants back often will keep them full and bushy and give you plenty of sprigs for fresh use or drying. Cold mint tea is refreshing on a hot summer day; hot mint tea is a great winter pick-me-up.

A BIT OF HISTORY

Mint was grown by the Romans and was part of English monastic gardens since the ninth century. Medieval homeowners would strew mint on the floor to freshen the air, and they used it as an insect repellant and in perfume. It was described by British garden writers as early as the fifteenth century. William Turner (1508–68) wrote that mint was good for the stomach and had a singular sweetness in sauces. During colonial times in North America, mint was the most widely grown herb after sage; it was used for teas and sauces and was distilled for its essential oil.

There are many mint species, the most common being spearmint (*Mentha*

Plant a variety of garden mints and you'll have the perfect ingredients for a refreshing glass of iced tea.

spicata) and peppermint (*M. × piperta*). Spearmint is the most widely grown mint and is used for mint juleps, the famous refreshing southern drink created in the 1800s. Peppermint is native to England, which is famous for its peppermint oil that has been produced commercially since the mid-1700s.

GROWING MINTS

Mints grow best in full sun to partial shade and in rich, moist, well-drained soil. If you have ever grown peppermint or spearmint, you know that it's hard to keep these voracious spreaders contained in a mixed bed. For best results, place mints in their own bed, or plant them in large, bottomless containers submerged in the soil to keep their roots from spreading. Start your mint bed from divisions or cuttings, as mint seed can be sterile or not grow true to type. To keep your mint patch vigorous, lift the plants every three to five years, divide them, and replant some of the divisions into the bed after you've worked compost into the soil. Give away the leftover plants, or toss them onto the compost pile.

PARSLEY

Petroselinum crispum
Biennial

SPECIAL FEATURES

Parsley's bright green foliage makes it an attractive addition to ornamental beds as well as herb gardens. The 12- to 18-inch clumps also grow well as potted plants on a sunny windowsill in winter. There are three varieties of parsley to choose from: curly leaf and flat leaf (or Italian) parsley, both of which are grown for their foliage, and parsnip-rooted (or Hamburg) parsley, grown for its root. If you leave parsley in your garden through the winter, it will bloom in late spring the second year with small, greenish yellow, Queen-Anne's-lace-type flowers.

A BIT OF HISTORY

This well-known culinary herb was used by the ancient Greeks to crown victors at the Isthmian Games, which were gymnastic, equestrian, and musical contests held in honor of Poseidon every two years. The Romans also grew parsley and used it as a culinary herb; Pliny wrote that every sauce and salad contained parsley. During Tudor times, parsley was thought to cure baldness if you sprinkled your head with parsley seeds three nights in every year. English farmers once thought parsley would prevent certain diseases in sheep, so they would grow whole fields of it. Today, gardeners raise parsley primarily for cooking or as an ornamental.

GROWING PARSLEY

Parsley thrives in full sun to light shade and rich, well-drained soil. The seed is notoriously slow to germinate (from three to four weeks), so it's best to start seed indoors in late winter, eight to ten weeks before your last frost date. You could also direct-sow the seed in the garden in spring, when there is still a chance of light frost, or in early autumn. Harvest the vitamin C–rich leaves at any time.

Let a few parsley plants overwinter, and then collect seed in late spring.

ROSEMARY

Rosmarinus officinalis
Zones 8 to 10

Rosemary is an attractive plant for container gardens.

SPECIAL FEATURES

This herb grows as a 5- to 6-foot shrub outdoors in warm climates; north of Zone 8, it usually reaches 2 to 4 feet and is grown as an annual or as a container plant. Rosemary is well-known for its green, needlelike leaves, which emit a unique, somewhat pinelike fragrance if you brush against them. It blooms in early spring with ½-inch blue flowers scattered throughout the plant. Snip leaves at any time for cooking or enriching potpourri. Besides giving you a useful harvest, regular pruning will help keep your plant full and bushy.

A BIT OF HISTORY

Rosemary has been used as a culinary and medicinal herb for centuries. The ancient Greeks believed this Mediterranean native improved memory, and students tucked sprigs in their hair as they studied for exams. The Romans probably introduced it to England. Rosemary has been known as the "herb of remembrance and fidelity," and it was traditionally included in wedding bouquets. It was also thought to cure depression, headaches, muscle spasms, and stomach problems. This highly aromatic herb flavors chicken, lamb, and pork dishes and is a pleasant scent in potpourris and soaps.

GROWING ROSEMARY

Grow rosemary in full sun and sandy, well-drained soil. Add lime or crushed oyster shells to acid soil every few years; the plants grow best in alkaline soil. Rosemary is an evergreen shrub where winter temperatures do not drop below 10°F. If you live north of Zone 8, grow this herb as an annual, or take cuttings of it in the fall and overwinter them indoors. (If you grow your rosemary in a pot, you don't even have to bother with cuttings; just bring the whole plant indoors.) Indoors, rosemary needs a spot with bright light and high humidity. Set plants out in your garden in spring, after the danger of frost has passed.

SAGE

Salvia officinalis
Zones 4 to 10

SPECIAL FEATURES

Sage is an aromatic, easy-to-grow herb that can reach 2 to 3 feet in height. The oblong, velvety, thick, gray-green leaves are attractive in dried herb wreaths. Sage flowers in summer, with ½-inch purple blooms arranged in whorls on the flower stalk. These handsome plants are equally at home in an herb garden or perennial border.

A BIT OF HISTORY

Native to the Mediterranean area, sage was considered a sacred herb by the ancient Romans. Specially appointed sage gatherers dressed in white and made sacrifices of bread and wine before gathering sage in a special ceremony. The seventeenth-century English herbalist Culpepper recommended sage for many medicinal uses, including "provoking urine, causing the hair to become black and for helping cure pains of all kinds in the head and of the joints." He also thought it helped the memory. Sage tea was at one time highly valued in China, and the Chinese traded with Holland—3 pounds of China tea for 1 pound of dried sage. In colonial America, sage was the most commonly grown kitchen herb to flavor foods (especially those that were beyond their prime), but it was also considered a useful medicinal herb for a number of ailments, including gastrointestinal upsets and mouth ulcers. Sage leaves are most often associated with turkey stuffing, but they are also delicious with omelets, yeast breads, and vegetable dishes.

Layering is an easy way to propagate sage and other herbs with woody stems. Simply bend a shoot to the ground, cover part of the stem with soil, and support the exposed part of the shoot with a stake. (If needed, anchor the buried stem to the ground with a rock.) In a few months, you can cut the rooted layer from the parent plant and transplant it.

GROWING SAGE

Choose a planting site with full sun and well-drained, moderately rich soil. Start seed indoors eight weeks before your last frost date. Set the seedlings outdoors when they are about 3 inches tall, after your last frost date has passed. Cut back established plants by about half in spring to keep them bushy and vigorous. To propagate existing plants, take cuttings in late summer or early fall, grow them indoors in winter, and set them out in spring. Or you can "layer" your sage (see the illustration on the opposite page). The portion covered with soil will take root within a few months. You can then cut the connecting stem to the old plant and transplant your new plant.

Sage has long-lasting, richly textured foliage, so it's a nice addition to perennial borders.

SUMMER SAVORY

Satureja hortensis
Annual

SPECIAL FEATURES

Summer savory grows 12 to 18 inches tall, with narrow, gray-green leaves and a few small, pinkish white flowers in late summer. It can become top-heavy and sprawl, so mound soil around the base of the clumps or set them about 6 inches apart so that the plants can support each other. Regular harvesting also helps keep plants bushy.

A BIT OF HISTORY

Another Mediterranean native, summer savory is one of the oldest European culinary herbs. It was also one of the strongest flavored until tropical spices like black pepper were imported into Europe. The Romans used it and probably brought it to England. In medieval times, savory leaves and flowers were steeped in hot water and the tea was used medicinally for stomach and intestinal disorders. Cooks from medieval times through the nineteenth century used summer savory and its perennial relative, winter savory (*Satureja montana*), for flavoring everything from soups and conserves to meat and vegetables. Lydia Marie

Child, author of *The American Frugal Housewife* (published in 1832), recommended savory as "excellent to season soup, broth, and sausages. As a medicine, it relieves the colic." Summer savory is one of the few culinary herbs the Shakers used in their kitchens, and they also grew and dried it for their commercial herb business. The fresh or dried savory leaves are especially recommended for flavoring beans—from fresh green beans to lentils. The Germans call it "bohnenkraut," or bean herb.

GROWING SUMMER SAVORY

This easy-to-grow annual herb needs full sun and light, well-drained soil in order to thrive. Summer savory transplants easily, so you can start seed indoors four weeks before your last frost date, or you can simply sow the seeds directly in your garden after your last frost date. If you leave some of the plants unharvested so that they can flower and set seed at the end of the growing season, summer savory will often self-sow in your garden.

THYMES

Thymus spp.
Zones 5 to 9

SPECIAL FEATURES

Common thyme (*Thymus vulgaris*), the thyme most often grown for culinary purposes, is a 1-foot-tall, shrubby perennial with small, aromatic, oval-shaped gray-green leaves and clusters of tiny purple flowers in summer. There are over 350 other species of thyme, ranging from ground-hugging types, such as creeping thyme (*T. praecox* spp. *articus*), that work well as groundcovers, to thymes with different scents, such as lemon thyme (*T.* × *citriodorus*), which is a bushy variety with small white flowers and dark green leaves that emit a strong lemony scent.

A BIT OF HISTORY

Numerous thyme species are native to the Mediterranean area. The ancient Etruscans and Egyptians used thyme for embalming. *Thymus* is from the Greek meaning "courage" or "to fumigate" because thyme was used as temple incense. Roman soldiers bathed in thyme water to give themselves vigor, and they thought it a useful medicinal herb. The Romans introduced it to England, where it was still a symbol of courage during the Middle Ages; ladies would embroider sprigs of thyme on scarves for their knights. On the more practical side, bunches of thyme were strewn on floors and burned to fumigate the dank dwellings of the time. Medicinally, an infusion of thyme was used to relieve breathing disorders such as asthma, bronchitis, and whooping cough. It was also used to expel hookworms, although the

Plant low-growing thymes between paving stones for a fragrant pathway.

dose needed could be fatal. (The essential oil of thyme can be a toxic compound when taken internally—as are the essential oils of most herbs—and skin irritations can occur from external use.) Now one of the most widely used culinary herbs, thyme works well with a wide range of dishes, including soups, eggs, meats, breads, tomatoes, and many other vegetables.

GROWING THYMES

Thyme prefers light, well-drained soil and a location in full sun. You can start seed indoors in early spring, or you can take cuttings from overwintered plants in late spring or early summer. Sow seeds in clusters in individual pots, as the seedlings are quite small and delicate. Bush thymes, with the exception of variegated cultivars, often self-sow freely.

Thyme will become woody and die out in the center of the plant after three to five years. When this happens, cut the center of the plant out, discard it, and divide up the outer, live roots, and transplant them. Water the transplants thoroughly. Mulch plants in fall to prevent frost heaving over winter.

C H A P T E R

S I X

Flavorful Old-Time Fruits and Berries

Fresh, sun-ripened fruit is such an exquisite treat that it's little wonder that gardeners have long pursued the best and most flavorful varieties. From the ancient civilizations of Persia, Greece, and Rome, where the nobility served fresh fruit as the grand finale to luxurious banquets, to the eighteenth-century Gooseberry Clubs of England, whose members strove to develop champion gooseberry varieties, growing and eating fine fruit has long been a passion. Today's fruit-growing enthusiasts can also experience the pleasure of finding the first sun-ripened strawberry, baking deliciously flavored blueberry cobblers, and growing an extraordinary range of antique varieties of apples and other tree fruits.

By raising your own heirloom and native fruits, you can enjoy a much greater diversity and much better flavor of fruit than you can find at your local supermarket. Old-time country gardeners in the seventeenth, eighteenth, and nineteenth centuries grew tree fruit in North America without the aid of pesticides. You can, too—just be sure to choose the best disease-resistant varieties for your area—and remember that blemishes on your fruit are okay. You'll find there's nothing to compare with the taste of a luscious, tree-ripened peach or the flavor of red raspberries straight off the bush!

OPPOSITE: *Select the best heirlooms for your growing area, and you'll be rewarded with a wonderful array of flavorful fruit.*

Selected Heirloom Fruits

Here's a gallery of some classic, old-fashioned fruits that are especially suited for today's home gardens. Some, like apples, are still widely grown; others, such as quince, are seldom seen nowadays but are still worth growing in an heirloom country garden.

APPLES

Malus × domestica
Zones 4 to 9

SPECIAL FEATURES

Apples have universal appeal and are a part of many fall harvest celebrations. And whatever size your yard, you should be able to find an apple tree to fit it. A "standard" (full-size) apple tree is a beautiful addition to a large landscape, while a dwarf apple tree trained along a garden fence will fit in even the smallest of yards. You can enjoy the petite 'Lady' apple, grown by Louis XIII in 1628 (it's beautiful in Christmas arrangements) or the huge, 1-pound 'Wolf River' apple originally found on a chance seedling tree in 1875 in Wisconsin (it's great for pies and baking).

A BIT OF HISTORY

Although apples may seem to be uniquely American (baseball and apple pie and all that), many cultures over the centuries have cultivated and consumed apples. Apples probably originated in the Caucasus, where forests of wild fruit trees still exist and are a plant breeder's paradise. The ancient Romans developed dozens of apple varieties and were responsible for bringing the domesticated apple to Europe and Britain.

In medieval times in Europe, apples were mainly used for cider and cooking rather than for fresh eating (most apple varieties were on the astringent side and eating raw fruit was thought to cause gastronomic havoc), but by the Renaissance, Italians were enjoying apples at lavish banquets where these and other kinds of fruit

You can choose from hundreds of varieties of heirloom apples in a range of sizes, colors, and uses.

were displayed in elegant, tall-stemmed glass containers.

Apple trees thrived in North America after being introduced by the first European settlers in the seventeenth century. The Europeans brought seeds, scions (grafting wood), and even young trees of their favorite apples for establishing new orchards. Because apples will not grow "true to type" from seed, planting seeds produced many new varieties, and regional favorites eventually became uniquely American varieties. At first, apples were grown throughout New England and Pennsylvania mainly for cider production. (Roughly one farmer out of ten had a cider mill, and well-to-do farmers put up 20 to 50 barrels of cider every autumn.)

But settlers soon became experts at baking with apples, too: pies, dumplings, fritters, and pancakes were favorites. Some of the popular varieties grown in early America included 'Black Gilliflower' (a very good baking apple), 'Roxbury Russet' (a favorite late-winter apple), and 'Westfield Seek No Farther' (considered to be one of the best all-purpose apples for cider and fresh eating).

Literally thousands of apple varieties were grown in North America in the nineteenth century. *Nomenclature of the Apple*, a 1905 government publication, lists 17,000 apple varieties from the nineteenth century! There were varieties for summer baking, for fresh eating and cider making in fall, and for storing in root cellars for winter use.

GROWING APPLES

When you're planning your home orchard, don't make the mistake of selecting only those varieties you're familiar with from the grocery store; investigate the incredible wealth of apple varieties available to home growers. Fortunately, there are several mail-order nurseries that specialize in heirloom cultivars; for their names and addresses, see "Seed and Plant Sources" on page 228. Be sure to check which varieties have good resistance to the disease problems in your growing area, and make sure the varieties you choose are compatible pollinators for each other (ask the supplier if you're not sure).

If you live where winters are severe (Zone 4 and colder), ask your nursery or extension agent about cold-hardy varieties and rootstocks. Hardy heirloom varieties include 'Baldwin', a crisp, juicy, fresh-eating variety from Lowell, Massachusetts in 1740; 'Golden Russet', an excellent keeper from New York State in the early 1800s that is used for cider, dried apples, fresh eating, and cooking; and 'Tolman Sweet', an 1845 Massachusetts introduction that has an attractive yellow skin with a trace of red and an excellent, sweet flavor. If you live in Zone 8 or parts of Zone 9, look for "low-chill" varieties that require fewer than 600 hours of temperatures below 45°F for their dormant rest period. 'White Winter Pearmain', an English variety dating back to about 1200, and 'Winter Banana', a good winter-keeper apple originating in Indiana in 1876, are two low-chill heirloom varieties.

Be aware that your chosen varieties will be grafted onto a rootstock that controls the size of the tree. Standard rootstocks are the most cold-hardy but produce a full-size tree (25 to 30 feet tall). More commonly grown today are semidwarf rootstocks, which produce trees that reach 12 to 15 feet at maturity, and full dwarf rootstocks, which are 6 to 8 feet tall. Full dwarf and some semidwarf rootstocks will need staking or trellising for support.

Plant your apple trees in full sun and fertile, well-drained soil. Be sure to avoid frost pockets—low-lying areas where cold air tends to settle on fall and spring nights. A late-spring frost can kill blossoms on your fruit trees, and an early-fall frost can nip your apples. Your trees will need training and pruning; see "Pruning Pointers" on page 181 for more information. Apply mulch around the base of the tree in spring to control weeds, but rake it off in autumn until the ground freezes; otherwise, you'll encourage rodents to make their winter homes next to your tasty trees. Thin the young fruits to 6 to 8 inches apart for good fruit size. You will need to monitor your orchard for pest problems and use insect traps and cultural controls to minimize insect damage; see "Coping with Pests" on page 177 for tips. Depending on the variety and rootstock, you can begin to harvest fruit in two to six years.

Try red currants! The fruit is wonderful in pies and preserves, and the plants are easy to grow.

CURRANTS AND GOOSEBERRIES

Ribes spp.
Zones 3 to 7

SPECIAL FEATURES

Currants and gooseberries are great for gardeners who'd like to grow heirloom fruit but have limited space. These small (3- to 5-foot-high), multistemmed shrubs produce clusters of luminous fruit that are ready for harvest during early to midsummer. Not widely grown in America but still popular in Europe, these fruits are wonderful for pies, jams, and preserves. One of my favorite vacation memories is one clear summer day in Norway when my sister and I visited a living history museum located high in the hills. We were returning via a walking trail that led through a beautiful meadow. As we walked, we ate the waffles layered with red currant jam and sour cream that we had purchased in the village. Life was good that relaxing sunny afternoon.

Favorite Fruits from Monticello

Peter J. Hatch, director of the gardens and grounds at Monticello, has written several books about Thomas Jefferson's gardens including The Fruit and Fruit Trees of Monticello. *I asked Peter for some of his recommendations for gardeners.*

Sarah: Which heirloom varieties of fruit would you recommend for gardeners just starting with fruit growing?

Peter: A number of the Jefferson varieties do well for us today and have superior qualities. The fruits of 'Newton Pippin' apple keep so well, and if you get the right strain, they are delicious. The taste of 'Spitzenburg' is unequaled. The 'Hewes Crab' is particularly hardy and makes a delicious and unique cider: It is indeed "ambrosia." The 'Seckel' pear does well in the East, and the sugary tasting fruit is special.

The 'Oldmixon Free' peach tastes like candy, and this year we had huge crop of 'Indian Blood' peaches, which were universally admired by everyone here. The 'Green Gage' plum, surviving centuries of cultivation, is still around because of its taste.

We make large quantities of wine from the 'Sangiovese' grape, and it equals Italian Chiantis I've admired. The 'Chickasaw' plum is always the healthiest tree in the south orchard here at Monticello. The 'White Pine' strawberries we grow have a subtlety of fragrance and flavor that has been lost in commercial varieties.

Sarah: Are there heirloom varieties that you caution gardeners not to grow?

Peter: European pears are hard in our Virginia climate; currants and gooseberries are impossible to grow in the South.

Sarah: In your book, you also discuss the two traditions of fruit growing that were prevalent in Jefferson's time: the American fruit farm and the European kitchen garden. Do you have suggestions for today's gardener who wants to grow heirloom varieties in an attractive garden?

Peter: I like gardens with a mix of fruits, flowers, and vegetables. Fruit trees— dwarf and even standards—are wonderful around the outside of kitchen gardens, in borders and allees (double rows of trees with a path between them). They provide height and structure, are beautiful in flower, and add a "pick-your-own-dessert" element to the garden experience.

A BIT OF HISTORY

Native to northern Europe and Asia, currants were first noted in a German herbal in 1488, when wild currants were gathered for medicinal use. By the mid-sixteenth century, currants had been domesticated by Dutch growers and were considered to be a garden plant. This beautiful fruit was introduced to Massachusetts in 1629. The growing conditions for currants were favorable in New England, and currants now thrive as far south as Virginia and as far north as British Columbia and Alaska. In 1782, Thomas Jefferson noted that a quart of currant juice "makes 2 blue teacups of jelly, 1 quart of juice to 4 of puree," and George Washington grew red, white, and black currants at Mount Vernon.

Currants retained their popularity as an easy-to-grow garden crop into the nineteenth century. The federal government's ban on growing *Ribes* species in 1918 put the crop into obscurity (it was thought to carry white pine blister rust), but since the ban was lifted in 1966, you can add this fruit to your garden and have wonderful pies and jellies from the berries. 'Red Lake' is a popular red currant that was introduced in 1933 by the University of Minnesota. 'Red Dutch' is the oldest known currant variety still being cultivated.

Gooseberries, which were cultivated plants in Europe since the thirteenth century, were finally introduced to North America in the seventeenth century. However, their intolerance of hot, humid weather and their susceptibility to powdery mildew proved to be problems for growers. Growing them under North American conditions became easier when a mildew-resistant seedling was discovered in 1833 by Abel Houghton of Massachusetts. 'Champion', an 1880 Oregon gooseberry, is a large, sweet gooseberry variety for Western growers. 'Poorman', a mildew-resistant gooseberry introduced in 1888, is considered to be one of the finest American gooseberries.

GROWING CURRANTS AND GOOSEBERRIES

Both currants and gooseberries are very hardy plants (to −20°F), and they prefer mild summers where temperatures do not routinely climb very much beyond 85°F. The best site for your *Ribes* is a north-facing slope with good air circulation. Mulching with compost, straw, or leaves will help keep the roots cool, retain moisture, and add organic matter to the soil. Both currants and gooseberries are usually grown as small shrubs, although you can also espalier them along a wall. Once your plants are several years old, you should prune out all stems more than three years old during dormant season pruning. Leave about six young shoots per shrub to bear fruit. You can propagate currants and gooseberries by taking hardwood cuttings in late fall or early spring.

'Concord' grapes are a good choice for Eastern, Midwestern, and Northwestern gardeners.

GRAPES

Vitis spp.
Zones 4 to 9
(depending on the species)

SPECIAL FEATURES

Full clusters of ripe, richly colored grapes are an integral part of the fall harvest. Grape arbors or trellises are attractive additions to the home landscape and can provide an abundant harvest for both you and the birds, such as cedar waxwings and bluebirds. And nothing beats the taste of jelly, jam, juice, or wine made from grapes grown right outside your own back door!

A BIT OF HISTORY

Grapes are one of the oldest of our food crops and have been grown by numerous cultures around the world. Valued as a fresh and dried fruit, a fermented drink, and a medicinal fruit, the oldest cultivated grapes (*Vitis vinifera*) were part of Egyptian, Jewish, Greek, and Roman cultures thousands of years ago. The Romans brought grapevines to Britain, and medieval European cultures made wine and verjuice (grape vinegar).

European colonists brought their grape varieties to North America and had great hopes for establishing vineyards in the new country. In California and Mexico, Catholic monasteries successfully grew the European varieties of *V. vinifera* that were favored for wine production. Elsewhere, however, the European grapes were susceptible to phylloxera (a root and leaf aphid) and fungal diseases, and they did not produce well.

Native grapes, on the other hand, were problem-free and grew abundantly in the wild. The native American or fox grape (*V. labrusca*) is both cold-hardy and tolerant of areas with hot, humid summers (Zones 4 to 8). It does have tougher skin than the European grapes for fresh eating, but it makes wonderful fresh juice, jelly, and jam. The 'Concord' grape, introduced in 1843, is the most famous descendant of the fox grape. Other *V. labrusca* varieties include 'Beta', a Minnesota variety dating to 1881 that is a very hardy and productive jelly and juice grape, and 'Buffalo', a disease-free early 'Concord' type that was introduced in 1938 and is an excellent table, jam, and wine grape.

Muscadine grapes (*V. rotundifolia*) do well in the humid Southeast, are disease- and pest-resistant, and are hardy from Zones 7 to 9. The most well-known and one of the oldest muscadine varieties is 'Scuppernong'. It has beautiful, large fruit with a reddish bronze cast and a musky, woodsy taste that is excellent for fresh eating and wine making. 'Scuppernong' needs a second muscadine variety, such as 'Higgins' (a cold-hardy, large, bronze muscadine introduced in 1955) to pollinate it.

GROWING GRAPES

American and muscadine grapes both need full sun and deep, well-drained soil rich in organic matter. Be sure to check with your local extension agent if you are not sure which grape varieties do well in your area. Grapes will need some type of support, in the form of a trellis, fence, or arbor. Mulch lightly to control weeds. Prune yearly when plants are dormant (see "Pruning Pointers" on page 181 for more information). Your vines will begin to bear fruit in two to three years.

Unlike some other fruits, grapes will not continue to ripen after they are picked, so only harvest when the fruit are mature. Cut off your clusters of American grapes when the fruit is fully colored, the seeds are brown, and the fruit has full flavor. Harvest early in the day, when possible, and store grapes in a cool area out of direct sunlight immediately after picking. While American grapes mature pretty much all at once, muscadine grapes ripen over a period of several weeks, so spot-pick ripe clusters and enjoy the extended harvest.

PEACHES

Prunus persica
Zones 3 to 9
(depending on the variety)

SPECIAL FEATURES

A juicy, sun-ripened peach is one of summer's best tastes. Heirloom peaches can have white or yellow flesh (some argue that white peaches have the best flavor). They can be either clingstone, where the fruit adheres to the seed, or freestone, which means the fruit separates easily from the seed.

A BIT OF HISTORY

First grown by the Chinese over 2,000 years ago, peaches were prized for their delicious fruit and their beautiful pink blooms. They were brought to the United States by Spanish settlers in 1565. By the time William Penn arrived in Pennsylvania, peaches were cultivated by Native Americans and had naturalized in many areas in the East. These wild or "Indian" peaches were so abundant in clearings that fruit covered the ground and made it slippery.

During the seventeenth century, peaches were so widely grown that the fruit was used to fatten the family hogs and make brandy, as well as being dried for winter use. Thomas Jefferson grew 38 varieties of peaches at Monticello. In the early nineteenth century, however, a mysterious malady hit peach orchards in Pennsylvania and gradually spread to other peach-growing areas.

The epidemic was peach yellows, a viral disease, which first caused the leaves to turn yellow and then quickly killed the tree. Today the problem can be avoided by growing varieties grafted onto virus-free rootstocks. A very old heirloom, 'Grosse Mignonne', was introduced in 1667 and is a rich, juicy, pale greenish white peach. Other old favorites include 'Early Crawford', a large, yellow, New Jersey peach from the 1880s, and 'Belle of Georgia', an old favorite from 1870 that is a semiclingstone white peach great for fresh eating and canning. 'Elberta', another Georgia peach from the 1870s, is a large, yellow, freestone peach still widely grown today. It is resistant to brown rot.

GROWING PEACHES

Ask your nursery expert or extension agent which varieties will perform best in your location, and find out if you need a high-chill or low-chill variety. (Chilling requirements refer to the number of hours below 45°F that a tree needs to break its rest period and bloom.) Tree height varies from 6 to 20 feet tall, depending on the rootstock. Check which diseases are common in your area, and select resistant varieties. Most peaches do not require a pollinator variety. Plant your peach tree in full sun and well-drained, fertile soil, and water during dry periods. Peach trees will bear fruit in 3 to 5 years, depending on the variety. The trees are not as long-lived as apples or pears, and you should plan on replacing them about every 12 years.

EUROPEAN PEARS

Pyrus spp.
Zones 5 to 8

SPECIAL FEATURES

Pear trees are not just beautiful in bloom, with their clusters of white blossoms—they're also one of the easiest fruit trees to grow, especially if you grow a fireblight-resistant variety. You can plant several varieties of this buttery-smooth fruit and have fresh pears from midsummer all the way through autumn. Pears are excellent for both fresh eating and cooking.

A BIT OF HISTORY

Native to western Asia, pears have been cultivated in Europe for thousands of years. They were a favorite fruit of the ancient Greeks and Romans, and the Romans cultivated several dozen varieties. During Medieval times, pears were used for medicinal and culinary purposes. When applied externally, wild pears were thought to heal fresh wounds and reduce inflammation. Culinary uses included jams, puddings, and perry, a fermented, ciderlike drink that was introduced to Britain by the Romans. European pears traveled to North America with the colonists but did not attain the early widespread popularity that apples enjoyed. Pears were apparently considered to be more the domain of "gentleman farmers" who enjoyed competing for honors at pear exhibits sponsored by local horticultural societies from about 1820 to 1870. The state of Massachusetts was the center of these pear competitions. Nurseries carried hundreds of varieties to provide growers with a good selection of choice pears.

Another reason that pear production was limited was fireblight, a serious bacterial disease first reported in the United States in 1794. By the early 1800s, it was nearly impossible to grow fireblight-susceptible pears south of New York. Fruit growers in the 1840s were happy to seize upon two fireblight-resistant cultivars: 'Le Conte' and 'Kieffer'. 'Le Conte' is a vigorous, consistently bearing variety that needs another variety for pollination. 'Kieffer' pears are excellent for canning and baking, but are gritty-tasting if eaten fresh.

Two excellent heirloom pear varieties are 'Seckel' and 'Bosc'. 'Seckel' pears, somewhat fireblight-resistant, originated as a chance seedling on a farm in the Philadelphia area around the time of the American Revolution. Its small fruit is wonderfully flavored. 'Bosc', a medium, dark yellow pear with russeted skin, also has a rich flavor. Introduced to North America from Belgium in 1807, it is susceptible to fireblight. 'Winter Nelis', a Belgian pear from the early nineteenth century, is a rough, russeted, dark brown pear that is juicy and aromatic. It is resistant to fireblight.

Growing European Pears

Plant your pear trees in a site that has full sun, good air circulation, and well-drained soil. Pears are bothered by very few pest problems other than fireblight. If fireblight is a problem in your area, be sure to choose a fireblight-resistant variety. Check with your local extension agent if you have questions about which varieties will do well in your area. The size of your tree will range from 10 to 30 feet high, depending on which rootstock you choose. Rootstocks in the 'Old Home' × 'Farmington' ('Oh' × 'F') series are fireblight-resistant. Pears are partially self-fruitful, but planting two varieties that cross-pollinate each other will ensure a good crop. (Check with your nursery to make sure that your varieties are compatible and will cross-pollinate.) It is easy to train pear trees to a central leader system (a central trunk with several sets of "scaffold" branches, much like a Christmas tree) because of their upright growth habit. If you have a fireblight-susceptible variety, you may want to train your tree to two trunks in case one trunk is hit by fireblight and needs to be removed. For more information, refer to "Pruning Pointers" on page 181.

QUINCE

Cydonia oblonga
Zones 6 to 9
(some varieties to Zone 5)

Special Features

Quince trees are 12 to 15 feet tall, with pretty pink or white blossoms in the spring. Quince fruits, approximately 5 inches long with a round or oblong shape, are not tasty fresh off the tree, but they impart a wonderful flavor to jams and pies. Many gardeners associate the word "quince" with flowering quince (*Chaenomeles* spp.), which is an entirely different plant, but the spring-flowering quince does produce a small, hard fruit that can also be used to flavor preserves.

A Bit of History

Native to the Middle East, quince was mentioned by the ancient Roman writer Pliny and was a favorite medieval fruit for pies and jellies. It was also popular with early North American colonists, and U. P. Hedrick, author of *A History of Horticulture in North America,* described quince as more commonly planted than apples and pears in the early eighteenth century. They were usually propagated from cuttings because planting from seeds would not produce the same variety as the parent. The most popular quince variety was 'Orange' quince, which is still available today. New England kitchen gardens often had this small spreading tree included in one corner. Other heirloom cultivars include 'Smyrna', introduced to

North America from Smyrna, Turkey, in 1897, and 'Pineapple', developed by the plant breeder Luther Burbank. 'Pineapple' has a distinctive pineapple flavor and tolerates wet soil.

GROWING QUINCE

Quinces need full sun and well-drained, moderately fertile soil. They are self-fertile, which means you only need to plant one variety and your tree will begin to bear fruit one to two years after planting. You can train a quince as a small tree with an open center or as a multistemmed shrub. (See "Pruning Pointers" on page 181 for pruning information.) If quinces receive too much nitrogen, they will produce lots of lush growth, which is more prone to fireblight, a serious bacterial disease that causes young shoots to turn black, wilt, and then die. Trim off any damage a foot below any visible sign of the disease, and destroy the prunings. Dip your pruners in bleach to disinfect them before making a new cut.

RASPBERRIES

Rubus spp.
Zones 3 to 9
(depending on the variety)

SPECIAL FEATURES

Several generations ago, most folks knew where wild hedgerows of berries were free for the picking, and there they gathered buckets of raspberries for pies and jellies. Today, shoppers know that fresh raspberries are expensive to purchase because they do not ship well and are highly perishable. Fortunately, it's easy to include raspberries in the home landscape, and you can enjoy berries from midsummer to fall. Plant black and purple raspberries for a midsummer treat, and extend your harvest season with summer- and fall-bearing red and yellow raspberries.

A BIT OF HISTORY

Native raspberries, as well as blackberries, blueberries, and other berries, were abundant in forest clearings in North America and played an important role in Native American diets. They ate the berries fresh and preserved them for winter use by drying them over a fire. The dried berries were added to breads, soups, puddings, and pemmican, which was made of dried meat and fat. Raspberries also had value as medicinal plants; the roots of the red raspberry were made into an eyewash, and the fruit itself was used as a flavoring for medicine. European colonists also had a tradition of using their varieties of berries for medicinal purposes, as ingredients in purgatives and laxatives.

The cultivation and improvement of black raspberries started around 1850 when H. H. Doolittle, a farmer from

Oaks Corners, New York, observed that in the autumn the tips of black raspberries would droop to the ground and root. He selected the best wild raspberries he could find growing along the edge of the woods and began propagating them by this natural tip layering. (Up to this point, black raspberry plants had been propagated by division, a slower and more difficult process.) Introduced before 1900, 'Cumberland' is a healthy, vigorous variety with excellent flavor for jams, jellies, preserves, and canning. The red raspberry 'Latham' is more than 60 years old and is also considered a standard for its vigor and fine flavor.

GROWING RASPBERRIES

Raspberries need fertile, well-drained soil. They prefer full sun, but in areas where summer daytime temperatures are often above 75°F, they will do better in light shade. They will grow best if trellised or otherwise supported. Look for a site where your plants will have good air circulation but not be exposed to cold winter winds. Make sure you start your patch with certified disease-free plants. Avoid planting black raspberries right next to red raspberries, since the red raspberries may transmit viruses to the more-susceptible black raspberries.

STRAWBERRIES

Fragaria spp.
Zones 3 to 10
(depending on the variety)

SPECIAL FEATURES

Who doesn't like luscious, fresh red strawberries? This low-growing perennial fruit is easy to cultivate in your garden, and most varieties are aggressive spreaders. You can choose from the tiny (½- to 1-inch-long), intensely flavorful fruits of the alpine strawberry (*Fragaria vesca* var. *sempervirens*)—try using them as a delicious edging for a perennial bed—or the heirloom varieties of garden strawberries for your favorite shortcake or strawberry jam.

A BIT OF HISTORY

Native to North America, the scarlet or Virginia strawberry (*Fragaria virginiana*) was introduced to Europe in the sixteenth century. It quickly became popular for its larger size, richer color, and longer fruiting season than the native European species, the alpine strawberry (*F. vesca*), which has small but wonderfully flavored fruit. In 1714, Lt. Colonel Frezier, an intelligence officer for King Louis XIV of France, shipped five plants of Chilean strawberry (*F. chiloensis*), a South American native, and they were carefully distributed to botanical gardens. The Chilean strawberry had larger fruit than the alpine strawberry and was a vigorous plant, but it was not hardy in many European locations. Today's garden

Strawberries can fit in any size garden and provide a tasty harvest the second growing season.

strawberry (*F.* × *ananassa*) is the result of North American and South American native strawberries from an early-eighteenth-century Dutch botanical garden collection accidentally crossing and producing a new strawberry hybrid.

Strawberries were one of Thomas Jefferson's favorite fruits, and he tried several species, including the alpine, which he rated high in flavor but disappointingly small, and Chilean, which he could not successfully establish at Monticello. (The Chilean strawberry does not do well in either very cold or hot and humid climates.) Victorian gardeners developed many new varieties of the cultivated strawberry, and plant breeders in the early twentieth century continued to develop new cultivars for gardens and commercial plantings. Several garden strawberries introduced from 1920 through the 1930s are still available, including 'Blakemore', 'Catskill', 'Dunlap', 'Fairfax', and 'Tennessee Beauty'.

GROWING STRAWBERRIES

Strawberries require full sun and rich, well-drained soil that's slightly acid (having a pH around 6.2). Avoid low-lying "frost pockets," so your berry blossoms don't freeze in the spring. Pick the blossoms off your garden strawberries during their first season so the plants will establish healthy root systems and send out plantlets on horizontal stems called runners. (These runners will root and form new plants.) Alpine strawberries are runnerless and are an attractive edging plant for perennial beds. Water during dry periods. Keeping your strawberry beds free of weeds is the biggest job; mulching between rows helps reduce weed problems. Birds enjoy ripe berries as much as people do. If your feathered friends are taking more than their share, drape bird netting over the patch. Mulch the bed with straw or leaves in the winter. Berry patches will lose their productivity over time, so plan to start new plantings every three to four years.

Part Three

GROWING and ENJOYING HEIRLOOM COUNTRY GARDENS

There's lots to do and enjoy in this section. Learn old-time advice on growing vegetables and flowers, plus how to prune heirloom fruit trees and grapes. In the projects section, you'll find instructions for a grape arbor and wattle fencing, and if you enjoy cooking, you'll have fun trying the variety of delicious old-time recipes.

Growing Great Gardens Grandma's Way

Good gardeners have always been a lively and curious lot. Over the centuries, our gardening forebears developed productive gardening techniques that have been passed on from generation to generation. We have much to thank past gardeners for, and we need to make sure that the best of the old ways are preserved, not forgotten. From preserving seeds to preserving the harvest, from enriching the soil to keeping weeds down, our ancestors have already tackled all the hard questions and worked out time-tested solutions, documenting—more or less!—the ways these problems have been handled for generations. And, of course, our gardening forebears were all

organic gardeners—they gardened before the advent of chemicals! At the same time, we can all use new information and biological controls to help us grow our gardens organically. This chapter contains a mix of old and new tips and techniques for your own heirloom country garden.

Getting Your Garden Started

A level, sunny, somewhat sheltered site is an ideal spot for starting a garden, since it will let you grow the widest range of vegetables, herbs, and flowers with a minimum of preparation. (Light shade is also good for growing

OPPOSITE: *Old-time country gardeners had productive organic gardens that were also lush and beautiful.*

many perennials, annuals, and bulbs.) Sure, there are solutions to problem sites, such as terracing a sloped area, planting a windbreak hedge for a windy area, and using raised beds for areas with poor drainage. But when you're just starting out, it's best to choose an easy site, if you can, even if it's small. Once you get that first garden going, you can turn your attention to fixing up those more challenging sites.

If you are unsure of what shape your soil nutrients are in, purchase a soil test kit from your Cooperative Extension agent. Follow the instructions for taking soil samples, and be sure to ask for organic fertilizer recommendations.

STARTING A KITCHEN GARDEN

No, it's not a garden *in* your kitchen—it's a garden *for* your kitchen! A kitchen garden is where you grow edible crops, including vegetables, fruits, herbs, and even edible flowers.

Kitchen gardeners of the past had more urgency to growing their vegetables than most of us do today. For country folk up through the mid-nineteenth century, their gardens were an essential, if not critical, part of their lives, because they grew all their own vegetables, fruits, and medicines. A bad year for crops meant a lean or even disastrous winter. Old-time country gardeners had to be knowledgeable horticulturists and work hard to fill their pantries and root cellars. Their lives were marked by the agricultural activities that went with each season.

Two priorities for old-time vegetable gardeners were maintaining soil fertility through crop rotation and maximizing harvests by planting successive crops in the same garden bed during the same growing season. Square or rectangular garden beds were and still are a good way to organize both crop rotations and successive plantings.

Understanding crop rotation. In simplest terms, crop rotation merely means not planting the same crop in the same spot two years in a row. Taking this a step further and planning rotations based on groups of crops that have similar needs will provide even more benefits, helping to maintain your soil's fertility while reducing pest and disease problems. I like to use a four-group system:

- "fruit" crops, such as tomatoes, peppers, corn, broccoli, and squash;
- leaf crops, like lettuce, spinach, chard, and cabbage;
- root crops, such as carrots, potatoes, beets, and onions; and
- legume crops, which include beans, peas, and leguminous cover crops (clovers, alfalfa, and vetches).

To use this system, simply plant a "fruit" crop in a particular garden bed one year, followed by a leaf crop the next year, a root crop the third year, a legume crop the fourth year, and back to a "fruit" crop in a cycle. The legume crop will help enrich the soil, providing ideal conditions for a heavy-feeding "fruit" crop to grow in. Crops in different groups also tend to have different pest

a

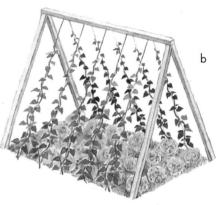

b

With a few time-tested planting techniques, you can double the harvests from your heirloom country garden. (a) Succession plantings, spaced about two weeks apart, mean that new crops are always coming along, so you get to harvest them as you need them, at their peak flavor. (b) Intercropping involves planting two or more crops with complementary growth habits, such as pole beans with lettuce. The lettuce fills the growing space under the beans, while the beans provide shade to extend your lettuce harvest.

and disease problems, so this system prevents these problems from getting out of hand.

The key to successful crop rotation is keeping track of what you plant where each year, so you know what to grow there the next. Way back in 1871, J. C. Loudon offered this excellent advice in his book *An Encyclopedia of Gardening*: "A studied rotation is advisable...so that no crop of the same class may immediately follow another. To facilitate this measure, the kitchen-ground should be divided into a number of portions, and a journal or note-book should be kept, with a reference to the numbers. In this journal, whatever relates to their cropping, manuring, trenching, or fallowing should be recorded, for reference

and guidance as to future cropping." Your records don't have to be fancy or extremely detailed—just complete enough to help you remember what you did and when you did it!

Getting the most from your space. While rotation keeps your garden healthy and thriving, successive plantings and intercropping can increase the harvest from your garden. Succession planting means growing two or more crops in sequence in a given garden bed in one year. You could start in spring with an early planting of a cold-tolerant vegetable (such as lettuce, radishes, spinach, or broccoli), then pull out that crop after harvest to make room for a warm-season crop, such as summer squash, tomatoes, peppers, eggplant, cucumbers, or sweet potatoes. Continue harvesting into fall with another planting of a cold-tolerant vegetable; these cool-season crops often produce even better in fall than in spring.

You can also modify this old-time technique to extend the harvest season of your favorite crop. Instead of planting all of your bush beans or radishes at one time, for instance, plant a small batch, then another batch every two weeks throughout the summer. Or choose several varieties that mature at different times, and plant them all at once. Either way, as one crop finishes producing, the next batch will be ready to harvest. You'll enjoy your vegetables for months without getting overwhelmed with picking and processing a large harvest all at once.

Intercropping—growing two or more crops in one bed at the same time—is another great way to boost your harvests. The trick is to pair crops that have different heights, habits, or maturity dates, so they don't interfere with each other's growth. One classic combination is radishes and carrots; simply mix radish seed in with your carrot seed when you plant the carrots in the garden. The radish seed germinates quickly and will mark the row, and you can harvest the radishes when you thin the carrot seedlings. Another effective grouping is

planting lettuce underneath a pole bean trellis; the beans will provide some season-extending shade for the lettuce when temperatures start to heat up. If you have a planting of sweet corn, try the Native American "three sisters" combination of corn, squash, and beans. (For more information, see "Gardening with the Three Sisters" on page 7.)

STARTING AN OLD-FASHIONED FLOWER GARDEN

Gardening isn't just about feeding your body—it's also about feeding your spirit. That's where flowers come in! While gardeners in times past were often very practical, even they made room for flowers where they could. Formal, carefully planned gardens had their place, but it's usually the free-for-all glory of the "cottage garden" that comes to mind when people think of old-time flower gardens. Cottage gardens aren't limited by particular design or color rules, and they can even include edible plants—vegetables, herbs, and fruits—as well as vines, roses, and other shrubs. Cottage gardens are as individual as the gardeners who nurture them.

Informal flower gardens usually incorporate a mix of perennials, annuals, and bulbs, so there's always something to admire, from earliest spring through fall frosts.

Perennials. Perennials—herbaceous plants that live for three or more years—provide a backbone of dependable color for the cottage garden. Many classic cottage garden perennials—including bellflowers, bleeding

An informal mix of heirloom perennials, annuals, and bulbs will give your garden an old-fashioned look.

hearts, irises, peonies, and primroses, to name but a few—are sturdy, reliable plants that can grow in one spot year after year with just a minimum of basic care. Biennials—plants that produce only leaves the first year, then die after flowering in their second year—are often treated as perennials as well, since they tend to return year after year from previous seasons' dropped seeds. Honesty (*Lunaria annua*) and sweet William (*Dianthus barbatus*) are two examples of beloved old-time biennials.

Old-time country gardeners didn't have the luxury of local garden centers and glossy mail-order plant catalogs, so they had two main ways of getting perennials to start a new garden—either as "slips" (cuttings) or divisions from friends, or by growing them from seed. Both of these methods are still good today, particularly if you have a small budget or a large space to fill. Seed-grown perennials tend to be somewhat variable in height and color, but that variety isn't a problem in an informal cottage-garden setting.

In his 1886 book *Gardening for Pleasure*, Peter Henderson offers this excellent advice to gardeners planning to grow perennials from seed: "As most of them do not bloom until the seedlings have one year's growth, the seeds should be sown in a reserve bed, from which at the end of the first summer, or in the following spring, they may be transplanted to the place where they are to flower. It is well to give the seedlings some protection the first winter, not because they are not hardy, but to prevent them from being thrown out of the soil by frequent freezing and thawing. A covering of evergreen boughs is most suitable, but if these are not at hand, use coarse hay or other litter, first laying down some brush, to keep the covering from matting down upon them." Remove the covering in spring. When the plants are big enough for the garden—usually after their second or third summer—transplant them to their final spot in spring or fall.

Mature perennials vary in their care needs, but most will perform well with just an annual mulch of compost and division every three to five years. For descriptions and detailed growing tips for these popular, old-fashioned flowers, turn back to "Perennials and Biennials" on page 102.

Annuals. Beautiful in their own right, annuals are also amazingly versatile for heirloom flower gardens. You'll use them to fill the space around young perennials, to cover bare soil left by dormant bulbs, and to provide quick color for pots, planters, window boxes, baskets, and trellises. Large-seeded annuals, such as sweet peas and nasturtiums, are easy to grow from seeds sown directly in the garden; just remember to thin the seedlings to the spacing recommended on the seed packet, so they don't get too crowded. For flowers with tiny seeds and those that need a long growing season, such as heliotrope (*Heliotropium arborescens*), it's best to sow the seeds indoors and transplant them to the garden as seedlings.

After planting, annuals generally need little care—just watering during dry spells. Pinching off the spent flowers can help extend the bloom season on many annuals. For specific growing tips for a variety of classic annuals, turn back to "Selected Heirloom Annuals" on page 86.

Bulbs. From spring to fall, bulbs add a finishing touch to any old-fashioned flower garden. Plant your spring-flowering bulbs in fall in loose, rich, well-drained soil. Summer- and fall-flowering bulbs appreciate the same soil conditions, but you'll generally plant them in spring. A simple rule of thumb is to dig the planting hole three to four times deeper than the height of the bulb itself.

After planting, put a thin layer of compost on the soil to provide valuable nutrients for the bulbs. Allow the foliage to turn yellow before cutting it off because the leaves provide nutrients for next year's flowers. For detailed growing tips for spring-, summer-, and fall-blooming bulbs, refer back to "Bulbs" on page 96.

Starting Seeds

In the days before garden centers and colorful mail-order catalogs, gardeners grew many of their plants from seed. While many seeds can be sown directly in the garden, annuals such as

Bottom-water seedlings by adding water to the tray rather than to the individual pots or containers. This moistens the medium more evenly and reduces the chances of diseases attacking your tender seedlings.

tomatoes, peppers, eggplant, pansies, and celosia, as well as many perennial flowers, grow best when you start them indoors or in a greenhouse or coldframe. Fluorescent lights are helpful when starting seedlings indoors, since seedlings produce weak, spindly stems if they do not get enough light. Temperatures between 60° and 70°F will suit most seedlings. To find out the best time to start your seeds, check the individual plant entries covered earlier in this book.

Here's how gardeners in the early twentieth century were getting their seeds growing, according to Peter Henderson's *Practical Floriculture,* published in 1911 (revised from the 1863 edition): "Boxes are filled with the prepared soil to the depth of one inch and one-half, which is gently and evenly pressed, so as to give an entirely level surface; the seeds are then sown, and a light covering from one-sixteenth to one-fourth of an inch thick, according to the size or strength of seed, is sifted over them, through a sieve having a mesh only one-tenth of an inch. The covering is gently pressed to prevent the air penetrating the loose soil and drying up the seeds; watering…is thus rendered less necessary. Be careful, however, not to let them suffer for moisture, as in the weak condition of seedlings, most plants are quickly injured by neglect of this kind."

This advice is still helpful, though modern gardeners tend to use plastic pots or trays, rather than the shallow wooden boxes of earlier times. We also use commercially prepared potting media, rather than actual garden soil, which can carry disease-causing organisms and weed seeds, and which packs down with regular watering.

It's best to moisten your chosen medium with warm water before filling your pots or trays—you want it to be evenly moist, but not so wet that it drips if you squeeze it.

After planting, you can either water the surface of the medium carefully, or else set the containers in a shallow tray of water and let the medium absorb the water from below. Remove the containers from the water when the surface of the medium looks moist.

When your seedlings are ready for the garden, expose them to outdoor conditions gradually (over a period of several days) by setting them in a coldframe or against a wall or sheltered area. Do this for few days before transplanting them permanently. Try to transplant on an overcast day or after the heat of the day has passed so your seedlings will suffer the smallest amount of stress.

Keeping Your Soil Healthy

Heirloom country gardens need the same basic care that regular gardens need to stay beautiful and productive—including regular attention to maintaining healthy, fertile soil. Until the past 50 years or so, animal manures were a mainstay of soil fertility management, as they were easily available. If you are lucky enough to have access to cow, horse, chicken, pig, or rabbit manure, it's still a great source of organic matter and nutrients. (Don't be tempted to use dog or cat droppings, as these materials can contain disease-causing organisms.) It's okay to add fresh manures to the garden in late fall, as they'll have the winter to break down somewhat; otherwise, they can be too rich and "burn" your plants. To prevent this problem, it's best to compost fresh manure for about three months before working it into your soil or using it as a mulch.

Many of today's gardeners do not have easy access to large quantities of animal manure, but we can still build and maintain fertile soil organically by making and using compost. Compost can include a wide range of materials, including grass clippings, weeds, garden trimmings, leaves, and kitchen scraps (excluding meat and dairy products, which break down slowly and attract animals to your pile). Mixed together, these materials will gradually decompose and break down into dark, rich humus. You will have finished compost more quickly if you have a mixture of carbon-rich materials (like dry leaves or straw) with nitrogen-rich materials (such as kitchen scraps, animal manures, and grass clippings).

Simply pile your organic materials as you collect them in an out-of-the-way spot. Turn over your compost pile once or twice a month with a pitchfork, and add water (if needed), so the materials are moist but not water-soaked. Compost is ready to use when it is dark and crumbly, with a rich, earthy smell. If your compost pile has a foul odor, it is probably either too wet or too high in nitrogen. To remedy either problem, mix in some dead leaves or straw as you turn the pile. Dig finished compost into your soil at planting time, or use it as a summer mulch to give crops and flowers a midseason nutrient boost.

Green manures are another excellent way to build and maintain garden soil. Green manures are plants that you grow in garden beds, then mow and dig or till into your soil. Popular green manure crops include leguminous plants such as clovers and vetches and nonlegumes like annual ryegrass, oats, and buckwheat. The nonlegumes add rich organic matter, while the legumes add both organic matter and nitrogen to the soil. Depending on the green manure crop and your planting scheme, you can fit it into your garden rotation at the end of the growing season to cover beds over the winter (oats are a good choice for this), or between spring and fall crops (try fast-growing buckwheat in this case).

Regular additions of organic matter—from animal manures, compost, or green manures—will go a long way toward keeping your soil healthy and crumbly, while providing a small but steady supply of nutrients to your soil. And be careful about *when* you work your soil. Way back in 1886, Peter Henderson's *Gardening for Pleasure* offered advice that's still valuable today: "Let me here caution that great care be taken never to plow, dig, harrow, rake, or hoe ground when wet; if work must be done, pull out weeds or set plants, if you will, but never, under any circumstances, stir the soil in preparation for a crop until it is dry enough not to clog. If stirred while wet, the particles stick together, and the crop is not only injured for the season, but in some soils the bad effects show for years."

Besides being great for building healthy soil, compost also makes an excellent liquid fertilizer. To brew your own "compost tea," just fill a burlap or coarsely woven sack with finished compost, tie it closed, plop it in a bucket or barrel of water, and let it steep for a few days. Dilute the resulting brew with water until it's the color of weak tea, and use it freely: Pour it around the bases of plants or spray it on their leaves.

An Old-Time Approach to Garden Problems

Gardeners have always been interested in effective ways of coping with garden problems. We can learn a lot from our forebears when it comes to combating the things that can go wrong in the garden. Weeds, which every gardener struggles with, can be controlled by pulling them when they're young, never letting a weed set seed, and mulching to prevent future generations from growing. I think the best pest management strategy is to be a diligent observer of your own garden and learn which insects are serious pests, which are helpful beneficials, and which are simply benign in the garden scheme of things. Hand-picking and trapping pest insects are two effective techniques that have been used for centuries. And planting appropriate varieties for a particular growing area, rotating annual crops, and maintaining healthy, vigorous plants are also good disease management techniques.

CONTROLLING WEEDS

Weeds have always been a bane of gardeners everywhere. In his 1806 *The American Gardener's Calendar*, Bernard McMahon sums it up nicely: "The utmost attention is necessary never to suffer weeds to perfect their seeds in any part, whether in cropped or vacant quarters, or in dung hills, or compost-heaps, as they would lay the foundation of several years trouble to extirpate them; for, as in digging and hoeing the ground, some of the seed would be buried near the surface, and others much deeper, at every time of stirring the earth, a fresh crop of weeds would arise from the same stock of seeds, which verifies the saying, 'one years seeding, makes seven years weeding'."

Gardeners from any time period would agree with McMahon that letting weeds form seedheads means more work the following year. Weeds compete with your garden plants for water and nutrients, and if you don't hoe or pull them out while they are still small, they can outcompete your vegetable or flower plants. Past generations believed in regularly hoeing weed seedlings out of their garden beds. Of course, with the large families of bygone years, the adult gardeners in these families also had a youthful labor force at their beck and call.

In those times, cultivating was pretty much the only option they had for weed control. Materials like hay and straw were more valuable for feeding and bedding livestock than for mulching. It took the advent of the reel lawn mower in the late nineteenth century to make grass clippings easily available to gardeners, and they remain a popular mulch to this day. Modern gardeners also have access to a wide range of other great mulches, from chopped leaves to conveniently bagged bark mulches. Besides greatly reducing weeding chores, mulches offer many other benefits, from keeping the soil evenly moist and moderating soil temperature to adding organic matter to the soil as the mulches break down. And they look great, too!

Spread a layer of straw, hay, grass clippings, or another mulch around the plants in your garden to suppress weeds and keep the soil evenly moist.

Even the best-laid mulches can't keep down all weeds, though, so it's important to manage your mulch properly. Before applying any mulch, first get rid of all the weeds you can see; don't expect the mulch to smother existing growth. During the growing season, pull any weeds that do manage to pop through the mulch while they are still small. You may also need to add more mulch once or twice during the growing season to keep it thick enough to smother weeds (it should be 1 to 2 inches thick, for most mulches). Fine-textured mulches, such as grass clippings and chopped leaves, tend to break down more quickly than coarse mulches, like bark chips, do.

COPING WITH PESTS

In the days before chemical pesticides were commonly available, gardeners relied on an arsenal of simple techniques for controlling pests. Dusting plants with lime and wood ashes, for example, is a time-honored technique for controlling a wide range of pests. Two newer products that also have wide-ranging effects include natural-grade diatomaceous earth (used as a dust) and insecticidal soap (used as a spray to control soft-bodied pests, such as aphids, leafhoppers, and slugs). When you are applying any dust or spray, always follow the label on commercial products. If you're using a "homemade" dust, like lime or wood ashes, wear a mask to avoid respiratory irritation.

For large-bodied pests like caterpillars, hand-picking is a simple but effective option. Drop the pests into a container of soapy water as you collect them.

Like our old-time counterparts, modern gardeners have found beneficial insects useful in reducing pest populations. An attractive way to encourage beneficial insects to patronize your garden is by providing pollen and nectar sources for them. Flowers such as alyssum (*Lobularia maritima*) and yarrows (*Achillea* spp.), and herbs like dill, catnip (*Nepeta cataria*), and tansy (*Tanacetum vulgare*) are good food sources for beneficial insects.

On page 178 is a rundown of some common garden pests, along with organic control measures. For more information on dealing with garden pests, turn to "Recommended Reading" on page 232.

Aphids and mites: Wash plants with a strong spray of water to rid leaves and stems of aphid colonies and to reduce mite colonies, which prefer hot, dry conditions.

Apple maggots: Red, apple-shaped sticky traps are a contemporary trapping technique for apple maggots, whose larvae leave numerous small tunnels around the inside of fruit. Hang two or three traps in each tree in early summer, and clean them off periodically.

Caterpillars: Sprays of BT (*Bacillus thuringiensis*) will control cabbage loopers, cabbageworms, European corn borer, and other similar larvae. BT, available at garden centers, is a microbial insecticide that is toxic only to specific pest larvae and is not toxic to humans.

Codling moths: Codling moths are common but serious apple and pear fruit pests whose larvae tunnel into the core of the fruit. Depending on your location, codling moths will have two to four generations per growing season. You can monitor codling moths with pheromone monitoring traps that have a pheromone bait and sticky cardboard tray. The pheromone bait in the trap is the scent the female codling moth emits to attract males. You can also try to trap the pest by hanging several traps in your trees. Also, wrap corrugated cardboard around the trunk of each tree to attract the codling moth larvae that have left the fruit and are looking for a place to pupate. Remove the traps every few weeks during the growing season and destroy the larvae.

Cutworms: To stop these caterpillars from chewing seedling stems at ground level, protect the bases of the stems with a homemade paper collar.

Flea beetles: Protect your plants with floating row cover, a lightweight material that lets air, light, and water through, but keeps pests out.

Plum curculio: Plum curculio, a fruit pest found east of the Rockies, will lay its eggs in the very small developing fruit right after the petals fall off. Damaged fruit will have crescent-shaped scars and be misshapen. In his 1859 book *Fruit, Flowers, and Farming*, Henry Ward Beecher suggests that by "giving the trees a sudden and violent blow with a mallet, the insects will drop and may then be gathered and destroyed. This should be performed while it is cool, as then, only, the curculio is somewhat torpid." Place an old sheet on the ground when you tap your trees so that you can locate the ½-inch-long, gray-brown beetles. Drop the collected beetles in a can of soapy water. You can also try trapping the insect with apple-shaped green traps coated with a sticky material, such as Tanglefoot (available at garden centers or through mail-order suppliers).

Slugs: Old-time gardeners reduced slug numbers by placing large cabbage leaves near plants that were being attacked and then collecting slugs from underneath the leaves early in the morning.

Squash borers and squash bugs: Protect young plants from attack by covering them with floating row cover. Remove the row covers when the crops begin blooming so that pollinators can visit the plants.

SALAD BIRD SCARECROW

WHILE SWALLOWS, BALTIMORE ORI-oles, chickadees, and many other birds are some of the best biological controls for garden insect pests, birds sometimes do raid the garden for freshly planted seeds or tender young seedlings, not to mention ripe strawberries! Many cultures have a tradition of placing scarecrows in the garden to deter birds, but one of the more unique scarecrows is the *tselaad fogel*, or salad bird scarecrow, used by Elizabeth Gottshall Kulp of Harleysville, Pennsylvania, in the vegetable garden she maintained from the 1930s through the 1960s.

Elizabeth followed the old traditions of the Pennsylvania Germans. She had a raised-bed garden planted with vegetables, herbs (mainly medicinal and aromatic herbs, as the Pennsylvania Germans did not use many culinary herbs), and flowers. She also grew small fruits in a perimeter border around the garden beds. Her son, Clarence Kulp, a historian with the Goschenhoppen Historical Society of Green Lane, Pennsylvania, remembers helping construct the scarecrow in the spring of each year. They would take a stake that was sharpened on each end, push a potato on one end, and use feathers from the chicken pen to shape the wings.

The salad bird scarecrow, meant to resemble a bird of prey, was placed in the corner of the raised bed planted with salad greens and was used to ward off birds interested in eating lettuce seeds or young seedlings. A salad bird scarecrow is included in the vegetable garden at the annual Goschenhoppen Festival, and it still works today!

You can make a salad bird scarecrow to guard tender lettuce seedlings in your spring garden by sticking chicken feathers into a potato.

DEALING WITH DISEASES

Until the late 1800s, disease management consisted of preventive measures—including healthy soil, proper watering, and crop rotation—and these are all still good ideas today. Other time-tested disease-control strategies include pruning out or removing diseased plant parts or whole plants. (Don't toss diseased plants into your compost pile, though, or you might spread the disease-causing organisms when you apply the compost to your garden!)

Today, we have an even more important tool in our disease-prevention programs: disease-resistant cultivars. Over the years, gardeners have noticed that some plants were quickly decimated by disease while others growing in the same area were disease-free or only slightly affected. By saving seeds only from their healthy plants, gardeners have developed disease-resistant strains of a wide range of popular crops. Plant breeders have also contributed by deliberately hybridizing plants for disease resistance. It's smart to take advantage of this benefit by growing crops that are resistant to disease problems that are common in your area.

If diseases do develop and pruning out the damaged parts isn't an option, you may choose to resort to sprays. In years past, dubious, even toxic, concoctions involving turpentine, tar, mercury, and urine were tried without any success. By 1885, sulfur-and-copper–based Bordeaux sprays were found to be effective on grapevine diseases. Today, sulfur sprays are still an effective last resort for fungal diseases on tree fruits, grapes, and roses. (When sulfur is sprayed on the plant before rain, it forms a barrier between the germinating fungal spores and susceptible leaves and fruit.) Do not apply sulfur when temperatures are above 80°F, though, or it will burn the foliage. For a milder fungicide, organic gardeners can also try baking soda sprays (1 teaspoon of baking soda to 1 quart of water, with ¼ teaspoon of vegetable oil). Spray affected plants thoroughly at the first sign of disease development, being sure to cover the undersides of the leaves as well as the tops.

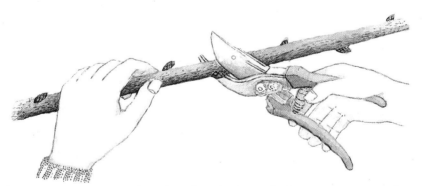

Make your pruning cuts at a slant about ¼ inch above a bud. In most cases, you'll want to cut above an outward-facing bud, to encourage growth away from the center of the plant.

Pruning Pointers

Yes, you will get fruit if you don't prune. But if you *do* prune, your plants will be healthier, and you'll be rewarded with a larger, higher-quality harvest. Pruning opens up the trees to sunlight for good fruit bud production and to ample air circulation so the leaves dry quickly and are less prone to disease. It also helps your trees develop a sturdy framework. So all in all, you're doing your trees a favor by pruning them.

In the colonial days of North American gardening, tree fruit plantings were either fields of large, unpruned, standard-size trees, or dwarf trees carefully trained to espalier systems along garden walls in the formal European tradition. Commercial orchardists today use a great variety of training systems. Many new plantings are of dwarf trees intensively trained to maximize production as land becomes a more expensive part of production.

Training young trees during the first few growing seasons is particularly important because you're establishing their basic framework. You will find that different varieties of a fruit crop, particularly apples, will have varying growth habits. One variety will tend to have an open framework, like 'McIntosh', while another variety, such as 'Northern Spy', will be a large tree with a lot of vigorous growth. The habit of your tree will determine which training and pruning style will work best for you.

CENTRAL LEADER TREES

The central leader system is a good choice for freestanding semidwarf apple and pear trees. The goal of training and pruning during the first two to four years after planting is to develop a tree with a Christmas tree–type framework—a single main trunk, with several well-placed tiers of branches. The tree should have an overall cone shape, with the bottom tier of branches the widest and the top tier the shortest. This allows maximum sunlight to reach all parts of the tree.

A central leader tree should have a pyramidal shape with an open framework of branches. This system is a good choice for most apples and pears.

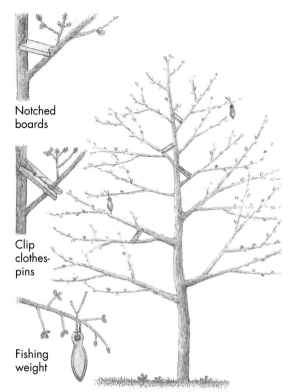

Notched
boards

Clip
clothes-
pins

Fishing
weight

Spread tree limbs with notched boards or clip clothes-
pins, or weight them with heavy fishing weights or
nuts and bolts, to encourage the development of a wide
branch angle that can support the weight of a heavy
fruit crop.

During early summer, look at how the "scaffold" branches—the branches coming out from the main stem—are developing. Choose two or three scaffold branches spaced about 6 to 8 inches apart that are growing in different directions; keep these, and prune off any remaining branches. You may not get a good selection of branches the first year, but work with what you have and select more next year.

Year two. In late winter, trim out shoots that are competing with the central leader (the main stem). If you did not have good scaffold branch development, cut the central leader back to a lower bud to stimulate more scaffold branch growth. Use limb spreaders or weights to train the scaffold branches at a 45- to 90-degree angle from the trunk.

Year three. Continue to select scaffold branches. Your mature tree should have five to eight scaffold branches well spaced along a straight, strong central leader.

Bearing trees. After you are finished training your tree, yearly late-winter pruning consists of cutting the scaffold branches back to maintain the pyramidal shape and removing dead wood or crossing branches. Also, prune out any "water shoots" or "water sprouts"— the vertical upright growths on scaffold branches—in the summertime.

MODIFIED CENTRAL LEADER TREES

Modified central leader training is a useful system for pear varieties that are susceptible to fireblight. If fireblight, a serious bacterial disease, infects the single trunk of a central leader

Year one. Cut the trunk of your newly planted, unbranched "whip" back to about 2½ feet tall. If your new tree arrived with branches, trim the branches back by about one-third. Growth hormones called auxins promote growth at the end of the shoot and inhibit shoot growth down the sides of the branch or main stem. When you remove the growing tip, buds further down on the stem are free to develop.

tree, it can kill the central leader and ruin the entire tree. Training a pear tree to have several leaders, however, gives the tree a better chance of survival. If you observe fireblight in time, you can prune out one infected leader, and the other leaders may survive the infection.

To use the modified central leader system, train the tree as in the central leader system for the first several years. When your tree has five to eight main scaffold branches, cut the main central leader back to the top scaffold branch in order for it to form several leaders. Head back the upper scaffold branches to keep them from shading the lower branches.

OPEN-CENTER TREES

This form of training and pruning is best for spreading trees like peaches that bear fruit on one-year-old wood.

Year one. At planting time, cut single-stemmed trees 2 to 2½ feet above the ground. If your tree already has branches, cut the main stem back to a bud 4 to 6 inches above the highest branch. During summer of the same year, choose four main scaffold branches that are growing in different directions and are separated along the trunk by 4 to 8 inches. Remove the rest of the branches. Cut off the main trunk just above the topmost main scaffold.

The open-center system lets ample light into the interior of the tree, encouraging the development of fruit buds. It's a popular choice for peach trees.

Year two. In late winter or early spring, trim the scaffold branches to encourage the growth of smaller side branches. Cut to an outward facing bud on the branch to direct growth away from the interior of the tree.

Years three and four. Continue trimming the scaffold branches in late winter or early spring to encourage new growth.

Bearing trees. Prune in late winter or early spring to maintain the structure of the tree. On peaches, cut about half the branches back about one-third in early spring to encourage the development of young fruiting wood. Thin crowded branches and remove water sprouts to maintain an open, airy tree.

ESPALIERED FRUIT TREES

Espalier-trained trees are an attractive way to fit a number of different varieties of tree fruit into a small space. Espaliered trees require support, so they are trained flat along a wall or a trellis of posts and wires. Dwarf apple and pear trees are the easiest trees to train as espaliers because they bear their fruit on short stems called spurs. There are quite a few espalier patterns to use, including the Belgian fence, candelabra espalier, palmette verrier, and cordon espaliers.

Year one. To begin a simple trellised espalier, plant your new tree about one foot in front of the support system. Cut your newly planted tree about 18 inches above the ground, just above the uppermost of three strong-looking buds. During the first summer, train the center shoot vertically to be the cen-

A simple but attractive method of espalier is to train branches to grow in horizontal tiers.

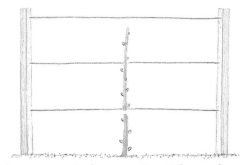

Plant a young, single-stemmed tree 1 foot out from a post-and-wire trellis. Cut off the top of the tree just below the bottom support wire. Train it vertically.

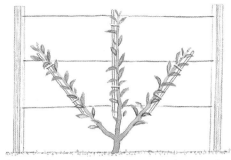

In the second year, select three vigorous shoots and remove the rest. Tie the remaining shoots to stakes, then fasten the stakes to the wires. During the season, gradually move the side arms down to a horizontal position.

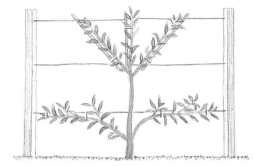

The following year, train the upper layer of arms the same way.

tral leader (tie it loosely to the support) and the two bottom shoots at 45 degree angles.

Year two. The following winter, cut the central leader back to three buds above the bottom tier of branches. Shorten the bottom branches to three buds also. During the growing season, train the bottom branches to 90-degree angles and the new top tier to 45-degree angles. Cut the branches growing from the horizontal tiers back to two or three leaves above the cluster of leaves at the base of the shoot.

Year three and bearing trees. Follow the same steps as in year two for each year until you have filled in your trellis. Continue cutting back shoots and trimming off the tips of main stems to maintain the framework of your tree. Remove shoots that are growing straight toward the wall or straight away from the wall.

TRAINING AND PRUNING GRAPES

Grapevines require sturdy support, so make sure you have some kind of support system in place before you plant. If you're growing just a few vines, an arbor is a nice choice, since it will be decorative as well as practical. If you are planting more than three or four vines, you will need to construct a post-and-wire trellis.

The first two years are the training time for your grapevines. Once the plants are established, regular pruning will keep the vines healthy and encourage good-size grape clusters. There isn't room to cover all the different pruning techniques, but here's some basic information on pruning and training American and Muscadine varieties.

Training newly planted grapes. During their first two years, your vines need more training than pruning. After planting, let your vines grow freely the first year so they develop good root systems. Each one will develop several stems. During the first winter, choose the thickest, stoutest stem, and cut it off above the third bud. This will form the trunk. Tie it loosely to a stake. The following growing season, let it grow until it reaches about one foot above the first wire on your trellis. Pinch off the growing tip to encourage the development of sideshoots. The next winter, choose four sturdy canes (sideshoots) for each lateral wire and attach them to the trellis with plastic-covered wire ties. Cut off and remove the other shoots. Pinch off any flowers the first two years to allow the vines to develop well.

Pruning American and American hybrid grapes. The American grape (*Vitis labrusca*) varieties produce grapes only on one-year-old wood, so they respond well to a technique called "cane pruning." This technique will give you one-year-old canes for this year's crop and also develop new canes each year for the coming year's crop.

In late winter, cut back the last year's fruiting canes and select two canes per trellis wire for the coming year. Tie this year's canes loosely to the wire and cut them back to leave 8 to 12 buds (nodes) on each. Also,

To cane-prune American grapes, cut off the canes that produced fruit the previous year. Then select two new canes per trellis wire for the coming season's crop, and trim them to leave 8 to 12 buds on each. Also, choose four new shoots and shorten them to 2 or 3 buds each—these will grow into canes during the coming summer and produce fruit the following year.

select four new shoots and shorten them to two or three buds. These shoots are the "renewal spurs" that will produce canes this year to become next year's fruiting canes. Each year, repeat the process to maintain a healthy, vigorous vine.

Pruning Muscadine grapes. Muscadine grapes are very vigorous growers and do well when trained on an arbor or pergola. To train Muscadine grapes on an arbor, follow the training outlined above, but allow the shoot to form a trunk that reaches to within 6 inches of the top of the arbor before pinching off the growing tip. Then allow fruiting canes to develop, and space them out across the top of the

arbor. Cane-prune the established vine annually by taking out dead wood and training young shoots as replacements. Remove shoots from the bottom part of the trunk unless you want to start a new plant by bending a shoot down to the ground and mounding soil on it.

TRAINING AND PRUNING BRAMBLES

Raspberries, blackberries, and other brambles have short-lived canes that die and are replaced by new, young growth. In the old days, gardeners with plenty of room let their brambles grow free in large patches, and you can still do that if you have the space. My family had a large patch of raspberries, both black and red, that was not trellised and was loosely grouped in rows. That patch is now over 30 years old, past the time when most plantings have been moved and renovated. The more disease-susceptible black raspberries have died out and the red raspberries have spread out and moved down the yard, but they still bear a good crop of fruit. The disadvantages of this untrellised patch are that picking raspberries in the center of a sprawling row is difficult, and ragweed can be a real problem to control, but I still like the old patch.

Bramble plantings are neater and easier to maintain if you establish them on trellises. You can provide good support with a simple trellis made from 4 × 4 posts sunk 2 to 3 feet deep in the ground, with horizontal wires strung at 2½, 3½, and 5½ feet, along with supporting guy wires. Tie the canes to the wires with plastic-coated wire ties or string. Besides looking more tidy, this system makes both picking and pruning a pleasure!

Summer-bearing red and yellow raspberries have a tall, upright growth habit and bear fruit on second-year canes. Each year, in late winter, prune out the canes that bore fruit the previous summer. (The old canes will be gray or brown, while the new canes will be green.) Also, cut out diseased or damaged canes. Thin out the remaining healthy canes to leave three or four canes per foot, and trim off the tops of these canes at about 5 feet. If you are using a trellis, fasten the canes to the wires.

Black raspberries do not sucker and spread like red and yellow raspberries, so they are easier to contain in row plantings.

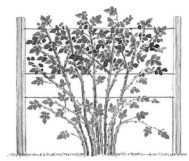

New growth appears each summer under the current year's crop.

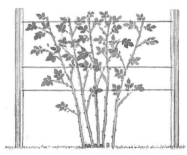

After harvest, prune out all of the fruited canes at ground level, and tie the new canes to the wire trellis. Also, trim off the tops of the new canes to encourage lateral branching.

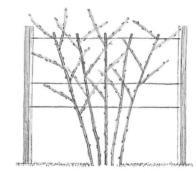

During the winter, prune the lateral branches back to 1 foot.

Black raspberries and blackberries need a slightly different approach. After the second-year canes finish fruiting, cut them to the ground and tie the new canes to the wire trellis. In early summer, trim off the tops of the one-year-old canes at about 30 inches to encourage the growth of lateral branches, which will bear fruit the next year. During dormant-season pruning, trim these laterals back to 1 foot long. Thin out the one-year-old canes to leave six to nine canes per plant.

Saving Seeds

Once you have plant varieties that interest you and do well in your garden, you can begin saving seeds from your own plants and sharing them with your neighbors over the fence. Not only is this a great way to propagate heirloom varieties, it's a great way to save some money when you go to plant next year's garden. Be warned, though: Once you start saving seeds, it may become a compulsion and you may not want to stop!

Part of the reason that seed saving is so addictive is that it's so easy. Saving flower seeds is simple for even a novice: Harvest the seeds when the plants have formed seedheads and turned light brown. Spread the seeds out on newspaper and clean off any plant debris, and then let the seed dry thoroughly. Store the seeds in paper envelopes in a cool, dry place.

The techniques for saving vegetable seeds are basically the same as for flowers,

although garden vegetables vary in the amount of time, effort, and expertise required to keep a variety "true to type" (meaning that it retains all the characteristics of the plant that produced the seeds). If this is your first project, start with one of the simpler self-pollinating annual vegetables, such as lettuce or tomatoes, rather than corn or another crop that cross-pollinates and needs to be isolated from all other varieties.

Biennial crops (such as cabbage), which don't flower and set seed until their second year, are also a bit tricky and better left until you have more seed-saving experience. It's also smart to start your seed-saving experiments with an heirloom variety that is available from numerous sources, such as the popular 'Brandywine' tomato. That way, you won't have the pressure of maintaining a precarious treasure on your first try.

SEED-SAVING BASICS

Whether you're saving one or dozens of heirloom varieties, the key points to remember are the same. Here are some basic guidelines to help you succeed:

1. Do not save seed from just one plant. Try to collect from as many plants as possible in order to preserve a healthy gene pool for the variety.
2. Never plant all of your seed of one variety in one year. Extreme weather or a hungry woodchuck could wipe out your crop during a growing season! If you set some seed aside, you can try again next year.

3. Try different varieties each year. It's better to grow larger plots of a few heirloom vegetable varieties one year and grow another group the following year, rather than save too small a sample of each variety each year. Adopting this plan will also reduce the risk of cross-pollination between varieties of the same vegetable.

4. Keep good records. Label plants from the seedling stage through seed saving and storage. Mislabeling (or worse still, not labeling at all) is frustrating if you're trying to preserve an heirloom variety.

5. Collect only from healthy plants. Rogue out (destroy) plants or seeds that have any symptoms of disease during the growing season to keep next year's crop a healthy one.

COLLECTING SEED

Seed-collecting methods are divided into two basic techniques: wet processing and dry processing. Choosing the appropriate technique for your crop is a key part of successful seed saving.

Wet processing. This is the method you'll use for fleshy fruits, such as tomatoes, cucumbers, muskmelons, and ground cherries. First, choose well-ripened fruit from your selected plants. Cut the fruit in half, and then squeeze or scrape the seeds and juice into a glass jar. (Make sure the jar is labeled with the correct variety name.) Let this mixture ferment for three to four days in an outbuilding protected from direct sun and temperatures above 95°F. (You don't want to do this in your house, as the odor is not exactly pleasant!) Cover with a piece of netting or floating row cover to keep insects out. A gross-looking layer of scum will develop on top of the liquid. This fermentation process kills seed-borne bacterial diseases. Do not continue this process for longer than the recommended three to four days, or the seeds may begin to germinate in the mixture.

When the fermentation period is over, add water to the jar (about twice as much water as there is seed mixture), stir vigorously, and let the mixture rest. When the scum and hollow seeds rise to the top, gently pour them off. Add water again and repeat the process. After cleaning off all the scum and bad seeds, pour the remaining liquid and seeds into a strainer and wash in cool water. Spread the seeds evenly on a screen or cookie sheet in low humidity to dry. If you're using a screen, prop it up on bricks to allow good air circulation around the seeds. If you're trying to dry seeds in humid weather, a fan set on low can help speed drying. Do not dry seeds in direct sunlight or in an oven, as temperatures above 96°F can damage them. Again, make sure the seeds are always labeled. Most small seeds, like tomatoes, should be dry in 8 to 12 days; larger seeds, such as squash, may take a few days longer. In her book *Seed to Seed*, Suzanne Ashworth recommends drying the seeds of all species to about 8 percent moisture. Seeds dried to 8 percent or less will break instead of bend when they're folded.

Once the seeds are dry, package individual varieties in paper envelopes or zipper-lock plastic bags before storing them in a large, airtight glass jar in a cool place. (Do not use lightweight plastic bags for storage, as they are not moisture-proof.) A freezer is the best choice, followed by a refrigerator. A low-temperature, dark, dry environment such as a basement or root cellar is good, as long as the temperature doesn't fluctuate.

Dry processing. To figure out when crops with dry seeds—such as beans, corn, lettuce, lima beans, radishes, and soybeans—are ready for harvest, take a look at the plants. You want to catch them after they have dried and turned brown, but before the pods have split open and the seeds have scattered. Collect seeds on a dry, sunny day. There are several ways to clean the seeds from the pods. For some, it's a simple matter to separate the seeds from the chaff by hand. If you're dealing with fine seeds, like lettuce seeds, rub them through a screen. (Use a screen with a mesh-size that allows the seeds to fall through while keeping the chaff on top.) With large quantities of large seeds, such as beans or peas, you can "thresh" them by putting the pods in a sack and hitting the sack with a stick. Don't mash the bag too vigorously, or you might damage the seed. Store the seed in a consistently cool, dry environment, as you would for wet-processed seed.

TESTING GERMINATION

If you collected and stored your seeds under good conditions, most should remain viable (able to sprout and grow) for three to five years—possibly even longer, depending on the vegetable and the variety. Tomato seed, for example, may retain its viability for up to ten years if stored under good conditions. However, there are some crops, including onions, leeks, and parsnips, that have short-lived seeds; they may last only a year or two. Testing the germination rate is a good way to check the viability of a particular seed batch, especially any you plan to share with fellow seed savers. Here's how to do it:

1. Choose a seed sample. Select 10 to 100 seeds of the batch you want to test. (It's easiest to use exactly 10 or 100, or at least some multiple of 10.) Place or scatter them evenly on a pad of dampened paper towels several layers thick. Roll up the paper towel pad and place it in a labeled plastic bag.

2. Set them aside to sprout. Store the bag in a warm place (70° to 80°F); the top of the refrigerator is a good choice. Check the bag every other day to make sure the paper towel is still damp, and mist it if it starts to dry out.

3. Take a sprout count. Seeds vary in the amount of time it takes for them to germinate, but most germinate within a week or two. (If you want to find the germination time for a specific vegetable, check *Rodale's All-New Encyclopedia of Organic Gardening*; otherwise, figure about two weeks.) Once the two weeks are up, unroll the towel and count how many seeds have sprouted. Divide the number of sprouted seeds by the total number of seeds, then multiply by 100 to get the percentage of seeds that germinated. If the germination rate is 50 percent or greater, the seeds are worth planting.

CREATING YOUR OWN HEIRLOOMS

WHILE MAINTAINING THE PURITY OF our existing heirloom varieties is important work, especially if you participate in a seed-saver exchange, it's also fun to think you might be able to develop an heirloom of your own! By keeping a close eye on your plants, you might find a unique characteristic worth keeping. First, look at the plants themselves. Do any seem to be more tolerant of stressful conditions such as drought, cold, or heat? Did you notice any that were particularly vigorous as seedlings? Or are there plants that don't seem to be troubled by the pests or diseases that are attacking their neighbors? Any of these differences can make it worthwhile to save seed.

Also look for special traits relating to the crop's production, such as especially large fruits or heads, unusual colors, or overall higher yields. Consider the crop's desired cooking qualities, as well. Especially meaty tomatoes, for instance, could be great for paste; particularly firm-headed cabbages would be a good choice for making sauerkraut. Maturity dates can also set a particular plant apart from others. Early-bearing tomatoes or sweet corn plants, for example, could be worth preserving, as these crops normally take a long time to mature. On crops you're growing for leaves, such as lettuce and other greens, you'd want to preserve any that were especially slow to send up a flowerstalk (a sign that your harvest of tasty leaves is over).

If you find plants you think are worth saving, mark them with colorful yarn or surveyor's tape to remind yourself and others not to harvest from them before the seeds are ripe. Be sure to save seed from a number of plants that have the characteristics you are selecting for in order to preserve genetic diversity. By selecting for the same characteristics each growing season, over time you will develop a strain of the heirloom variety that is especially adapted to your special growing conditions and preferences.

Another way to develop your own heirloom is to actively cross two or more varieties, then grow out the seedlings and select for the traits you desire, as described above.

If you want to learn more about developing and evaluating your own backyard plant breeding projects, I suggest reading Carol Deppe's book *Breed Your Own Vegetable Varieties*.

Garden Projects for That Country Look

For me, the appeal of heirloom country gardens is that they reflect a wonderful combination of creativity, thriftiness, regional character, and the love of gardening. And often, that historical flavor is provided by a garden accent—a bench, gazing ball, or rose-bedecked arbor. The projects in this chapter will help you give your garden that same old-time charm, with rustic trellises and fencing or accents such as colorful planters. The projects also include pretty gifts you can create from old-time herbs and flowers grown in your garden.

Look over the projects and see what sparks your interest. You might decide to arrange a bouquet of flowers from your garden and drop it off with a neighbor, or you may want to grow your own broom corn and try your hand at making brooms.

Don't feel bad if you don't have time right now to create lots of homemade gifts from your garden. (I must confess that I tucked away a box of pressed flowers several years ago and still haven't made them into note cards!) Try one or two of the projects that interest you the most, and earmark a few for next season. Whether you garden to cook with flavorful heirloom vegetables, to experience the fragrance of herbs, or to cut beautiful bouquets of antique flowers, the important thing is to enjoy all the bounty your garden has to offer.

OPPOSITE: *This wonderful wattle fence and mixed flower planting is a charming example of how you can give a country garden your own personal touch.*

RUSTIC GRAPE ARBOR

There's nothing like a rustic arbor to add an old-time touch to your country garden. Here's a simple structure based on a grape arbor at the Genesee Country Museum, a living history museum in Mumford, New York, that depicts nineteenth-century village life.

MATERIALS

Shovel or posthole digger

Gravel

Cement

Four 10-foot posts, 4 to 5 inches in diameter, each with a fork at one end

Trowel

Two 12-foot straight lengths of wood, roughly 3 inches in diameter

5-inch nails and hammer, or twine

Five 10-foot straight lengths of wood, roughly 3 inches in diameter

Step 3

1. Measure an 8 × 10-foot site for the arbor. Dig postholes 2½ feet deep at each corner with the shovel or posthole digger. Put a 3-inch layer of gravel at the bottom of each hole for drainage.

2. Mix the cement according to the package directions and fill each hole. Set a post in each hole. (Make sure the forks face each other on the 10-foot sides so that you can install parallel supports for the crosspieces.) Use the trowel to slope the cement in the postholes slightly away from the posts for rainwater drainage.

3. Fit the two 12-foot lengths of wood (the main crosspieces) in the forked posts. Use nails or twine to secure the crosspieces. (The twine gives a more rustic look, but nails are more secure.)

4. Lay a 10-foot length on top of the crosspieces at each end to form the corners. Secure with nails or twine. Finish the grape arbor by placing the remaining three 10-foot-long supporting pieces at evenly spaced intervals along the top. Secure them to the crosspieces.

PROJECT POINTERS: The four forked posts and crosspieces need to be made of rot-resistant wood such as cedar or black locust. Each one needs a fork large enough to hold a piece of wood 3 inches in diameter.

MOSAIC POTTERY CONTAINERS

They sell these containers at auctions, but you can make them for the cost of a few flea-market dishes. My dad remembers that his mother and aunt saved their broken dishes and glasses to make these for their houseplants.

1. Break your china and pottery into small pieces with a small hammer. (You can wrap the dishes in an old towel or pillowcase first, to contain the pieces and prevent injury.) Be sure to wear protective eye gear and gloves when you do this, and always handle the broken pieces with great care, as the shards can have jagged edges.

2. Mix a small amount of plaster of paris with hot water until it is the consistency of thick cake batter. Plaster of paris will harden in half an hour, so only mix enough to coat one container at a time.

3. Working rapidly, apply a coat of plaster about ½ inch thick to the outside of half the container. Choose china or pottery fragments and push them into the plaster, making sure that any sharp edges are coated with plaster.

4. Coat the other half of the container with plaster and finish choosing and placing the pieces on it. Allow the container to dry overnight, and then insert a plant to fill your colorful new pottery.

PROJECT POINTERS: If you're short on broken dishes, take a trip to a local flea market and collect a mixed assortment of inexpensive, colorful—sometimes already chipped or broken—china and vases. Yard sales and second-hand stores are other good places to scout for cheap, fun dishes.

MATERIALS

Assorted pottery and china
Small hammer
Protective eye gear
Gloves
Plaster of paris
Hot water
Stirring stick
Clay pots of various sizes and/or tin cans
Small trowel

Step 3

WATTLE FENCING

In medieval times, gardeners and farmers created strips of woodland planted with trees like hazel, ash, and willow. They cut the trees to the ground every seven to ten years, and straight new stems quickly regrew. These stems were harvested for a variety of purposes, including fencing materials. Today, we can use our tree prunings to recreate a low wattle fence.

MATERIALS

Stakes of 10-inch-long, straight prunings, 1 inch in diameter

Long, straight, flexible grapevine, trumpet vine, or willow prunings, about a finger thick

Twine

Pruning shears

1. Drive the stakes 5 inches into the soil of the garden bed. Space them 12 to 14 inches apart.

2. Weave the first layer of vine or willow prunings at ground level, alternating weaving in front of and in back of the stakes.

3. Continue with a second layer. This time, weave the opposite front to back pattern of the first row. Attach your horizontal prunings to the stakes with twine as needed.

4. Add as many layers as needed until your fence is the desired height. Trim the prunings at each end to finish your wattle fencing.

PROJECT POINTERS: The upright "watersprouts" that often appear on fruit trees make excellent stakes for this project. Gather the long, straight weaving stems no more than a few days before making your fence, since they will lose their flexibility as they dry.

Step 3

HERBAL SOAPS

You can easily make fragrant, pretty herbal soaps by using castile soap and adding fragrant herbs and a few drops of essential oils. Castile soap is a pure soap made from vegetable oils, without any added colorings or perfumes.

1. Bring water to a boil. Add ground herbs, and steep for 15 minutes.

2. Pour the steeped liquid into the enamelware or glass container, set over a saucepan of water, and reheat. Add the soap and a few drops of essential oil. Stir on low heat until the soap mixture is the consistency of softened butter.

3. Knead the soap mixture together and shape into plum-size balls. Dry on waxed paper for two to five days, and then store in plastic bags.

PROJECT POINTERS: Avoid using metal containers or spoons when you are making herbal soaps because the metal can react with herbal ingredients.

Although natural, some essential oils may irritate sensitive skin. Test the essential oil by putting a drop or two on the pad of an adhesive bandage strip and placing the strip on your inner arm between the wrist and the elbow. Leave the strip on for 24 hours, then check your skin for any redness or irritation.

MATERIALS

¼ cup water

2 tablespoons dried fragrant herbs, finely ground

Saucepan and enamelware or glass container to use as a double boiler

2 bars of castile soap, grated (approximately 2 cups)

Essential oils

Waxed paper

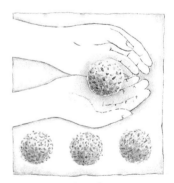

Step 3

HOMEMADE FLOWER PRESS

This simple flower press is a snap to make. It provides uniform pressure for drying flowers, petals, and leaves. The pressed, dried materials make elegant accents for decorating note cards, picture frames, and other home-crafted gifts. It's a wonderful way to enjoy the fruits of your garden throughout the year—and to share those fruits with friends and family.

MATERIALS

Two 1-foot squares of ½-inch-thick plywood

Clamps

Drill with 5/16-inch bit

Sandpaper

Varnish

Four ¼-inch bolts, 3 to 6 inches long

Fast-drying glue

Blotting paper

Newspaper

Corrugated cardboard

Scissors

Assortment of flowers and leaves

4 wing nuts

1. Clamp the two pieces of plywood together and drill a 5/16-inch hole 1 inch in from each of the four corners. Unclamp the pieces and lightly sand all surfaces of both pieces. Apply a coat of varnish; let dry. These pieces will form the top and bottom of your press.

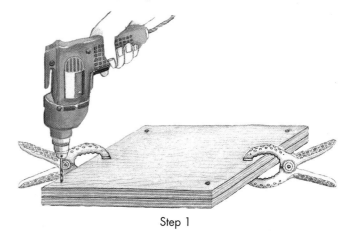

Step 1

2. Thread the bolts through the holes of one piece of plywood. Apply a drop of glue to the underside of each bolt to help secure it to the wood.

3. Cut a dozen 11-inch squares each of the blotting paper, newspaper, and cardboard. Cut off the corners so that the papers clear the bolts.

4. Assemble the press by layering one sheet of cardboard, two or three sheets of newspaper, two sheets of blotting paper, several more sheets of newspaper, and another layer of cardboard. Continue until your press is filled. Add the top plywood piece, and attach the wing nuts.

5. After completing your press, gather the best-looking flowers and foliage you can find, and get it in your press before the plant material begins to wilt. Remove petals from thicker flowers like roses or sunflowers; also remove thick stems (and remember—thicker pieces take longer to dry).

6. Open your press, and arrange the flowers between the pages of blotting paper so that they lie flat and don't touch each other. I tag the page with the date and type of flowers, so when I check the press, I'll know what is finished drying.

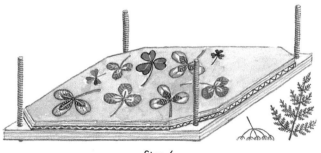

Step 6

PROJECT POINTERS: Store pressed flowers between pieces of waxed paper in a dry place to prevent molding. Shallow drawers or shallow cardboard boxes will work fine.

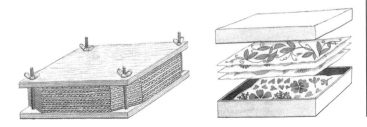

BEST BETS FOR PRESSING

Choose flowers that have just opened and have not yet produced pollen. Here are some of my favorites.

Bachelor's button (*Centaurea cyanus*): flowers

Bleeding heart (*Dicentra spectabilis*): flowers

Borage (*Borago officinalis*): flowers

Columbines (*Aquilegia* spp.): flowers, seedheads

Cosmos (*Cosmos* spp.): flowers, petals, foliage

Garden phlox (*Phlox paniculata*): individual flowers

Hollyhock (*Alcea rosea*): whole flowers, petals

Johnny-jump-up (*Viola tricolor*): whole flowers, foliage

Larkspurs (*Consolida* spp.): individual flowers, buds, foliage

Lavenders (*Lavandula* spp.): flower stalks

Lily-of-the-valley (*Convallaria majalis*): flowers

Oxeye daisy (*Leucanthemum vulgare*): flowers

Primroses (*Primula* spp.): flowers, foliage

Roses (*Rosa* spp.): flowers, petals, buds

Sweet William (*Dianthus barbatus*): flower heads

Violets (*Viola* spp.): flowers, foliage

PRESSED FLOWER NOTE CARDS

Preserving fresh flowers by pressing them is a charming and inexpensive method of capturing the fleeting beauty of old-time flowers. Here we discuss how to make greeting cards, but you can also work on a larger scale to create framed compositions.

1. Measure and cut your paper to the size you want. The fold for the card can be either at the top or the side. You may want to ink in a gold or black border to create a rectangular or oval frame before you add any flowers.

2. Review your collection of pressed flowers and plan your design. Lay a sheet of waxed paper on top of your card and arrange and rearrange the flowers until you're happy with your design; then carefully slide the waxed paper sheet off your card and begin gluing the flowers to the card paper.

Step 2

3. Apply a dot of glue to the back of individual flowers or leaves, and gently press them into place on the paper. Use tweezers or a small paintbrush to help you position the flowers.

4. If desired, spray your finished design with a clear acrylic fixative spray to help protect the delicate blossoms.

PROJECT POINTERS: The design can be simple—such as a single flower with its foliage and a hand-labeled Latin name, as on a botanical print—or a collage of flowers. Fun ideas for collages include seasonal groupings (such as all spring flowers) or color themes. Try shades of pink and purple for a dainty, romantic card, or strong reds and oranges for a dramatic look. Use varying textures and shapes to add interest to the design. Your design can be a simple garland of individual blossoms, petals, and leaves, or a wreath of small flowers that fills the frame.

PERFECT PRESSED FLOWERS

Here are some tips to help you have beautiful pressed flowers:

✳ Uniform pressure produces the best pressed flowers. A flower press is easy to make (see "Homemade Flower Press" on page 198), but an old phone book or any heavy book that does not have glossy paper also works well. If you do use a book, place a heavy brick or block on the cover once you place the flowers inside.

✳ Experiment to find out which of your flowers retain their color best. Blue or yellow flowers usually remain quite vivid, while reds darken and pink colors fade and soften. White flowers will take on an ivory hue.

✳ Depending on the flower shape, press the bloom either in full face or profile. Bleeding heart blooms, for instance, look best in profile, while larkspur looks great either in profile or full face.

✳ Don't limit yourself to open flowers; try buds and leaves, too. Fern fronds, ivy leaves, chervil leaflets, young rosemary sprigs, carrot or Queen-Anne's-lace foliage, and grasses work very well. Just avoid materials that are thick or succulent; they are difficult to press effectively.

✳ Keep pressed-flower designs out of direct sunlight to prevent fading.

HOMEGROWN POTPOURRI

*In medieval times, people scattered herbs on their floors
to mask unpleasant odors. Even though our living conditions are vastly
more hygienic today, a mix of dried, fragrant, and colorful herbs
and flowers combined with aromatic spices or essential oils is a soothing
and pleasant addition to the kitchen, bath, or bedroom. Potpourri created
from your garden is invariably more beautiful and subtly fragrant
than most commercial potpourris.*

MATERIALS

Dried leaves or scented
flowers for fragrance

Dried flowers, flower petals,
and seedheads for color

Large glass or ceramic bowl

Nonmetal spoon

Tablespoon

Aromatic spices (optional)

Essential oils (optional)

Fixative

Storage container
with tight lid

Pretty containers for display
or fabric bags for sachets

1. Decide on the combination of color and scent for your potpourri mix. You could create a mix of dried culinary herbs such as rosemary, thyme, and sage, plus bay leaves and cloves, for the kitchen, or you could make sachets of rose petals and lavender to add to dresser drawers. You can also take a seasonal approach by using herbs and flowers gathered from spring (such as violets, peony petals, lily-of-the-valley, and sweet peas), summer (bee balm, flowering tobacco, lavender, and mints), or fall (pot marigold petals, rose hips, rosemary, sage, and interesting seedheads).

Step 2

2. Mix your choice of flower petals and leaves together in the bowl. If you will be displaying your potpourri in a glass container or open bowl, you will want ⅓ to ½ of your mix to be colorful materials, but if you are putting your potpourri in fabric sachets, you'll only need fragrant materials. You don't need to be exact: Sprinkle your fragrant and colorful materials into the bowl until you are pleased with the combination.

3. Mix the potpourri with a nonmetal spoon. Add spices or essential oils until you are pleased with the fragrance. A general guideline is 1 tablespoon of spice or 6 to 8 drops of an essential oil to each quart of potpourri. Also add 1 tablespoon of a fixative (see "Project Pointers," below) for every quart of potpourri, and mix thoroughly.

Step 3

4. Store your finished potpourri in a container with a tight lid in a cool, dark spot for a month, so that the fragrances will blend well. Then display the potpourri in pretty containers or tie it into sachets to put in dresser drawers or closets.

PROJECT POINTERS: Throughout the growing season, harvest flower petals and herb foliage regularly for drying. Store thoroughly dried materials in airtight containers. Pick a dreary fall or winter day to open up your stash of

PETALS AND PODS FOR POTPOURRI

Making potpourri isn't an exact science—just use what you have on hand. But if you're looking for ideas for ingredients, here are some suggestions:

✳ **Plants for color** (individual flowers, unless otherwise indicated): bachelor's button (*Centaurea cyanus*); bee balms (*Monarda* spp.); borage (*Borage officinalis*); calendula (*Calendula officinalis*); foxglove (*Digitalis purpurea*); globe amaranth (*Gomphrena globosa*); larkspurs (*Consolida* spp.); lavenders (*Lavandula* spp.); love-in-a-mist (*Nigella damascena*), seedheads; pansy (*Viola x wittrockiana*); peonies (*Paeonia* spp.), petals; roses (*Rosa* spp.), petals; sages (*Salvia* spp.); tansy (*Tanacetum vulgare*); tulips (*Tulipa* spp.), petals; zinnias (*Zinnia* spp.).

✳ **Plants for fragrance** (individual leaves, unless otherwise indicated): angelica (*Angelica officinalis*), leaves and ground roots; basil; bee balm (*Monarda didyma*); dill, leaves and seeds; lavender; lily-of-the-valley (*Convallaria majalis*), flowers; mints; rosemary; sweet pea (*Lathyrus odoratus*), flowers; tansy (*Tanacetum vulgare*); thyme; sweet violet (*Viola odorata*), flowers.

**Don't restrict your potpourri se-
lections to sweet-smelling flowers
and colorful flower petals. Try
mixing some of these fragrant
spices to make a wonderful
kitchen potpourri.**

Bay: leaves

Cinnamon: sticks or ground

Cloves: whole or ground

Coriander: seeds or ground

Ginger root: pieces

Nutmeg: whole or ground

Mace: ground

materials and relive the glory of summer by blending a few batches of potpourri.

Finishing your customized mix with a fixative will enhance and retain the scent of your potpourri. Orris root, made from the roots of the Florentine iris (*Iris* × *germanica* var. *florentina*), is the most commonly used plant-based fixative. You can buy it in a pharmacy, at a craft store, or from an herbalist. You can make your own orris root fixative by digging up a section of the Florentine iris root, washing and drying it, and grinding it with a grater or blender into a fine powder while it's still slightly moist. (Make sure to wear a dust mask, since some individuals have an allergic reaction to orris root. Allergy-prone people can develop swollen eyes and an itchy nose.)

Other plant-derived fixatives that you can purchase are vetiver root (an East Indian grass), rose attar (an oil or perfume made from rose petals, particularly damask roses), liquid amber (*Liquidambar styraciflua*), benzoin (*Styrax benzoin*), and violet root powder (*Viola odorata*).

You can also use purchased wood shavings or natural cellulose fiber (which is actually ground-up corncobs), scented with a few drops of an essential oil as a fixative material in your potpourri. Be careful not to overwhelm your potpourri with essential oils, though, since they are very concentrated fragrances that have been distilled from large quantities of herbs or flowers. You can find these materials at most craft stores.

You may see animal-derived fixatives listed in some herb books as traditional potpourri and perfume ingredients. Ambergris is from sperm whales; civet is from the civet cat found in Africa, India, Malaysia, and China; and musk is obtained from the Asian male musk deer. These fixatives are very costly, and the animals that they are produced from are endangered species, so stick with plant-derived fixatives.

CANDIED FLOWERS

For a really spectacular dessert for a special occasion, try a Victorian favorite and decorate a layer cake with delicate candied Johnny-jump-ups or violets.

1. Pick a small quantity of edible flowers right before you are ready to work on this project. The flowers should not have any moisture on them.

2. Lightly beat an egg white until frothy. Holding the flower or flower petals with tweezers, carefully brush the flower on all sides with the egg white. (The egg white will form a barrier coating to preserve the flower.)

3. Sprinkle superfine granulated sugar over the flower with a spoon, or dip the flower in a shallow bowl of the sugar. Gently shake the flower to remove the excess sugar.

4. Lay the coated flowers on a baking sheet or wire rack covered with waxed paper or baking parchment. Let them dry overnight in a warm, dry place, until they're crispy.

5. Carefully layer the flowers in an airtight glass container between sheets of waxed paper or baking parchment. The flowers will keep for several months.

PROJECT POINTERS: You may prefer to use a powdered egg white product instead of fresh egg white because of health concerns. An old-time option is to use gum arabic, an edible binder made from the acacia tree. It's sometimes available from candy-making or cake-decorating suppliers, or from pharmacies in powder form. You'll need to dissolve several teaspoons of the gum arabic powder in a small jar of water several days before you plan to coat the flowers. Egg white is usually easier to work with, in my experience.

MATERIALS

Fresh, edible flowers

Fresh or powdered egg white

Tweezers

Small paintbrush

Superfine granulated sugar

Waxed paper or baking parchment

Baking sheet or wire rack

Step 2

Step 3

CHAPTER

N I N E

Favorite Old-Time Recipes

Old-time country cooks were intimately linked to the land and keenly aware of the seasons and their cycles, sowing, growing, harvesting, and preserving foods they prepared as hearty meals for their families. Old-time recipes also reflect regional foods and the cultural traditions of the cook. Our foremothers were industrious and creative, and they gave us a richly diverse heritage of American cooking. From Native American dishes to traditional African and European foods, we've inherited the skills and knowledge of generations of cooks.

Gardeners today can also have that link from the earth to the table and know the satisfaction of growing vegetables, fruits, and herbs, and the enjoyment of a good meal. I find that preparing old-time recipes connects me with my roots and gives me a sense of community and tradition.

This chapter features a sampling of some classic, old-time recipes. Many of the recipes here were contributed by living history museums and festivals where visitors have the opportunity to see heirloom gardens and demonstrations of old-time cooking. Living history museums are important players in the effort to keep our heirloom varieties alive, and many offer heirloom seeds and plants through their museum catalogs. For a listing of living history museums, turn to "Historical Gardens" on page 226.

OPPOSITE: *A large part of the pleasure of kitchen gardening is the end result—having delicious, fresh, organic vegetables and fruit at your fingertips.*

207

CORN PUDDING

This filling and delicious Shaker corn pudding recipe
from Pleasant Hill, Kentucky, is one that you'll want to make often!
It's adapted from We Make You Kindly Welcome
by Elizabeth C. Kremer.

Ingredients

3 tablespoons butter

2 tablespoons sugar

2 tablespoons flour

1 teaspoon salt

3 whole eggs

2 cups corn (fresh, canned, or frozen)

1¾ cups milk

1. Preheat oven to 325°F. Blend butter, sugar, flour, and salt.

2. Add eggs to this mixture and beat well. Stir in corn and milk.

3. Pour ingredients into a buttered, 1-quart casserole dish and bake for 45 minutes.

4. Stir once halfway through cooking. When done, the pudding will be a golden brown and a knife inserted into the center will come out clean.

OPTIONS: You can also prepare this recipe early in the day and keep it in a jar in the refrigerator until you're ready to cook it. When you're ready to cook the pudding, shake the jar well and pour the contents into a buttered casserole dish; bake as above.

YIELD: 6 SERVINGS.

The Pleasant Hill, Kentucky, Shaker community was active for over 100 years. Today, the restored village is a living history site, raising heirloom varieties of vegetables, herbs, and fruit in the nineteenth-century Shaker manner.

ESCALLOPED CORN AND TOMATOES

This simple vegetable casserole is a popular dish in the farmhouse restaurant at Living History Farms in Urbandale, Iowa.

Ingredients

2 cups whole tomatoes, skinned, peeled, and chopped

One 15-ounce can creamed corn

2 cups cooked corn

2 eggs, slightly beaten

1 teaspoon pepper

2 teaspoons sugar

2 tablespoons flour

Topping:

1 medium onion, finely chopped

1 clove garlic

½ cup butter

½ cup Parmesan cheese

4 cups bread crumbs

1. Preheat oven to 350°F. Thoroughly mix tomatoes, corn, eggs, pepper, sugar, and flour together. Pour this mixture into a 13 × 9-inch casserole dish.

2. To prepare the crumb topping, sauté the onion, garlic, and butter. Take off the stove and add the remaining ingredients.

3. Sprinkle the crumb topping on top of the tomato-and-corn mixture. Bake for 1 hour.

YIELD: 10 SERVINGS.

Living History Farms in Urbandale, Iowa, tells the story of Midwestern agriculture and rural life from the eighteenth century through the twentieth century on its 600-acre site.

BUBBLE AND SQUEAK

This traditional English dish derived its name from the noise the cabbage and potatoes make when you press your spoon on the mixture as it cooks. The Genesee Country Village and Museum in Mumford, New York, contributed their favorite version of this classic dish.

Ingredients

½ pound bacon

1 large onion, sliced

1 head cabbage, cut into
1-inch-wide wedges

½ cup water

1 small sprig of fresh lovage

1 teaspoon each of salt, pepper,
and caraway seed

4 or 5 raw or cooked potatoes,
quartered

1. Brown the bacon and onion in a large saucepan.

2. Add the cabbage and water. Season with lovage, salt, pepper, and caraway seed. Cover and keep over heat.

3. If you are using raw potatoes, add them when the cabbage begins to wilt and soften. If you're using cooked potatoes, wait until the last 10 minutes to add them.

4. Add more water as needed to keep the bottom of the pan covered as this dish cooks. Bubble and Squeak is ready to serve when the cabbage and potatoes are tender and fully cooked. Total cooking time is approximately 40 minutes.

YIELD: 6 TO 8 SERVINGS.

The Genesee Country Village and Museum in Mumford, New York, is a recreated nineteenth-century community with a dozen heirloom gardens that provide produce for daily cooking demonstrations.

SISTER MARY'S ZESTY CARROTS

Horseradish and onion add the zest to this easy carrot recipe created by Sister Mary, a member of the Hancock Shaker Village in Pittsfield, Massachusetts, in the late 1800s. This recipe is excerpted from The Best of Shaker Cooking *by Amy Bess Miller and Persis Fuller.*

Ingredients

6 carrots, cleaned and cut into thin strips

2 tablespoons grated onion

2 tablespoons horseradish

½ cup mayonnaise

1 teaspoon salt

¼ teaspoon pepper

¼ cup water

¼ cup buttered breadcrumbs

1. Cook the cleaned and sliced carrots in salted water until tender. Place in a 6 × 10-inch baking dish.

2. Preheat oven to 375°F. Mix grated onion, horseradish, mayonnaise, salt, pepper, and water. Pour over carrots. Sprinkle with buttered breadcrumbs. Bake for 15 minutes.

YIELD: 4 TO 6 SERVINGS.

Now open to the public, Hancock Shaker Village in Pittsfield, Massachusetts, showcases gardens growing heirloom vegetables using various nineteenth-century Shaker gardening techniques.

Roast Corn Soup

This hearty soup is a traditional Iroquois recipe and a favorite of the Rickard family of the Iroquois tribe in New York.

Ingredients

2 gallons water
1½ pounds pork or bacon
2 cups dry roast corn
½ pound dry beans, cooked
2 teaspoons salt
½ teaspoon pepper

1. Bring water to a boil in a large pot. Cut pork or bacon into small pieces. Add pork or bacon and roast corn to boiling water. Cook at a slow boil for about 3 hours.

2. Add cooked beans. Add salt and pepper. Cook at a slow boil for one more hour, adding water periodically as the soup boils down.

YIELD: 6 TO 8 QUARTS.

Root Cellar Soup

This soup includes less-familiar root vegetables such as turnips and parsnips.

Ingredients

3 tablespoons butter
½ pound ham, cut into ½-inch cubes
2 large onions, chopped
3 large carrots, diced
3 parsnips, diced
3 medium turnips, peeled and diced
5 cups water
1 teaspoon dried thyme

1. Melt butter in a saucepan over medium heat. Add ham and onions, and sauté until ham begins to brown and onions are translucent.

2. Add diced carrots, parsnips, and turnips, and water and thyme to the saucepan. Cover and cook until the vegetables are very tender.

3. Remove the saucepan from heat. Mash soup mixture until vegetables are blended together. Return soup to the stove, and simmer on low until you're ready to serve it.

YIELD: 6 TO 8 SERVINGS.

PRESERVING IROQUOIS TRADITIONS

Norton and Marlene Rickard, members of the six-nation Iroquois people, are keeping their traditions alive by growing the ancient Iroquois corn, beans, and squash, and other heirloom vegetables and fruit, and by teaching their children how to prepare time-honored dishes. Norton is especially concerned about preserving the Tuscarora white flour corn, and he grows seven acres of it each year. The Rickards have a traditional corn husking bee in October, after the corn has dried down. Family and friends gather to harvest the corn, eat good food, and celebrate the harvest.

Roasting is one of the ways that the Rickards prepare their Tuscarora white flour corn. Earlier in the season—about the middle of August—they pick some of the corn at the "green" stage. (Marlene compares this stage to a blackberry being red right before it turns black.) You can test for the green stage by taking your fingernail and poking a kernel of corn: If a little milk comes out, it is ready to pick for roasting.

After picking and husking the corn, the Rickards roast it on a large grate over an open fire. They turn the corn until it is nice and brown on all sides, and then they remove it and set it aside until it is cool enough to handle. Marlene finishes the roasting process by shelling the corn into large cake pans. She fills the pans about half-full and places them in the oven at 250°F to dry, turning the corn periodically with a spatula. Marlene knows the corn is dried when it has a dried appearance and makes a dry sound when it hits the pan. When the corn has cooled, Marlene stores it in the freezer in plastic bags. The corn has a wonderful roasted flavor that's a welcome addition to winter recipes such as "Roast Corn Soup" on the opposite page.

HOPPIN' JOHN

The New Year is welcomed in with hearty bowls of Hoppin' John all through the South. Originating with African-American cooks from the Caribbean, there are many versions of this dish.

Ingredients

2 cups dried black-eyed peas

Water

½ pound bacon

1 green bell pepper, cut into strips

1 large onion, chopped

4 cups cooked rice

Hot pepper sauce

1. Wash the black-eyed peas and remove any debris. Soak in 6 cups of water overnight in a large cooking pot.

2. Cut the bacon into small pieces. Sauté the bacon with the green pepper and onion until the bacon is crispy.

3. Drain the water off the black-eyed peas and rinse. Add the sautéed bacon, pepper, and onion along with 6 cups of water. Simmer on low heat until the beans are soft, approximately 1½ hours. Stir occasionally and add water if dry.

4. Add the cooked rice. Season with hot pepper sauce to taste.

YIELD: 6 SERVINGS.

TEPARY CHILE

Here's a flavorful Southwest chile recipe from the Native Seeds/SEARCH organization, based in Arizona. Part of its zesty flavor comes from chipotle chiles, which are actually dried smoked jalapeños.

Ingredients

2 cups dried tepary beans

Water

2 chipotle chiles (optional if you prefer mild chile)

1 large onion, chopped

4 cloves garlic, chopped

1 red bell pepper, chopped

1 teaspoon cumin seed

1 tablespoon vegetable oil

1½ teaspoons salt

2 teaspoons dried lemon basil

1 teaspoon dried Mexican oregano

2 tomatoes, chopped

1. Rinse and drain tepary beans. Bring 6 cups water to a boil in large pot. Add beans and chipotles.

2. Simmer on low heat 3 to 4 hours until cooked, adding more water as necessary to keep beans covered.

3. A half-hour before the beans are done (when the beans have softened), sauté onion, garlic, pepper, and cumin seed in vegetable oil until tender. Stir in salt, basil, oregano, and tomatoes. Add this to the beans, and simmer for half an hour.

OPTIONS: You can also cook this in a Crock-Pot on low for 6 to 8 hours, adding the sautéed vegetables for just the last half hour.

YIELD: 6 SERVINGS.

Native Seeds/SEARCH in Tucson, Arizona, works to conserve the traditional crops, seeds, and farming methods of native peoples of the southwestern United States and northern Mexico. They specialize in heirloom crops such as corn, beans, squash, melons, gourds, chiles, chiltepines, desert greens, and teosinte.

CLARA'S PATTY PAN SQUASH

Patty pan squash is a favorite with the staff at the National Colonial Farm in Accokeek, Maryland. Clara Moran, the staff librarian, devised this recipe and likes to serve it with corn on the cob and sliced tomatoes.

Ingredients

1 medium onion or 6 green scallions

2 or 3 garlic cloves, minced

1 tablespoon fresh thyme leaves, chopped

2 tablespoons olive oil or butter (or a mixture of the two)

3 or 4 patty pan squash (each 4 inches in diameter), cubed

Salt and pepper

¼ cup fresh parsley

¼ cup Parmesan cheese

½ cup dry breadcrumbs

1. Cut onions or scallions into thin slices from stem to root. Sauté onions, garlic, and thyme in olive oil or butter for 2 to 3 minutes.

2. Add the cubed squash and salt and pepper to taste. Toss frequently, as for stir-fry, cooking until the squash cubes are translucent but not mushy. Add parsley.

3. Transfer to a casserole dish or Pyrex pie plate. Sprinkle with Parmesan cheese and breadcrumbs, and brown under the broiler for a few minutes.

OPTIONS: Instead of using the cheese and breadcrumbs, top with ¾ cup grated Swiss cheese. Place under the broiler until the cheese is melted. Sprinkle with paprika.

YIELD: 6 SERVINGS.

The gardens at the National Colonial Farm of the Accokeek Foundation, in Accokeek, Maryland, showcase crops grown during colonial times. Different gardens include crops from the Americas, Europe, Africa, and gathered wild plants. Gardeners tend each using traditional methods.

BASIC PIE CRUST

Believe it or not, lard really does make the best flaky pie crust!

Ingredients

2 cups flour
½ teaspoon salt
⅔ cup lard
⅓ cup water

1. Combine flour and salt in a mixing bowl. Cut lard into flour mixture with a pastry blender.

2. Add water gradually, tossing the mixture lightly with a fork. If the dough mixture is too dry, it will be too crumbly to roll; if it's too wet, the dough will stick to the rolling pin.

3. Shape dough into a round ball, handling it as little as possible. Divide in half and roll each half into a circle ⅛ inch thick. Press one circle into a 9-inch pie plate, and reserve the other to top the filling.

YIELD: 1 TWO-CRUST PIE OR 2 OPEN PIE SHELLS.

SWEET DOUGH

Sweet dough is a popular top crust for pies at the Goschenhoppen Folk Festival in East Greenville, Pennsylvania.

Ingredients

1 cup flour
1 cup brown sugar
½ teaspoon baking soda
½ teaspoon cream of tartar
1 egg

1. Stir together flour, brown sugar, baking soda, and cream of tartar. Beat egg in a separate bowl, and then add to dry ingredients.

2. Roll dough into a circle, using additional flour if it's sticky, and use as a lid to top a pie or cut into strips to make a lattice top.

YIELD: 1 TOP CRUST.

ELDERBERRY-APPLE PIE

Elderberries and apples are a wonderful combination in this recipe from
Farm Journal's Country Cookbook.

Ingredients

2 cups elderberries, stemmed

1½ cups tart apples,
peeled and chopped

1½ cups sugar

3 tablespoons tapioca

1 unbaked, 9-inch pie shell

Sweet dough for top crust,
cut into strips

1. Preheat oven to 425°F. Combine elderberries, apples, sugar, and tapioca. Fill pie shell with mixture and top with sweet dough strips in a lattice pattern.

2. Bake at 425°F for 10 minutes. Reduce heat to 350°F, and bake for 20 minutes.

YIELD: 1 PIE (8 SERVINGS).

OPTIONS: Having trouble removing elderberries from their stems? I find that it works well if I hold the stem with one hand and gently roll my thumb over the berries to take them off the stems. Another effective technique is to use a fork and gently tug at the berry clusters to remove the berries.

GRAPE PIE

This is a tasty adaptation of an old recipe by my sister, Alice Keppley, the premiere fruit-pie baker at the Goschenhoppen Folk Festival.

Ingredients

3 cups 'Concord' grapes
1 cup sugar
3 tablespoons flour
1 tablespoon lemon juice
1 unbaked, 9-inch pie shell

Topping:
1 cup flour
½ cup sugar
¼ cup butter

1. Wash, drain, and stem grapes. Cook in saucepan (do not add water) until soft (about 5 minutes).

2. Preheat oven to 350°F. Combine the sugar, flour, and lemon juice in a large mixing bowl.

3. Strain the cooked grapes through a food mill or sieve into the mixing bowl. Mix together and pour into the pie shell.

4. Mix flour, sugar, and butter with a pastry blender. Sprinkle crumb topping over pie. Bake for 40 minutes.

YIELD: 1 PIE (8 SERVINGS).

SCHNITZ PIE

This dried-apple pie is one of the most popular pies at the annual Goschenhoppen Folk Festival in East Greenville, Pennsylvania.

Ingredients

2 cups dried apples (schnitz)
2 cups warm water
⅔ cup sugar
¼ teaspoon ground cloves
½ teaspoon cinnamon
1 orange rind, grated
1 unbaked, 9-inch pie shell
Sweet dough for top crust

1. Put the dried apples in warm water overnight. In the morning, cook the apples in the soaking water until they're soft (about 45 minutes).

2. Preheat oven to 375°F. Stir the apples to mash them, and add remaining ingredients. Pour into the pie shell, top with a lid of sweet dough, cut slits in the top, and bake for 45 minutes.

YIELD: 1 PIE (8 SERVINGS).

GREEN TOMATO PIE

This unusual but flavorful pie is served at the Goschenhoppen Folk Festival.

Ingredients

1 unbaked, 9-inch pie shell
3 cups green tomatoes, washed and thinly sliced
1 teaspoon cinnamon
½ teaspoon cloves
1 tablespoon flour
¾ cup brown sugar
Sweet dough for top crust

1. Preheat oven to 425°F. Fill pie shell with the sliced green tomatoes.

2. Combine cinnamon, cloves, flour, and brown sugar, and sprinkle over green tomatoes.

3. Cover tomatoes with sweet dough crust. Bake for 10 minutes at 425°F and then reduce heat to 350°F and bake for 40 minutes.

YIELD: 1 PIE (8 SERVINGS).

RHUBARB-STRAWBERRY COBBLER

Rhubarb and strawberries are a winning taste combination in this delicious cobbler from the Shaker Village at Pleasant Hill, Kentucky. This recipe is adapted from Welcome Back to Pleasant Hill *by Elizabeth C. Kremer.*

Ingredients

½ cup flour

3 cups granulated sugar

1 teaspoon salt

6 cups rhubarb, sliced

2 cups strawberries (slice large berries in half)

4 tablespoons butter

1 tablespoon lemon juice

Pie crust to cover 9 × 13-inch pan

1. Preheat oven to 450°F. Combine flour, sugar, and salt. Sprinkle over rhubarb and strawberries, and toss well.

2. Lightly butter a 9 × 13-inch pan. Heap mixture into greased pan and spread evenly. Sprinkle the mixture with lemon juice and dot with butter.

3. Top with pie crust. Either prick the crust with a fork, or use a knife to cut slits in it. Bake for 1 hour.

YIELD: 12 SERVINGS.

PUMPKIN MUFFINS

*This moist muffin recipe from the Shaker Village at Pleasant Hill,
Kentucky, works equally well with either pumpkin or butternut squash.
It's adapted from* We Make You Kindly Welcome
by Elizabeth C. Kremer.

Ingredients

¾ cup brown sugar

¼ cup molasses

½ cup soft butter

1 beaten egg

1 cup mashed cooked pumpkin, strained

1¾ cups flour

1 teaspoon baking soda

¼ teaspoon salt

¼ cup pecans

1. Preheat oven to 375°F. Thoroughly blend sugar, molasses, and butter. Add egg and pumpkin, and blend well.

2. In a separate bowl, mix the flour, baking soda, and salt; beat this mixture into the pumpkin batter.

3. Fold pecans into the mixture.

4. Fill well-greased muffin pans about half-full with batter; bake for 20 minutes.

YIELD: 15 MUFFINS.

WATERMELON RIND PICKLES

This unusual old-time favorite is a Shaker recipe from Pleasant Hill, Kentucky. It's excerpted from Welcome Back to Pleasant Hill *by Elizabeth C. Kremer.*

Ingredients

20 tablespoons salt

Water

5 quarts 1-inch watermelon rind cubes (each with a little pink)

5 quarts granulated sugar

2 cups cider vinegar

2 teaspoons whole cloves

2 teaspoons whole allspice

4 to 6 sticks cinnamon

½ teaspoon ground pepper

1. Prepare brine by mixing the salt with 5 quarts of water. Pour brine over the watermelon rind cubes and let sit overnight.

2. Pour off brine, wash the cubes in clear water, and drain. Cover with fresh water and cook slowly until tender (about 1 hour). Drain again.

3. Make pickling syrup of sugar, vinegar, and 4 quarts of water. Tie spices in a cloth bag and add to syrup. Bring all to boiling and pour over the watermelon cubes.

4. Boil until watermelon cubes are clear and syrup is honey-thick (about 1 hour).

5. Put in sterilized pint canning jars, leave ½ inch of space, and process in a hot-water bath for 10 minutes.

YIELD: 10 PINTS.

SALMAGUNDI

This arranged salad of colorful vegetables was popular in the eighteenth and nineteenth centuries. It's a beautiful addition to a summer luncheon. Compose your salmagundi from whatever vegetables are freshest in the garden; the vegetables suggested here are from a spring garden. The salad size can vary with the number of people you're serving.

Ingredients

Snow or sugar snap peas
Baby carrots
Scallions
Radishes
Red leaf lettuce
Green leaf lettuce or watercress
Hard-boiled eggs
Chive flowers
Parsley or chervil
Violet or pansy flowers
Vinaigrette dressing

1. Wash and trim vegetables. Trim each of the vegetables to roughly the same size so that you can easily arrange them.

2. Peel the hard-boiled eggs and separate the yolks from the whites. Chop each very finely.

3. Begin your salmagundi by placing an oval of chopped egg yolks surrounded by the chopped egg whites in the center of a large, shallow, oval platter.

4. Arrange your vegetables in concentric rings around the eggs, using the different colors and shapes to create patterns.

5. Finish the platter with decorations of herbs and flowers. Serve immediately with a vinaigrette or other dressing.

OPTIONS: For an equally beautiful summer salad, try slices of cucumber, summer squash, peppers, blanched beans, baby beets, and nasturtium and borage flowers, with a cold, sliced chicken breast in the center.

YIELD: ONE LARGE SALAD (VARIES WITH AMOUNT OF VEGETABLES USED).

EARLY AMERICAN COOKBOOKS

If you look through old cookbooks, you'll find that the directions are not exactly precise. Women grew up helping their mothers in the kitchen, and by the time they established their own households, they had learned their mother's specialties and seldom referred to a cookbook. My mother's notebook of recipes that she had copied from my grandmother had notations like "lard like an egg," "flour to stiffen," and the very helpful "bake until done." This can be challenging for modern cooks trying to recreate old-fashioned favorites, but it can also provide some exciting culinary adventures.

I asked Joe Carlin, a nutritionist and food historian, about vegetable recipes in early American cookbooks. (Joe is the owner of Food Heritage Press, P.O. Box 163, Ipswich, MA 01938, which carries facsimiles of early-American and British cookbooks. Food Heritage Press also carries international cookbooks and food history titles.)

"Cookbooks in the first half of the nineteenth century do not have many vegetable dishes, and when they do, the instructions are for making pickles out of them and turning them into pies and puddings," says Joe. "All cooks knew how to prepare vegetables, and my guess is that few people followed recipes directly, but rather improvised.

"Nothing was wasted from kitchen gardens. There is even economy in the way a recipe is written. Modern recipe writers would develop a recipe for a specific green, but not writers of the period. You used whatever was available at that time of year."

An example of this is the following recipe from *Miss Beecher's Domestic Receipt Book, Third Edition.* : "Beet tops, turnip tops, spinach, cabbage sprouts, dandelions, cowslips, all these boil in salted water till they are tender, then drain in colander, pressing hard. Chop them a little, and warm them in a sauce-pan, with a little butter. Lay them on buttered toast, and if you like, garnish them with hard boiled egg, cut in slices. If not fresh, soak them half an hour in salt and water."

Resources for Heirloom Country Gardens

Historical Gardens

INDIANA

Corner Prairie
13400 Allisonville Rd.
Fishers, IN 46038
Phone: (317) 776-6000
Fax: (317) 776-6014

IOWA

Living History Farms
2600 NW 111th St.
Urbandale, IA 50322
Phone: (515) 278-5286
Fax: (515) 278-9808

KENTUCKY

Shaker Village at Pleasant Hill
3501 Lexington Rd.
Harrodsburg, KY 40330
Phone: (800) 734-5611

LOUISIANA

Rosedown Plantation & Gardens
12501 Hwy. 10
St. Francisville, LA 70775
Phone: (504) 635-3332

MARYLAND

National Colonial Farm
Accokeek Foundation
3400 Bryan Point Rd.
Accokeek, MD 20607
Phone: (301) 283-2113
Fax: (301) 283-2049

MASSACHUSETTS

Hancock Shaker Village
P.O. Box 927
Pittsfield, MA 01202
Phone: (413) 443-0188
Fax: (413) 447-9357

Old Sturbridge Village
1 Old Sturbridge Village Rd.
Sturbridge, MA 01566
Phone: (508) 347-3362

Plimoth Plantation
P.O. Box 1620
Plymouth, MA 02362
Phone: (508) 746-1622
Fax: (508) 746-4978

NEW JERSEY

Howell Living History Farm
101 Hunter Rd.
Titusville, NJ 08560
Phone: (609) 737-3299

NEW YORK

**Genesee Country Village
& Museum**
P.O. Box 310
1410 Flint Hill Rd.
Mumford, NY 14511
Phone: (716) 538-6822
Fax: (716) 538-2887

North Carolina

Historic Lotta Plantation
5225 Sample Rd.
Huntersville, NC 28078
Phone: (704) 875-2312

Old Salem, Inc.
Box F, Salem Station
Winston-Salem, NC 27108
Phone: (336) 721-7350

Pennsylvania

Bartram's Garden
54th St. and Lindbergh Blvd.
Philadelphia, PA 19143
Phone: (215) 729-5281
Fax: (215) 729-1047

Landis Valley Museum
2451 Kissel Hill Rd.
Lancaster, PA 17601
Phone: (717) 569-0402

Quiet Valley Living Historical Farm
1000 Turkey Hill Rd.
Stroudsburg, PA 18360
Phone: (570) 992-6161

Virginia

Colonial Williamsburg Foundation
P.O. Box 1776
Williamsburg, VA 23187
Phone: (800) 447-8779

Monticello
P.O. Box 316
Charlottesville, VA 22903
Phone: (804) 984-9821
Fax: (804) 977-6140

Mount Vernon
George Washington Pkwy.
Mt. Vernon, VA 22121
Phone: (703) 780-2000

Canada

Annapolis Royal Historic Garden
P.O. Box 278
Annapolis Royal, Nova Scotia,
  Canada B0S 1A0
Phone: (902) 532-5104

King's Landing Historical Settlement
Exit 259, Rte. 2
Prince William, New Brunswick,
  Canada E0H 1S0
Phone: (506) 363-4999
Fax: (506) 363-4989

Seed-Saving Organizations

Eastern Native Seed Conservancy
222 Main St.
P.O. Box 451
Great Barrington, MA 01230
Phone: (413) 229-8316

The Flower and Herb Exchange
3076 North Winn Rd.
Decorah, IA 52101
Phone: (319) 382-5990
Fax: (319) 382-5872

Garden State Heirloom Seed Society
c/o Joe Cavanaugh
P.O. Box 15
Delaware, NJ 07833

The Maine Seed Saving Network
P.O. Box 126
Penobscot, ME 04476

Native Seeds/SEARCH
526 N. 4th Ave.
Tucson, AZ 85705
Phone: (520) 622-5561
Fax: (520) 622-5591
Web site:
   http://desert.net/seeds/home.htm
E-mail: nss@azstarnet.com

Seeds of Diversity Canada
P.O. Box 36
Station Q, Toronto, ON
Canada M4T 2L7
Phone: (905) 623-0353

Seed Savers Exchange
3076 North Winn Rd.
Decorah, IA 52101
Phone: (319) 382-5990
Fax: (319) 382-5872

Seed and Plant Sources

Abundant Life Seed Foundation
P.O. Box 772
Port Townsend, WA 98368
Phone: (360) 385-5660
Fax: (360) 385-7455
Catalog: $2.00
Vegetables, flowers, herbs

The Antique Rose Emporium
9300 Lueckmeyer Rd.
Brenham, TX 77833
Phone: (800) 441-0002
Fax: (409) 836-0928
Catalog: Free
Antique roses

Archias' Seed Store
106 East Main St.
Sedalia, MO 65301
Phone: (816) 826-1330
Catalog: $1.00
Vegetables, flowers

Boone's Native Seed Company
P.O. Box 10363
501 Cleveland St.
Raleigh, NC 27605
Catalog: Free
Tomatoes, chile peppers

Bountiful Gardens
18001 Shafer Ranch Rd.
Willits, CA 95490
Phone: (707) 459-6410
Catalog: Free
Vegetables, flowers, herbs

Classical Fruits
8831 AL Hwy. 157
Moulton, AL 35650
Phone: (205) 974-8813
Catalog: Free
Tree fruit, small fruit

The Cook's Garden
P.O. Box 535
Londonderry, VT 05148
Phone: (800) 457-9703
Fax: (800) 457-9705
Web site: www.cooksgarden.com
Catalog: Free
Vegetables, flowers, herbs

Down on the Farm Seed
P.O. Box 184
Hiram, OH 44234
Catalog: Free
Vegetables, flowers, herbs

Fedco
Rt. 2, Box 275
Clinton, ME 04927
Phone: (207) 426-9005
Fax: (207) 426-9005
Catalog: $2.00
Vegetables, flowers, herbs, small fruit, tree fruit

The Fragrant Path
P.O. Box 328
Fort Calhoun, NE 68023
Catalog: $1.00
Flowers

Greenmantle Nursery
3010 Ettersburg Rd.
Garberville, CA 95440
Phone: (707) 986-7504
Catalog: $3.00
Tree fruit

Henry Leuthardt Nurseries, Inc.
Montauk Hwy., Box 666
East Moriches, NY 11940
Phone: (516) 878-1387
Variety and price listing: Free
Small fruit, tree fruit

High Mowing Organic Seed Farm
R.D. 1, Box 95
Derby Line, VT 05830
Phone: (802) 895-4696
Catalog: Free
Vegetables

Historical Iris Preservation Society
Andrea Desiree Wilson, Membership
   Secretary
15 Bracebridge Rd.
Newton Centre, MA 02459
Annual membership dues: $5.00
Web site: www.worldiris.com

J. L. Hudson, Seedsman
P.O. Box 1058
Redwood City, CA 94064
Catalog: $1.00
Vegetables

Johnny's Selected Seeds
310 Foss Hill Rd.
Albion, ME 04910
Phone: (207) 437-9294
Fax: (207) 437-2165
Catalog: Free
Vegetables, flowers, herbs

**Landis Valley Museum Heirloom
   Seed Project**
2451 Kissel Hill Road
Lancaster, PA 17601
Phone: (717) 569-0401, ext. 204
Fax: (717) 560-2147
Catalog: $4.00
Vegetables, herbs

Old House Gardens
536 Third St.
Ann Arbor, MI 48103
Phone: (734) 995-1486
Fax: (734) 995-1687
Web site: www.oldhousegardens.com
Catalog: $2.00
Antique bulbs

Perennial Pleasures Nursery
P.O. Box 147
63 Brickhouse Road
East Hardwick, VT 05836
Phone: (802) 472-5104
Fax: (802) 472-6572
Web site:
   www.kingcon.com/hyssop/index.htm
Catalog: $3.00
Flowers, herbs

Pinetree Garden Seeds
Box 300
New Gloucester, ME 04260
Phone: (207) 926-3400
Fax: 1 (888) 52-SEEDS
E-mail: superseeds@worldnet.att.net
Web site: www.superseeds.com
Catalog: Free
Vegetables, herbs, flowers

Redwood City Seed Co.
P.O. Box 361
Redwood City, CA 94064
Phone: (415) 325-7333
Catalog: Free
Herbs, vegetables

Richters
357 Hwy. 47
Goodwood, Ontario
Canada LOC 1AO
Phone: (905) 640-6677
Fax: (905) 640-6641
Web site: www.richters.com
Catalog: Free
Herbs

Sand Hill Preservation Center
1878 230th St.
Calamus, IA 52729
Phone: (319) 246-2299
Catalog: Free
Vegetables, flowers, and heirloom poultry

**Santa Barbara Heirloom
  Seed Nursery**
P.O. Box 4235, Ste. I
Santa Barbara, CA 93140
Phone: (805) 968-5444
Fax: (805) 562-1248

Web site:
  www.heirloom.com/heirloom/
Catalog: $2.00
Vegetables, herbs

Seeds Blüm
HC 33 Idaho City Stage
Boise, ID 83706
Phone: (800) 527-3337
Fax: (208) 338-5658
Web site: www.seedsblum.com
Catalog: $3.00
Vegetables, herbs, flowers

Seeds of Change
P.O. Box 15700
Santa Fe NM 87506
Phone: (505) 438-8080
Fax: (505) 438-7052
Web site: www.seedsofchange.com
Catalog: Free
Vegetables, herbs, flowers

Select Seeds—Antique Flowers
180 Stickney Rd.
Union, CT 06076
Phone: (860) 684-9310
  or (800) 653-3304
Web site: www.selectseeds.com
Catalog: $1.00
Flowers

Shepherd's Garden Seeds
30 Irene Street
Torrington, CT 06790
Phone: (860) 482-3638
Web site: www.shepherds.com
Catalog: Free
Vegetables, herbs, flowers

Sonoma Antique Apple Nursery
4395 Westside Rd.
Healdsburg, CA 95448
Phone: (707) 433-6420
Fax: (707) 433-6479
Web site: www.applenursery.com
Variety and price list: Free
Small fruit, tree fruit

Southern Exposure
  Seed Exchange
P.O. Box 170
Earlysville, VA 22936
Phone: (804) 973-4703
Fax: (804) 973-8717
Catalog: $2.00
Vegetables, herbs

Southmeadow Fruit Gardens
P.O. Box 211-10603 Cleveland Ave.
Baroda, MI 49101
Phone: (616) 422-2411
Fax: (616) 422-1464
Variety and price listing: Free
Full catalog: $9.00
Tree fruit, small fruit

St. Lawrence Nursery
R.R. 5, Box 324
Potsdam, NY 14240
Phone: (315) 265-6739
Catalog: Free
Tree fruit, small fruit

Thomas Jefferson Center
  for Historic Plants
Monticello
P.O. Box 316
Charlottesville, VA 22903
Phone: (804) 984-9821
Fax: (804) 977-6140
Web site: www.monticello.org/shop
Catalog: $2.00
Vegetables, flowers, antique roses, bulbs

Tomato Growers
  Supply Company
P.O. Box 2237
Fort Myers, FL 33902
Phone: (941) 768-1119
Fax: (941) 768-3476
Catalog: Free
Tomatoes

Underwood Gardens, Ltd.
4N381 Maple Ave.
Bensenville, IL 60106
Fax: (888) 382-7041
Web site:www.grandmasgarden.com
Catalog: $1.00
Vegetables, flowers, herbs, specialty potatoes

Vintage Gardens
2833 Old Gravestein Hwy. South
Sebastopol, CA 95472
Phone: (707) 829-2035
Catalog: $5.00
Antique roses

Recommended Reading

Historic References

Beecher, Henry Ward. *Fruit, Flowers, and Farming.* New York: Derby & Jackson, 1959.

Breck, Joseph. *The Flower Garden.* Boston: John P. Jewett and Co., 1851.

Burr Jr., Fearing. *The Field and Garden Vegetables of America.* Chillicothe, IL: The American Botanist, Booksellers, 1994. (Reprinted from the second edition, 1865)

Child, Lydia Marie. *The American Frugal Housewife.* Bedford, MA: Applewood Books, 1989.

Coats, Alice M. *Flowers and Their Histories.* London: Hulton Press, 1956.

Downing, Andrew Jackson. *Victorian Cottage Residences.* New York: Dover, 1982. (Reprint of 1873 edition.)

Henderson, Peter. *Gardening for Pleasure.* New York: Orange Judd Co., 1888.

———. *Practical Floriculture.* New York: Orange Judd Co., 1869.

Hottes, Alfred. *A Little Book of Annuals.* New York: A.T. DeLa Mare Company, Inc., 1925.

Jekyll, Gertrude. *Annuals and Biennials.* London: Country Life, 1911.

———. *A Gardener's Testament.* London: Antique Collector's Club, 1982 (first published by Country life, 1937).

McMahon, Bernard. *The American Gardener's Calendar.* Charlottesville, VA: Thomas Jefferson Memorial Foundation, Inc., 1997. (Reprint of 1806 work.)

Vilmorin-Andrieux, M. M. *The Vegetable Garden.* Berkeley, CA: Ten Speed Press, 1981. (First published in 1885.)

Gardening History

Favretti, Rudy and Joy. *For Every House A Garden: A Guide For Reproducing Period Gardens.* Hanover, NH: University Press of New England, 1990.

Hedrick, U. P. *A History of Horticulture in America to 1860 With an Addendum of Books Published from 1861-1920.* Portland, OR: Timber Press, 1988.

Hill, May Brawley. *Grandmother's Garden: The Old-Fashioned American Garden 1865–1915.* New York: Harry Abrams, 1995.

Landsberg, Sylvia. *The Medieval Garden.* New York: Thames and Hudson, 1995.

Leighton, Ann. *American Gardens in the Eighteenth Century: "For Use or for Delight."* Amherst, MA: The University of Massachusetts Press, 1986.

————. *American Gardens of the Nineteenth Century: "For Comfort and Affluence."* Amherst, MA: The University of Massachusetts Press, 1987.

————. *Early American Gardens: "For Meate or Medicine."* Amherst, MA: The University of Massachusetts Press, 1986.

Verey, Rosemary. *Classic Garden Design: How to Adapt and Recreate Garden Features of the Past.* New York: Random House, 1984.

Welch, William, and Greg Grant. *The Southern Heirloom Garden.* Dallas, TX: Taylor Publishing Company, 1995.

Westmacott, Richard. *African-American Gardens and Yards in the Rural South.* Knoxville, TN: The University of Tennessee Press, 1992.

Wilson, Gilbert L. *Buffalo Bird Woman's Garden: Agriculture of the Hidatsa Indians.* St. Paul, MN: Minnesota Historical Society Press, 1987.

Seed-Saving

Ashworth, Suzanne. *Seed to Seed.* Decorah, IA: Seed Saver Publications, 1991.

Bubel, Nancy. *The New Seed-Starters Handbook.* Emmaus, PA: Rodale Press, 1988.

Rogers, Marc. *Saving Seeds: The Gardener's Guide to Growing and Storing Vegetable and Flower Seeds.* Pownal, VT: Storey Communications, 1990.

Turner, Carole B. *Seed Sowing and Saving: Step-by-Step Techniques for Collecting and Growing More Than 100 Vegetables, Flowers, and Herbs.* Pownal, VT: Storey Communications, 1998.

Heirloom Gardening and Heirloom Varieties

Bender, Steve, and Felder Rushing. *Passalong Plants.* Chapel Hill, NC: The University of North Carolina Press, 1993.

Buchanan, Rita. *The Shaker Herb and Garden Book.* New York, NY: Houghton Mifflin, 1996.

Deppe, Carol. *Breed Your Own Vegetable Varieties.* Boston: Little, Brown, and Co., 1993.

Gardener, Jo Ann. *The Heirloom Garden: Selecting and Growing Over 300 Old-Fashioned Ornamentals.* Pownal, VT: Storey Communications, 1992.

Hatch, Peter J. *The Fruit and Fruit Trees of Monticello.* Charlottesville, VA: University Press of Virginia, 1998.

Jabs, Carolyn. *The Heirloom Gardener.* San Francisco, CA: Sierra Club Books, 1984.

Male, Carolyn. *Heirloom Tomatoes for the American Garden.* New York, NY: Workman Press, 1999.

Martin, Tovah. *Heirloom Flowers.* New York: Fireside, 1999.

Stickland, Sue. *Heirloom Vegetables: A Home Gardener's Guide to Finding and Growing Vegetables From the Past.* New York: Fireside, 1998.

Stuart, David. *Gardening with Heirloom Plants.* Pleasantville, NY: Reader's Digest Association, 1997.

Talbot, Rob, and Robin Whiteman. *Brother Cadfael's Herb Garden: An Illustrated Companion to Medieval Plants and their Uses.* New York: Bullfinch Press Book, Little, Brown, 1997.

Watson, Benjamin. *Taylor's Guide to Heirloom Vegetables.* New York: Houghton Mifflin, 1996.

Weaver, William Woys. *Heirloom Vegetable Gardening: A Master Gardener's Guide to Planting, Seed Saving, and Cultural History.* New York: Henry Holt, 1997.

Whealy, Kent. *Garden Seed Inventory, Fifth Edition.* Decorah, IA: Seed Saver Publications, 1999.

Whealy, Kent, and Steve Demuth. *Fruit, Berry, and Nut Inventory, Second Edition.* Decorah, IA: Seed Saver Publications, 1993.

Zeeman, Anne. *Fifty Easy Old-Fashioned Flowers.* New York: Henry Holt, 1995.

————. *Fifty Easy Old-Fashioned Roses, Climbers, and Vines.* New York: Henry Holt, 1995.

Garden Crafts

Black, Penny. *The Book of Pressed Flowers.* New York: Simon & Schuster, 1988.

Emery, Carla. *The Encyclopedia of Country Living.* Seattle, Washington: Sasquatch Books, 1994.

Newdick, Jane. *Victorian Flowercrafts.* Emmaus, PA: Rodale Press, 1994.

Heirloom Cooking

Miss Beecher's Domestic Receipt Book, Third Edition. New York: Harper & Brothers, 1858.

Kremer, Elizabeth C. *We Make You Kindly Welcome.* Harrodsburg, KY: Pleasant Hill Press, 1977.

————. *Welcome Back to Pleasant Hill.* Harrodsburg, KY: Pleasant Hill Press, 1977.

Miller, Amy Bess, and Persis Fuller. *The Best of Shaker Cooking.* New York: Macmillan, 1985.

Nichols, Nell B. *Farm Journal's Country Cookbook.* New York: Doubleday, 1959.

For a large selection of cookbook fascimiles, contact the Food Heritage Press, P.O. Box 163, Ipswich, MA 01938; www.foodbooks.com. There is a $1.00 charge for their printed catalog.

Acknowledgments

Many individuals were a part of creating this book, and I am very grateful for their participation.

Thank you to the good people at Rodale: Ellen Phillips, executive editor, who believed in the concept for the book and kindly encouraged me, and Nan Ondra, freelance editor, for her tremendous patience and editing skill. Thanks, too, to Marta Strait, designer, for her wonderful creative abilities, and to Tom Gettings, who provided photographs, contacts, and enthusiasm.

I also want to thank the talented gardening experts and heirloom specialists who generously contributed to the book: Joe Carlin, Jo Ann Gardener, Peter Hatch, Rachel Kane, Skip Kauffman, Clarence Kulp, Scott Kunst, Carolyn Male, Jeff McCormack, Norton and Marlene Rickard, Nancy Roan, Felder Rushing, Lee Stolzfus, Tom Wagner, Ben Watson, William Woys Weaver, and Diane and Kent Whealy.

Thanks are also due to James Weaver of Meadow View Farms, Bowers, Pennsylvania; Dick Frecon of Frecon Orchards, Boyertown, Pennsylvania; and Eileen Weinsteiger of The Rodale Institute in Maxatawny, Pennsylvania, for providing beautiful heirloom produce for photographs. The Jean and Alexander Heard Library of Vanderbilt University in Nashville was very helpful with its wonderful collection of historical cookbooks.

Most of all, I thank my family—all talented and supportive in many ways—John, Pop, Bill, Nancy, Susy, Mike, Joe, Alice, Meryl, and my co-author, Buster.

Photo Credits

Index

Note: Page references in **boldface** indicate illustrations.

New England gardens, 4
    traditional, 6–8, **7, 8**
New York gardens
    formal, 9, **9**
    traditional, 6, 9
Nicotiana alata, 92–93, **92**
    in Country Cottage Garden, 23
Nicotiana species, 92–93, **92**
Nigella damascena, 92
    in Old-Fashioned Parlor Garden, 40
Note cards, pressed flower, 200–201, **200, 201**

O

Ocimum basilicum, 132–33, **132**
    in Medieval Herb Garden, 28
Old-Fashioned Fruit Garden, 42–45, **43, 45**
Old-Fashioned Parlor Garden, 36–41, **36, 37, 39**
Onion, 65–67, **66**
    Bubble and Squeak, 210
    'Early Yellow Globe', 67
        in Bountiful Kitchen Garden, **33,** 34
    Hoppin' John, 214
    'Red Wethersfield', **66,** 67
    Root Cellar Soup, 212
    'Southport White Globe', 67
    'White Portugal', 67
Oswego tea, 110

P

Paeonia species, 111–12, **111**
    in Country Cottage Garden, 23
Pansy, wild, **94**
Papaver orientale, 112
Papaver rhoeas, 112
Parlor gardens, 4
    Old-Fashioned Parlor Garden, 36–41, **36, 37, 39**
Parsley, 142, **142**
    in Bountiful Kitchen Garden, **33,** 35
    in Medieval Herb Garden, **26,** 28
Parsnips, Root Cellar Soup, 212
Paths, width of, 41
Pea(s), 67–69, **68**
    'Alderman', 69
    'Golden Sweet Edible-Podded', 69
    'Homesteader', 69

'Lancashire Lad', 68
'Lincoln', **68,** 69
'Mammoth Melting Sugar', 69
    in Bountiful Kitchen Garden, **33,** 34
'Tall Telephone', 69
Peaches, 158
    grown at Monticello, 154
    pruning system for, 183–84, **183**
Pears
    espaliering of, 184–85, **184**
    European, 154, 159–60
    and fireblight, 159, 160, 182–83
    pruning, 181–83, **181, 182, 183**
Peonies, 111–12, **111**
    in Country Cottage Garden, **21,** 23
Pepper(s), 69–72, **70**
    'Bull Nose', 71
    'Cherry Sweet', 72
    'Chimayo', 71
    'Corno di Toro', 72
    'Cyklon', **70,** 71
    'Czechoslovakian Black', 71
    Hoppin' John, 214
    'Horn of the Bull', 72
    'Long Red Cayenne', 71
    'Sweet Banana', 72
        in Bountiful Kitchen Garden, **33,** 35
Peppermint, 141
Perennials, 4
    in informal flower gardens, 170–71, **171**
    selected ones discussed, 102–15, **103, 105,**
        107, 109, 111, 113, 115
    starting from seed, 171–72
Petroselinum crispum, 142, **142**
    in Medieval Herb Garden, 28
Phaseolus coccineus, 127, **127**
    in Country Cottage Garden, 22
Phaseolus vulgaris, 50–52, **51**
Pheromone monitoring traps, 178
Phlox, garden, 113–14, **113**
    in Country Cottage Garden, **21,** 22
Physic gardens, 24–29, **25, 26, 27**
Pisum sativum, 67–69, **68**
Plant breeding, 191
Plant of forgetfulness, 108
Pleasant Hill Shaker Village, 208
Plum curculio, controlling, 178
Plums, grown at Monticello, 154

Poppies, 112
Potagers, 30
Potato(es), 72–75, **73**
　　'All Blue', 74
　　'Anna Cheeka's Ozette', 74
　　'Banana', 74–75
　　'Bintje', 74
　　Bubble and Squeak, 210
　　'Cow Horn', 74
　　'Garnet Chile', 74
　　'Green Mountain', 74
　　'Russian Banana', 74–75
Potpourri, making, 202–4, **202, 203**
Pressed flower note cards, 200–201, **200, 201**
Primroses, 114
Primula species, 114
Propagation
　　by layering, 144, **144**
　　by seeds, 172–74, 188–90
Pruning
　　of bramble fruits, 186–88, **187**
　　central leader system, 181–82, **181, 182**
　　of grapes, 185–86, **186**
　　how to cut, 180, **180**
　　modified central leader system, 182–83
　　open-center system, **183,** 183–84
　　of raspberries, 186–88, **187**
Prunus persica, 158
Pumpkin(s), 77–80, **78**
　　Pumpkin Muffins, 222
Pumpkin 'Connecticut Field', 77, 80
Pumpkin 'Rouge Vif d'Etampes', 80
Pyrus species, 159–60

Q

Quince, 160–61

R

Radish(es), 75–77, **76**
　　'China Rose', 76
　　'French Breakfast', 76, **76**
　　　　in Bountiful Kitchen Garden, **33,** 34
　　intercropping and, 170
　　'Long Black Spanish', 77
　　'White Icicle', 77

Raphanus sativus, 75–77, **76**
Raspberries, 161–62
　　in Old-Fashioned Fruit Garden, 44, **45**
　　pruning, 186–88, **187**
　　training, 187, **187**
Recipes, 207–25
　　Basic Pie Crust, 217
　　Bubble and Squeak, 210
　　Clara's Patty Pan Squash, 216
　　Corn Pudding, 208
　　Elderberry-Apple Pie, 218
　　Escalloped Corn and Tomatoes, 209
　　Grape Pie, 219
　　Green Tomato Pie, 220
　　Hoppin' John, 214
　　Pumpkin Muffins, 222
　　Rhubarb-Strawberry Cobbler, 221
　　Roast Corn Soup, 212
　　Root Cellar Soup, 212
　　Salmagundi, 224
　　Schnitz Pie, 220
　　Sister Mary's Zesty Carrots, 211
　　Sweet Dough, 217
　　Tepary Chile, 215
　　Watermelon Rind Pickles, 223
Recommended Reading, 232–34
Regional heirloom garden styles
　　creating, 6, 14
　　mid-Atlantic, 9–10, 11, **11**
　　New England, 6–8, 7, **7, 8**
　　New York, 6, 9, **9**
　　southern, 10, 12–13, **13**
　　western dryland, 13–15, **14**
Resources for Heirloom Country Gardens, 226–31
Ribes species, 153, **153,** 154, 155
Rocket larkspur, 88–89
　　in Old-Fashioned Parlor Garden, **39,** 40
Roman chamomile, 134
Rosa alba, 116
Rosa × *borboniana,* 117, **117**
Rosa carolina, 123
Rosa centifolia, 118
Rosa chinensis, 118
Rosa damascena, 119, **119**
Rosa gallica, 120, **120**
Rosa gallica var. *officinalis,* in Medieval Herb Garden, 28
Rosa nitida, 123

USDA Plant Hardiness Zone Map

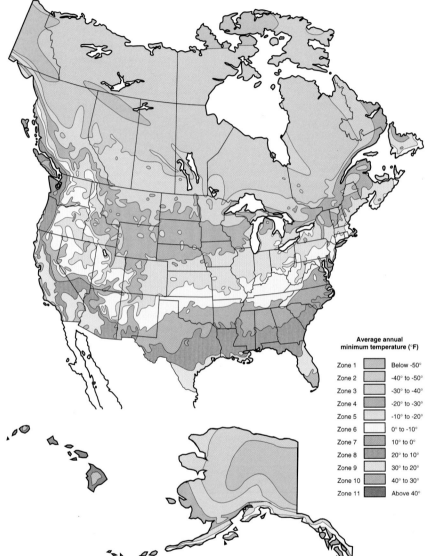

Average annual minimum temperature (°F)

Zone 1	Below -50°
Zone 2	-40° to -50°
Zone 3	-30° to -40°
Zone 4	-20° to -30°
Zone 5	-10° to -20°
Zone 6	0° to -10°
Zone 7	10° to 0°
Zone 8	20° to 10°
Zone 9	30° to 20°
Zone 10	40° to 30°
Zone 11	Above 40°

This map was revised in 1990 to reflect the original USDA map, done in 1965. It is now recognized as the best indicator of minimum temperatures available. Look at the map to find your area, then match its pattern to the key above. When you've found your color, the key will tell you what hardiness zone you live in. Remember that the map is a general guide; your particular conditions may vary.